Learning and Forgetting in Development NGOs

AF834969

Learning and Forgetting in Development NGOs draws on a range of theoretical approaches and empirical evidence to explore how development organisations learn or fail to learn from experience. Despite the overwhelming discourses of NGOs as learning organisations, little is known about the phenomenon of learning within NGOs. As constantly changing buzzwords and institutional approaches abound and old ideas and concepts are "re-discovered", development NGOs are often accused of trying to reinvent the wheel as they struggle to escape from the challenges of development amnesia.

Based on detailed empirical data on the everyday practices and accounts of development practitioners, this book moves between the boundaries of organisational institutionalism, learning theories, management and ethnographies of NGOs' practices to investigate the many faces of organisational learning in an attempt to counteract development amnesia. *Learning and Forgetting in Development NGOs* will be an essential guide for students, scholars and development practitioners with an interest in development management and organisational theory.

Tiina Kontinen is an Academy of Finland Research Fellow at the Department of Social Sciences and Philosophy, University of Jyväskylä, Finland.

Routledge Explorations in Development Studies

This Development Studies series features innovative and original research at the regional and global scale. It promotes interdisciplinary scholarly works drawing on a wide spectrum of subject areas, in particular politics, health, economics, rural and urban studies, sociology, environment, anthropology and conflict studies.

Topics of particular interest are globalisation; emerging powers; children and youth; cities; education; media and communication; technology development; and climate change.

In terms of theory and method, rather than basing itself on any orthodoxy, the series draws broadly on the tool kit of the social sciences in general, emphasising comparison, the analysis of the structure and processes, and the application of qualitative and quantitative methods.

Chinese Hydropower Development in Africa and Asia
Challenges and Opportunities for Sustainable Global Dam-Building
Edited by Giuseppina Siciliano and Frauke Urban

Youth, Gender and the Capabilities Approach to Development
Rethinking Opportunities and Agency from a Human Development Perspective
Edited by Aurora Lopez-Fogues and Firdevs Melis Cin

Democratic Rural Organizations
Thresholds for Evolution in Africa and Asia
Esbern Friis-Hansen, Janki Andharia and Godfrey Suubi

Aid and Technical Cooperation as a Foreign Policy Tool for Emerging Donors
The Case of Brazil
Déborah Barros Leal Farias

Learning and Forgetting in Development NGOs
Insights from Organisational Theory
Tiina Kontinen

Learning and Forgetting in Development NGOs

Insights from Organisational Theory

Tiina Kontinen

Routledge
Taylor & Francis Group
LONDON AND NEW YORK

First published 2018
by Routledge
2 Park Square, Milton Park, Abingdon, Oxon OX14 4RN

and by Routledge
52 Vanderbilt Avenue, New York, NY 10017

First issued in paperback 2020

Routledge is an imprint of the Taylor & Francis Group, an informa business

© 2018 Tiina Kontinen

The right of Tiina Kontinen to be identified as author of this work has been asserted by her in accordance with sections 77 and 78 of the Copyright, Designs and Patents Act 1988.

All rights reserved. No part of this book may be reprinted or reproduced or utilised in any form or by any electronic, mechanical, or other means, now known or hereafter invented, including photocopying and recording, or in any information storage or retrieval system, without permission in writing from the publishers.

Trademark notice: Product or corporate names may be trademarks or registered trademarks, and are used only for identification and explanation without intent to infringe.

British Library Cataloguing-in-Publication Data
A catalogue record for this book is available from the British Library

Library of Congress Cataloging-in-Publication Data
Names: Kontinen, Tiina, author.
Title: Learning and forgetting in development NGOs : insights from organisational theory / Tiina Kontinen.
Description: Abingdon, Oxon ; New York, NY : Routledge, [2018] |
Series: Routledge explorations in development studies |
Includes bibliographical references and index.
Identifiers: LCCN 2018005539 (print) | LCCN 2018019556 (ebook) |
ISBN 9781315108988 (eBook) | ISBN 9781138089808 (hbk) |
ISBN 9781315108988 (ebk)
Subjects: LCSH: Non-governmental organizations–Management. |
Non-governmental organizations–Developing countries. |
Economic assistance–Developing countries. | Organizational learning.
Classification: LCC HD62.6 (ebook) | LCC HD62.6 .K665 2018 (print) |
DDC 352.1/106–dc23
LC record available at https://lccn.loc.gov/2018005539

ISBN 13: 978-0-367-66636-1 (pbk)
ISBN 13: 978-1-138-08980-8 (hbk)

Typeset in Times New Roman
by Out of House Publishing

Contents

List of illustrations vi
Acknowledgements vii
List of abbreviations viii

1 Introduction 1

2 Categorising learning in development: towards organisational institutionalism 23

3 Learning as a search for a shared meaning for empowerment 46

4 Learning as a change in organisational epistemology 71

5 Unlearning, forgetting and ignorance 100

6 Learning as legitimation and synchronisation 128

7 Conclusions 149

Index 162

List of illustrations

Figures

4.1 The organisational learning trajectory concerning story-based M&E in ISF 77
4.2 An example of a change path in regard to attitude change in an FGM project 94

Tables

1.1 A list of research projects and material used in this book 13
2.1 Suggestion for categories of learning in development 33
3.1 Structure of workshop sections on empowerment in Kenya and India 2012 54

Acknowledgements

The book is based on a number of research projects over an extended period of time. I especially would like to acknowledge with gratitude the funding received from the Finnish Funding Agency for Innovation, TEKES for the project "Empowering Leadership in an international NGO" (2012–2013, decision no 2420/31/2011) and from the Academy of Finland for the project "Counteracting Development Amnesia" (2013–2015, decision no 260359). I would like to thank Sara Robinson-Moncada, Anna Pörsti and Suvi Baloch in the former project, and Oona Timonen and Veera Joro in the latter project, for their valuable contributions in collecting and transcribing the research material. I also want to thank my former employer, the Finnish umbrella organisation KEPA for an opportunity to combine research with my duties in the "Towards Evaluation for Everyday Use" project (2009–2010), and my colleagues at that time, Anja Onali and Laura Lager for co-implementing the project. My warmest thanks go to all the NGOs that invited me to work with them and allowed access to their internal events, discussions and documents. They also provided me a chance to get to know a number of committed, smart and funny people always ready to work for improvements across the globe.

List of abbreviations

ADP	Area Development Programme (World Vision)
CSO	Civil Society Organisation
DFID	Department of International Development, United Kingdom
FGM	Female Genital Mutilation
FINGO	Finnish International Non-Governmental Organisation
FRC	Finnish Refugee Council
GLM	Green Living Movement
HRBA	Human Rights-Based Approach
IDP	Integrated Development Programme (World Vision)
INGO	International Non-Governmental Organisation
ISF	International Solidarity Foundation
IT	Information Technology
KEPA	A Platform for Finnish Civil Society Organisations and an Expert on Global Development Issues
LFA	Logical Framework Approach
M&E	Monitoring and Evaluation
NGO	Non-Governmental Organisation
OD	Organisational Development
ODW	Operation a Day's Work Finland
OM	Outcome Mapping
PME	Planning, Monitoring and Evaluation
PRA	Participatory Rural Appraisal
RBM	Results-Based Management
TUO	Student Union in Turku University of Applied Sciences
UMWA	Uganda Women Media Association
UNHCR	The United Nations Refugee Agency
WV	World Vision

1 Introduction

Lessons learned = An expression appearing in evaluations. Often it means only lessons.

An irrelevant glossary in Smillie (1995)

We would like to really learn… not just keep on repeating that we are a learning organisation.

A research interview in 2015

In our sector, you have to have PME, and sometimes even R for research. It is part of what we should do as NGOs. And technically, most of the NGOs do. But it does not necessary mean that organisations would learn something. It is just done in order to be a kind of professional organisation.

A research interview in 2015

Learning in development organisations

"Lessons learned" and "learning organisation" are terms that appear frequently in the vocabularies of non-governmental organisations (NGOs) engaged in development cooperation. The strategic plans of NGOs, from large international non-governmental organisations (INGOs) to small local ones, include aspirations to be a learning organisation. Every monitoring and evaluation (M&E) report includes a section on lessons learned that are expected to be taken into account when adjusting activities or designing new initiatives. A great number of institutional learning events such as training, workshops, seminars and organisational development (OD) are continuously conducted all over the world.

International development, in general, has for a long time taken pride in being a learning institution that draws lessons from its past and effectively produces new knowledge for learning purposes (Carlsson & Wolgemuth 2000; King & McGrath 2004; Powell 2006).The recent trends of evidence-based policymaking and results-based management have increasingly emphasised the role of knowledge and learning at different levels of development,

development NGOs included (Hayman et al. 2016). Increased emphasis on learning has led to establishment of sophisticated knowledge-management systems (Ferguson et al. 2010) and systematic M&E procedures and impact assessment approaches that encourage combining accountability and learning (David et al. 2006; Guijt & Roche 2014). Learning in partnerships between northern and southern NGOs is especially called for (Mougeout 2017). NGOs continuously maintain their aspiration of being learning organisations (Senge 1990), flexible and engaged in continuous learning from their so-called beneficiaries and local knowledges (Roper & Pettit 2002). Organisational capacity building and OD processes in both northern and southern NGOs promote organisational learning and change (Kühl 2009; Ubels et al. 2010). Literature on organisational learning in NGOs has tackled the question of how to create organisational culture supportive of learning, what kind of leadership is needed to maintain learning NGOs, and how to promote continuous cycles or spirals of learning (Britton 1998, 2005, 2012; Fowler 1997; Hailey & James 2002).

At the same time, critical accounts have pointed to NGOs' difficulties to learn (Lewis 2007, 116). Despite their claimed flexibility, development NGOs are not seen to have the required adaptability in the face of changing development architecture and the world in general (Ronalds 2010). It has been also argued that NGOs have a tendency to forget their past rather than draw lessons from it (Lewis 2009, 2016; Smillie 1995, 158). The activist culture typical to NGOs is hindering learning. The NGO staff might prefer action over reflection, and organisations know how things should be on the basis of their world view rather than having the patience to engage with new knowledge (Edwards 1997). The learning potentialities of M&E are lost when they are reduced into mechanical performance of required accountability techniques (Lister 2003). A lot of documentation and information might be collected, but the challenge is to get the members of staff to actually read or use this (Matturi 2016). Continuously changing development fads and fashions can result in a kind of "perpetual present" in which no lessons are drawn from the past, and the future is "a place that is promised, and on which present activities are premised, but which never arrives" (Lewis 2016, 84). Learning from the past feels irrelevant as the next project, next annual plan, and next M&E system is already on its way.

In this book, I aim neither to provide straightforward advice for learning in NGOs, nor to offer a cynical critique of impossibility of learning in them (Biggs & Smith 2003). Rather, I will contribute to the continuous analysis of the very concepts and practices of learning in development (Johnson & Wilson 2009, 13–18). Drawing from organisation theory literature, my objective is to provide an empirically grounded and theoretically informed account of how learning takes place in organisations. I also pay attention to unlearning, forgetting and ignorance as phenomena closely related to learning but less investigated in regard to development NGOs. The idea for this book emerged during more than 20 years of research on and with development NGOs of different sizes and objectives. During these years I have met a large number of NGO practitioners both in the global south and north, who are committed to fighting inequalities and supporting improvements in the lives of those being marginalised, and who have allocated countless hours of their time to ensuring the success of NGO initiatives.

I have also met the most self-critical practitioners among the most motivated. The slow pace of envisaged changes and the endless project management procedures easily result in frustration and even cynicism. Some practitioners really feel they have been captured in what ethnographers call "aidland" (Mosse 2011). A land where certain knowledge practices, terminologies and performances determine the success of an NGO. Much time and energy allocated for learning is used for adoption of these practices. It is common, for example, that in institutionalised learning events such as workshops, the focus is on transmission of information about managerial tools rather than joint engagement in critical reflection on the goals, means and consequences of the work done. Traditionally, NGOs have had a strong ethos of voluntarism. Increasingly, however, working in a development NGO is a career choice and source of professional identity. Accordingly, practitioners' enthusiasm is not geared only to "making things right" in consideration of the people they work with, but also to doing things in the "right way", according to the professional standards of the industry. This kind of professionalisation is argued to lead to a loss of NGOs' connection with the grassroots and a depoliticising of their agendas (Banks et al. 2015). After all, NGOs have been seen as harbingers of democracy, grassroots development, global solidarity and transformative change towards more just and equal world, rather than professional entities whose job is to do development.

With the professionalisation, capacity building and organisational development, NGOs in different parts of the world have learned a lot during the last 30 years. The question frequently asked, however, is whether they have learned "wrong" things; those related to management rather than those closely connected with the lives of people they work with. In this book, I deliberatively focus on learning that is internal to NGOs. I am interested in seeing what kinds of learning take place in contemporary organisations and how these learning processes could be conceptualised. Instead of offering success stories of exceptional learning events in NGOs, I understand learning as part of a continuous change in organisations (Weick & Quinn 1999). The book scrutinises the "muddling through" of everyday practices and continuous organisational sense-making that takes place in NGOs that have paid staff to allocate their working time for fulfilling the organisational purposes (Powell & Rerup 2017; Weick 2001, 2009). In this effort, I will draw from management and organisational theory literature. In so doing, I connect organisational learning with management practices and conceptualise development NGOs as organisations. Therefore, one explicit aim of the book is to explore the conceptual possibilities offered in these literatures in analysing development NGOs.

Learning and development management

When we look at the job titles, it seems that what people in NGOs do is to *direct, advise, facilitate, coordinate* and *manage*. Organisations employ plenty of project coordinators, project managers and monitoring offices, where the substantial knowledge for activities is often provided by external experts or volunteers when it comes to community development (Brown & Green 2015; Green 2012). NGO staff typically arrange meetings, workshops and training sessions. They conduct mobilisation missions, baseline studies, monitoring visits, and fill Excel sheets and write reports. They contribute to annual planning, annual reporting and, at times, revising the Mission, Vision and Strategy. Staff are trained on issues such as results-based management (RBM), outcome mapping (OM), the human rights-based approach (HRBA) and the logical framework approach (LFA). Until today, the main model of NGO work has been a project with a starting point and an end, and it has to be managed – planned, implemented, monitored and evaluated. With the introduction of a programmatic approach, individual projects have to be further connected with larger programme goals and strategic objectives. These institutionalised management practices often seem to occupy most of the working time of NGO staff.

Development practice, thus, is full of terminologies and procedures that come from general management literature. In a similar vein, development management literature widely discusses organisational learning and organisational change in development NGOs (Edwards & Fowler 2002; Fowler & Malunga 2010; Lewis 2008). Learning is an integral part of most development management approaches. For instance, each stage in project management should ideally include learning: from past experience, from other NGOs, from beneficiaries and other stakeholders, and from the continuous feedback received in the course of project implementation. However, much development research on NGOs has been quite reluctant to draw from theoretical insights of management or organisational theory. Rather, it has been critical towards these fields that have been perceived as harbingers of neoliberal managerialism and as means to strengthen the legitimacy of certain kinds of modern organisations that appear to straightjacket organisational life and hinder real self-reflection (Dar & Cooke 2008; Roberts et al. 2005). It has been argued that development management is a continuation of colonial administration, and thus, reconstructs the power unjust power relations it claims to address (Cooke 2008). Management approaches circulating in the international development systems have been seen as examples of a Gramscian hegemony of managerialism (Girei 2016), Foucauldian technologies of governance (Mueller-Hirt 2012) and outcomes of mechanisms of institutional isomorphism (Claeyé & Jackson 2012) that privilege certain donor accountability modes over local ones (Dar 2014).

Thus, management approaches that focus on projects and organisations easily sideline the wider task of development management; managing for development as a "progressive social change" that takes place without such intentional efforts (Thomas 1996; 2000). While the everyday life in NGOs tends to be geared towards the management of deliberate development efforts, the critical reflection of the kinds of development that occur outside interventions and the overall assumptions behind their organisational idea of development are less focused on. NGO workshops infrequently concentrate on critical analysis of how colonial legacy or global managerialism is shown in their own conduct. More often, NGOs focus on learning prevalent approaches and become more competent development professionals within the existing framework. For instance, when improving their monitoring and evaluations, NGOs tend to opt to develop better indicator-based tools rather than trying to find alternative approaches that would better suit the complexities in the context (Horton 2010).

Obviously, both the adoption of existing management techniques and critical reflection on organisational goals fall under the general banner of organisational learning. However, their scope and dynamics are different. Using the much-cited distinction between single-loop and double-loop learning in organisational learning literature (Argyris & Schön 1978; Ebrahim 2003), the adoption of existing technologies is of the former type of learning, and critical reflection might lead to the latter type. Both kinds of learning have their own time and place in organisational functioning, as they address different learning needs. Through single-loop learning, organisations aim to be more effective and learn to do better what they do. As a consequence of double-loop learning, organisations might learn to do different, perhaps better, things. Moreover, organisations are not isolated islands. Organisational learning and organisational change are related to their institutional environments, and particularly to that of international development that shapes learning through mechanisms of institutional isomorphism (DiMaggio & Powell 1983; Lister 2003). Moreover, there are institutional tendencies beyond international development such as the global spread of the model of modern organisation (Meyer et al. 2006) and the overall managerialism typical of our times (Roberts et al. 2005) that effect changes in the organisational characteristics of development NGOs.

In the current institutional environment, an urge to learn in order to be able to manage better within the existing approaches is an almost taken-for-granted goal. Critical development management literature has, however, advocated for more fundamental reflection. For example, instead of aligning with the global managerialism in NGO relationships, "global solidarity" that includes democratic, self-critical analysis and action has been suggested (Cooke & Dar 2008, 3). The proposal, thus, is to be critical and abandon the very ideas of management in development, and to seek alternatives from the post-development discourse. In this scenario, the assumed implication might be that NGOs in their current forms and with their overall belief in the manageability of development should cease to exist and, instead, new forms of more democratic social organising and mobilising should emerge. This "radical" view has been contrasted with a "reformist" stance (Guljarani 2010). The reformist agenda maintains a belief in planning and seeks for "a non-rationalist idea of modernisation" and a "non-managerialistic practice" (Guljarani 2010, 142). In this new vision based on romantic social ideology, organic vocabularies, anchored in concrete historical and political realities, would be at the core of the reflexive professional practices, replacing the universalistic, rationalistic tools used today. Such "post-rationalist" learning would acknowledge that knowledge is always partial, contextual and produced in practices (McFarlane 2006). Reformist ideas about contextuality of knowledge go beyond the current management demands for "baseline studies" and "context analysis" which, on one hand emphasise the need to contextualise development interventions, and on the other require doing so by means of universal, non-contextualised tools and approaches.

Therefore, I suggest that there are at least three ways that organisational learning connects with the debates on development management. First, organisational learning can refer to adoption of the management systems and practices typical to field of development in any given time. This kind of learning aims for organisations to change into directions of being more effective in planning, implementing and reporting their development initiatives according to the quite universalistic approaches such as LFA and HRBA. Second, in their interaction with different contexts, organisations can learn to critically reflect and question the prevalent approaches. In accordance with the reformist approach, this kind of learning aims not only to better management within existing approaches but also learning to design different ones drawing from professional flexibility and collaborative relationships. Third, as suggested by the radical approach, NGOs should critically reflect and perhaps abandon their fundamental beliefs concerning the possibility of planned change implemented by organisations formed according to the principles of modern organisation. Such fundamental reconsideration would lead to radical reformulation of NGO identities, and perhaps an end to "NGO" as currently known. It is quite evident that in the empirical realities of NGOs today, learning mostly revolves around the two first options of learning as adoption of and adaptation to the existing approaches or as reformation in search for approaches better suitable for specific organisational purposes.

Development NGOs as organisations

Development NGOs have been widely discussed in development literature. Especially, in the mid-1990s and early 2000s, partly as a consequence of the growing emphasis of the goal of strengthening civil society in international development, development research showed a lot of interest in analysing the growing field of development NGOs in different parts of the worlds. Among others, the themes such as NGO performance and accountability (Edwards & Hulme 1995; Hulme & Edwards 1997), partnerships between northern and southern NGOs (Fowler 1998; Ebrahim 2003), the emergence of new international field of development NGOs (Tvedt 1998), and the relationship between NGOs and the concept of civil society (Howell & Pearce 2002; Lewis 2002) were discussed. Ethnographic studies showed the everyday dynamics of organising in a variety of contexts (Hillhorst 2003; Igoe 2003; Mercer 2002) and revealed the mechanisms of transnational governance that aligned the agendas of newly established southern NGO with international human rights trends (Englund 2006).

Much of the critical research revolved around different conceptualisations of civil society. It was argued that the interpretation of the civil society held by the mainstream development agencies mainly drew from a neo-Tocqeuvillian understanding of civil society as an associational sphere where individuals voluntarily organise around certain issues and thus, contribute to bottom-up democracy. However, in order to be able to promote aspired societal change, the notion of civil society should rather draw from a Gramscian anti-hegemonic space where people are mobilised to undertake collective action (Edwards 2004; Howell & Pearce 2002; Mitlin et al. 2007). In practice, support for civil society mostly turned to increasing funding for NGOs. The increased opportunities for financial support, in turn, led to a wave of establishing new NGOs in many parts of the world, and strengthened the position of the already existing organisations.

Therefore, at the core of the critique was and continues to be the "NGOization" of civil society (Choudry & Kapoor 2013). The typical organisational elements, such as bureaucratisation and professionalisation of development NGOs are seen as hindrances for their authenticity and ability to function as agents of transformation and global solidarity (Banks et al. 2015; Cooke & Dar 2008). The management practices borrowed from the private and public sectors have been also under critical scrutiny, as they are considered not to fit with the value-based aspirations of NGOs (Lewis 2003). Nevertheless, there is no question that many constellations of people all over the world, who call themselves NGOs, have learned to be modern, professional organisations. They have learned to define their missions and visions, plan their work, and account and report accordingly. Therefore, the potential contributions of management and organisation research are worth exploring when it comes to understanding the dynamics of organisational learning and organising in development NGOs (Lewis 2014, 127–159; Roper & Pettit 2002).

In this book, I approach development NGOs as organisations (Watkins et al. 2012). Development NGO is difficult to define, as Lewis and Schuller (2017, 58) argue, it is a "productively unstable" category that escapes any precise definition. My definition is quite pragmatic: the organisations under scrutiny are defined as development NGOs, as they enjoy funding from the so-called NGO channel in international development (Tvedt 1998). They also define themselves as NGOs, and in some instances, as civil society organisations (CSOs) in reference to their position as not being governmental bodies (although receiving funding from donor governments) nor private sector organisations, and basing their action on certain missions as typical of any third sector organisation (Billis 2010). Therefore, rather than searching for an all-encompassing definition of what an NGO is, I am interested in how *NGO-ing* is carried out as everyday practice in these constellations (Hillhorst 2003).

When it comes to defining organisation, it is obvious that organisation theory is rich with different theoretical approaches and definitions. For example, Morgan (1986) differentiates eight metaphors for organisations, including those of machines, cultures, brains or political systems; each used by a number of theories. In general, organisations can be defined as formal entities that have a certain shared orientation, organisational positions and rules that their members are supposed to follow (Blau & Scott 1962). They are also cultures and practices revolved around a certain purpose (Tsoukas 2005, 70). Moreover, they interact with wider regulative, normative and cultural-cognitive institutional elements that partly define their status, forms and goals (Scott 2014). They typically experience organisational phenomena such as resource dependency (Pfeffer & Salancik 1978) or decoupling between formal structures and actual practices (Meyer & Rowan 1977).

In this book, I combine my interest in *NGO-ing* with a practice-based perspective to organisation. I focus on what is done in NGOs rather than on how they are structured. The practice-based approach emphasises organisations as sites of negotiations where different perspectives and interpretations meet, and where organisational meanings, practices and routines are continuously created in this interaction (Gherardi 2000; Feldman & Orlikowski 2011; Orlikowski 2002). According to the practice-based perspective, organisational structures, positions and rules are applied and enacted by members of the community in particular situations (Tsoukas & Vladimirou 2001, 980). Methodologically, in this book, I define organisations as practices that take place within certain structures constructed around shared tasks. When it comes to development NGOs, the organisational borders are often fluid as the "shared task" is extended to partnerships and not addressed by one organisation only, and further, the organisational goals are finally completed, if they are, by the so-called beneficiaries.

Beyond organisations: organisational institutionalism

Organisations are not isolated entities as they are always located in a certain context. Much of the organisational learning literature understands learning as an interaction between an organisation and its environment. For private sector organisations, environment can refer to market, clients and competitors. Information gathered from these environments might lead to organisational learning, the goal of which is better efficiency, and thus enhanced survival in market environments. In the case of development NGOs, the question of relevant organisational environments can be more complicated. First, they are situated in certain societal contexts of certain countries. However, for international ones, the location of the headquarters is different from those where field offices are situated and where most of the organisation's activities take place. Often, conducting development projects is a joint effort of different autonomous organisations located in different environments. In development partnerships, the international community of "development" offers an important joint point of reference, and further, global trends in general effect the forms and goals of NGOs. A wealth of ethnographic work on NGOs, especially in the southern hemisphere, has shown how local contextual dynamics and the relationship with the international discourses intertwine in NGO formation and practice (see Crewe & Harrison 1998; Englund 2006; Hillhorst 2003; Igoe 2003; Mercer 2002; Riles 2001).

To conceptualise the relationship between organisations and their environments, I draw from the tradition of organisational institutionalism (Greenwood et al. 2008; 2017; Scott 2008). It has become one of the most prevalent approaches in organisation studies, but has not yet been widely applied in development research (see Claeyé & Jackson 2012; Ebrahim 2003; Fejerskov 2016; Tvedt 1998). I connect organisational learning and organisational institutionalism through two notions: organisational change and micro-foundations of institutions.

First, I suggest that organisational change is part of a process of organisational learning. Organisational institutionalism argues that change in organisations does not take place only in order to be more effective, but also in an effort to be more legitimate in their environments (Meyer & Rowan 1977). Environment is typically conceptualised as an organisational field that refers to a "community of organisations that partake of a common meaning system" (Scott 2014), and further, "organisations that constitute a recognised area of institutional life" in which they produce similar goods or services (DiMaggio & Powell 1983, 148). In seeking legitimacy, organisations engage in practices and use vocabularies "appropriate" in this particular field. An international organisational field of "development NGOs" constitutes a significant organisational environment for individual NGOs (Tvedt 1998, 2002, 2006; Watkins et al. 2012). For example, through organisational learning, NGOs may change their practices in order to convince their donors, government officials, beneficiaries or the general public of being "real", "efficient" and "legitimate" organisations that align with the historically evolved perceptual frames of the field (Ebrahim 2003).

The organisational field of development NGOs is characterised, for example, by the physical distances between organisations, dependence on changing donor priorities, and on local partner organisations for access to grassroots that provides legitimacy to goals such as empowerment (Watkins et al. 2012, 288–295). The typical resource transfer channels, as well as the rhetoric and discourses used in the system are the main ways through which NGOs interact with the field (Tvedt 2002; 2006; Watkins et al. 2012, 370). For instance, learning to be a legitimate development NGO includes discoursive internationalisation of the appropriate rhetoric (Tvedt 2002, 369). In order to get access to resources circulating in the field, using the language adapted from donors is extremely important for the southern NGOs, but similar pressures apply to northern NGOs as well (Watkins et al. 2012, 370).

Second, I argue that the organisational change and learning in interaction between NGOs and the organisational field is a mutual process. While the institutional pressures direct organisational change, organisational practices, on their part, provide micro-foundations for institutions (Powell & Colyvas 2008). According to this perspective, organisations do not mainly adapt to institutional pressures, but play an important role in constructing institutions through everyday interactions and micro-level practices. NGOs often follow the institutionalised taken-for-granted scripts in their action (Lister 2003), and might contribute to their change through small modifications. Organisational practices are continuously constructed in discoursive and material interaction between members (Feldman & Orlikowski 2011), while making sense of the organisational environments (Weick 2001, 2009). Therefore, the perspective of micro-foundations of institutions encourages to study organisational change and learning in the "fairly mundane" everyday activities that are geared to "sense-making, alignment, and muddling through" (Powell & Rerup 2017, 312), rather than searching for radical transformations in organisations.

Finally, organisational institutionalism provides ideas that go beyond the field of international development. For instance, a "world culture" approach (Meyer et al. 2006) provides an additional, wider perspective to organisational change and learning in development NGOs. From the world culture perspective, the professionalisation and modernisation of organisations is a global cultural process that operates far beyond the field of development. This process has globally spread the model of a modern organisation, different from more traditional collective entities. The model of a modern organisation is that of a purposeful entity which coordinates and manages its activities. Typical to modern organisation is that it talks about its goals, has an elaborate technical structure, and traces its resource use through counting and accounting. (Meyer et al. 2006, 25; 44–45). While the world culture approach identifies such organisations in different levels of society, as well as in multiple fields, these characteristics resonate extremely well with those typical of development NGOs all over the globe (Watkins et al. 2012).

Learning and power in development NGOs

Every attempt to conceptualise learning in development, at some point, encounters the issues of power. The very existence of international development is based on global asymmetries that it explicitly seeks to tackle, or often implicitly reconstructs through its own discourses and practices rich with paternalism (Eriksson Baaz 2005) and hierarchical control mechanisms (Groves & Hinton 2004; Wallace 2006). Moreover, NGOs often explicitly aim to address local power relations through the promotion of empowerment of hitherto marginalised groups of people (Kabeer 1999) or the transformation of societal power relations (Mitlin et al. 2007). There are also power issues internal to NGOs related to organisational hierarchies and challenges in internal democratic decision making. Moreover, organisations have also been considered to be subject to power effects of development discourse (Lister 2003) and the hegemony of overall trends such as managerialism (Girei 2016).

The Foucauldian (Foucault 1991) development literature, in general, has pointed out the power of development discourse in producing its objects (Escobar 1995), and in depoliticising development interventions (Ferguson 1994). Moreover, development has been seen as Foucauldian governmentality, with consequences of both production of certain kinds of NGOs (Mueller-Hirth 2012), and further, neoliberal subjectivities and citizens (Lazar 2012). In response to the idea that development is merely a technical effort, the urge for bringing politics back in development has been articulated (Hickey 2009; DFID 2010). The idea that all development is political implies that power is embedded, in different ways, to any development initiative. NGOs and civil society in general have been attached to the role of transforming societal power relations and hegemonies (Gramsci 1971; Mitlin et al. 2007). Different conceptualisations of power relate to the notion of learning in different ways. However, both Foucauldian and Gramscian ideas emphasise the importance of the power/knowledge nexus. Learning, thus, can refer to taken-for-granted alignment with, adaptation of, and consent to hegemonic discourses and practices, or, as critical perspectives would argue, becoming aware of and reflecting on these hegemonies, and undertake action to resist and contest them.

In development practice, one of the learning needs constantly identified is the acknowledgement and reflection on the power relationships in north-south partnerships (Contu & Girei 2016; Eyben 2006; Johnson & Wilson 2009; Lister 2000). Learning to reflect on the power effects is often seen as the first step in a process of effective collaboration and mutual learning. For NGO collaboration, learning on power includes being sensitive to what kinds of organisational forms and practices are supported through so-called capacity-building programmes (Kühl 2009). As organisational development and capacity building are central ways to promote intentional organisational learning within NGOs, central questions should be how the "best practices" transmitted by these efforts are defined, and where do they come from. Therefore, it is important to locate power relations within theoretical perspectives on organisational learning (Ebrahim 2003), and reflect on what limitations or possibilities for learning the power relations imply. For example, through an innovative combination of Habermas' theory of communicative action and Foucault's ideas of regimes of truth, Johnson and Wilson (2009) assert that learning in development takes place in social relations, including those of power, and they coin the idea of "action learning space" as an analytical tool to understand learning as it occurs in communication, and where a tendency to regard certain types of knowledge as more "truth" than others is acknowledged.

Organisational learning theories, for their part, have often been criticised for not adequately addressing the issue of power. For example, learning theories might treat individuals as part of the organisational system, and take it for granted that individuals are always ready and willing to learn practices and ideas that are best for the organisation. However, as Schein (1999) suggests, much individual learning in organisational settings can be merely that of coercive persuasion, in which learning new ways of working and participating in organisational change is not exactly a choice for an individual, as "not to learn means loss of job" (ibid. 171). Accordingly, social learning theories that perceive organisations as communities of practice might overlook the organisational hierarchies in the practical organisational learning situations, as well as ignore the effects of general societal asymmetries (Contu 2014). Thus, an analysis of how the seemingly shared ideas, meanings and practices are embedded in relations of power, and through which kind of processes they are made hegemonic in organisations is needed (Contu & Willmott 2003). Therefore, in each instance of analysing organisational learning, it is necessary to ask what role power plays in the learning process, and thus, engage with the politics of learning.

Methodological note

I draw from a series of research projects and long-term collaboration with development NGOs (see Table 1.1). Over the past 20 years I have participated in, observed or facilitated a considerable number of seminars and workshops conducted in, for or about NGOs in development. Although the topics and locations have varied from gender budgeting in Tanzania and north-south partnerships in Zambia to monitoring of empowerment in India, the events have, at least implicitly, revolved around organisational learning and change. My "workshopping" started in the early 1990s when I was affiliated with some Finnish voluntary organisations that later became the subjects of my PhD along with their Tanzanian partners (Kontinen 2007). It continued with my participation in a number of "capacity-building workshops" and my implementation of capacity-building needs assessments in Tanzania in the early 2000s when the idea of an "NGO" was mushrooming in the country. Later, as an organisational development expert in a Finnish umbrella organisation KEPA, I arranged and facilitated a number of training courses and designed and implemented OD initiatives such as *Towards Evaluation for Everyday Use* (2009–2010), where we worked with ten NGOs in improving their M&E approaches (Kontinen 2012; Kontinen & Onali 2017).

Table 1.1 A list of research projects and material used in this book

Project	*Research material*
NGO Quality Performance and Collaboration Improvement through Capacity Building (2001)	Participatory performance analysis in 11 small NGOs Two NGO workshops with 17 NGOs Morogoro, Tanzania
Towards Evaluation for Everyday Use (2009–2010)	OD workshops in ten Finnish NGOs (5–10 workshops in each organisation) Documents
Empowering Leadership in an International NGO (2012–2014)	OD workshops with World Vision Finland (n=8) Workshops with partners in Kenya and India, Individual interviews with both the Finnish staff and staff in the partner organisations in Kenya, Uganda, India, Sri Lanka and Peru (n=40) Documents
Counteracting Development Amnesia (2012–2015)	Organisational meetings with FINGO (n=3) Participation in five-day learning workshop with the field staff from different locations in 2014 Individual interviews with the Finnish staff (n=16) Individual interviews with field staff (n=12) Organisational meetings (n=5) in International Solidarity Foundation (ISF) Individual interviews with Finnish field staff in Uganda, Somaliland, and Nicaragua Annual plans, reports and memos

After returning to academia in 2010 as a postdoctoral researcher and later, a senior lecturer in an international Master's Degree Programme, I continued interacting – and at times, workshopping – with NGOs. Within the framework of two separate research projects, *Empowering Leadership in an International NGO* (2012–2014), and *Counteracting Development Amnesia* (2013–2015), I collaborated for varying periods of time with NGOs of different sizes and with different objectives. As part of the Empowering Leadership project, I was involved in co-design of an approach to monitor empowerment with World Vision Finland (Kontinen & Robinson-Moncada 2014). In Counteracting Development Amnesia, organisational learning and forgetting in two professional development NGOs were examined. The observations and arguments I present in this book are based on all these experiences, while particular case material analysed in different chapters illustrates specific arguments.

Each of these research projects had their own specific approach to learning and knowledge production. However, they all shared a principle according to which researchers, NGO staff, together with partner organisations when possible, co-produced knowledge in the course of a shared learning process.

In each organisation, we entered ongoing processes and, thus, did not initiate an adoption of a particular approach. Therefore, research projects were based on the conceptualisation of continuous rather than episodic organisational change in which researchers did not play a major role as change agents (Weick & Quinn 1999). Rather, we spent a certain period of time with NGOs, observing their learning and contributing to it through analysis and dialogue. For me, researching organisational learning meant merely seeing what people do, listening to how they interact, and tell about their work in interviews (Yanow 2000, 253). As a researcher, though, I was able to identify some repetitive patterns and, thus, to provide kind of "sideway perspective" while engaging in dialogue between theoretical literature and the practice (Yanow 2000).

It is obvious that in qualitative research an "objective" stance is impossible, and not a desired one. I have been part and parcel of the knowledge produced for the research projects. However, during the phase of analysis, I took some epistemic distance from the everyday life of the staff and engaged analytically with the material. The analysis was done from selected perspectives in organisational theory; it therefore does not cover the richness of the organisational life in its entirety. Naturally, people I have worked with or interviewed in the course of the research projects are not just neutral research material. They are human beings whose voices, smiles, ideas, frustrations and enthusiasm I remembered while making inferences from the material. For them, I would like to offer this book as an appreciation of their commitment, patience, enthusiasm and endurance in everyday life in organisations. In the chapters of the book I will give space for the voice of practitioners in the forms of direct quotes from discussions and interviews. In accordance to our agreements and consent forms, the names and exact positions of the individual interviewees are not revealed, if not otherwise agreed, in order to ensure anonymity, whereas most of the names of the organisations are provided. The individual interviewees are identified with running codes that facilitate reader's evaluation of the variety of respondents.

The contributions of the chapters

The main question addressed in this book is: What kinds of learning take place within development NGOs and in their interaction with their international institutional environment? Furthermore, I ask what the potential manifestations of unlearning, forgetting, and ignorance are in these instances. Each chapter discusses the everyday practice of NGOs from slightly different analytical perspective and is, therefore, more or less an independent contribution. I do not provide one comprehensive theoretical framework for organisational learning, forgetting and change. Rather, in the course of the book, I contribute to problematisation of these notions in order to trigger more empirical and theoretical research on the issues.

How to conceptualise learning in development NGOs? To answer this question Chapter 2 suggests a categorisation of learning in development. The categorisation draws, on the one hand, from Gregory Bateson's (1987/1964) logical categories of learning and, on the other, from a review of literature discussing learning in development. The chapter suggests an analytical distinction between four qualitatively different levels of learning, namely zero, I, II and III. It then identifies individuals, projects, partnerships, organisations and institutions as potential learners in development. On the basis of the categorisation presented, the chapter introduces the focus of learning in this book as change in organisational knowledge, practices and routines on the basis of an organisation's experience and interaction with its institutional environment of international development.

Chapter 3 embarks from the notion of learning as a search for shared organisational meaning (Cook & Yanow 1993). Shared meanings are essential for organisation. In order to be able to coordinate their actions, members of the organisation should use shared language and make sense of events and activities in a similar way. The chapter analyses organisational learning as a search for a shared meaning of empowerment in World Vision Finland and its partners in Kenya, Uganda, India and Sri Lanka in the context of organisational workshops. The chapter analyses scripts of NGO workshops and a variety of schemata of empowerment emerging in the organisational discussions. The chapter shows how institutionalised learning events tend to reinforce the organisational roles and meanings rather than provide spaces for their modification and critical reflection. It also illustrates how organisational schemata of empowerment include tensions between understanding empowerment as an intervention approach or an indigenous process, between the locus of empowerment in individuals or communities, and between empowerment being merely a change in structural power relations or an increase in individual strengths.

Chapter 4 continues to discuss organisational meanings but scrutinises organisational knowledge and organisational epistemology (Seirafi 2012). NGOs continuously produce, use and disseminate knowledge. At the same time, they continuously judge what counts as knowledge and what are the appropriate means for knowledge production in their particular organisation. The chapter analyses learning as a change in the organisational knowledge criteria, in other words organisational epistemology, in the context of one of the most institutionalised knowledge production practices of M&E. The chapter also analyses a learning trajectory in the International Solidarity Foundation when it developed a form of story-based monitoring in parallel with an indicator-based one. Chapter 4 shows how a change in organisational epistemology from initial ideas to institutionalised practice requires time, negotiation and experimentation. It discusses how introducing the story-based M&E method included negotiations in regard to the organisational goals, structure and different methodological questions such as trustworthiness and conceptualising change, and further, struggled to align with the existing institutional knowledge criteria.

Chapter 5 acknowledges that organisations do not only learn, they also unlearn, forget, and leave certain things in the sphere of organisational ignorance (Martin de Holan & Phillips 2011; Roberts 2012). Inspired by the claims that NGOs have a particular tendency to forget and be unable to learn from their past (Lewis 2016), the chapter introduces the notions of organisational forgetting and ignorance and provides illustrative empirical examples of their occurrence. It identifies personnel turnover, an activist culture and accountability as elements contributing to organisational forgetting, and shows how organisational memory systems and their use as well as internal power relations and organisational identity play roles especially in forgetting how to be a global organisation. It also shows how NGO ignorance is constructed vis-á-vis uncertainty in development, unpleasant issues and everyday practice in the field. The chapter argues that organisational forgetting and ignorance support learning at level I rather than critical reflection and change of the strategies and assumptions and, thus, contribute to reproduction of the institutional features of development.

A more institutional perspective is provided in Chapter 6 (Alasuutari & Qadir 2014; Alasuutari 2015; Meyer et al. 2006). Organisations can learn in order to be more effective and to critically reflect upon their strategies, but they also change in order to be legitimate, and "real NGOs". The chapter analyses learning in development NGOs as legitimation vis-á-vis the international institutional field of development NGOs. Further, the chapter pays attention to learning to be a modern organisation in general. The chapter first argues that learning in development NGOs is not simply a case of adaptation to isomorphic pressures, but involves editing, translating and synchronising these trends with other ongoing processes internal or external to organisations. First, drawing from an example of improving monitoring and evaluation in a number of different Finnish NGOs, the chapter argues that M&E learning included synchronisation of activities internal to organisations, and those of partner organisations, and, finally, attempts to be a better organisation. Similar processes of learning to be a modern organisation with established visions, goals and means of measurement are also illustrated by an example of "learning to be an NGO" in small Tanzanian organisations in early 2000 in which the emerging model of "NGO" intertwined with other forms of organising.

The concluding Chapter 7 brings together key lessons. It presents three messages for further investigation of learning in development NGOs. First, it argues for taking into account the many faces of learning and forgetting, and for paying special attention to gradual learning in everyday organisational life. Second, it suggests combining different faces of learning with the key dilemma of balancing between organisational control and contextual flexibility in development management. Third, it proposes to understand learning as political and intertwined with different power relations. In the end, the chapter suggests that the categorisation of learning provided in the book could be applied and further developed to investigate learning also among so-called NGO beneficiaries – citizens – in an attempt to contribute to the debates concerning incremental and transformative change and the role of learning in active citizenship in these.

References

Alasuutari, P. (2015) The discoursive side of new institutionalism. *Cultural Sociology*, 9(2), 162–184.1–23.

Alasuutari, P. & Qadir, A. (eds) (2014) *National Policy-Making: Domestication of Global Trends*. London: Routledge.

Argyris, C. & Schön, D. (1974) *Organizational Learning: A Theory of Action Perspective*. Reading: Addison-Wesley.

Banks, N., Hulme, D. & Edwards, M. (2015) NGOs, states, and donors revisited: Still too close for comfort? *World Development*, 66, 707–718.

Bateson, G. (1987/1964) The logical categories of learning and communication. In: Bateson, G. *Steps to an Ecology of Mind*. New Jersey: Jason Aronson Inc.

Blau, P.M. & Scott, R.W. (1962) *Formal Organization. A Comparative Approach*. Stanford, CA: Stanford University Press.

Biggs, S. & Smith, S. (2003) A paradox of learning in project cycle management and the role of organisational culture. *World Development*, 31(10), 1743–1757.

Billis, D. (ed.) (2010) *Hybrid Organisations and the Third Sector. Challenges for Practice, Theory and Policy*. London: Palgrave.

Britton, B. (1998) *The Learning NGO*. Occasional papers series no 17. UK: INTRAC.

Britton, B. (2005) *Organisational Learning in NGOs: Creating the Motive, Means, and Opportunity* Praxis Paper No 3. UK: INTRAC.

Britton, B. (2012) Barefoot Guide 2: Learning practices in organisations and social change. *Development in Practice*, 22(3), 427–429.

Brown, H. & Green, M. (2015) At the service of community development: The professionalization of volunteer work in Kenya and Tanzania. *African Studies Review*, 58(2), 63–84.

Carlsson, J. & Wolgemuth, L. (eds) (2000) *Learning in Development Co-operation*. Expert Group on Development Issues (EGDI) Studies 2000:2. Stockholm: Ministry of Foreign Affairs.

Choudry, A. & Kapoor, D. (2013) *NGOization. Complicity, Contradictions and Prospects*. London: Zed Books.

Claeyé, F. & Jackson, T. (2012) The iron cage re-revisited: Institutional isomorphism in nonprofit organisations in South. *Journal of International Development*, 24(5), 602–622.

Contu, A. (2014) On boundaries and difference: Communities of practice and power relations in creative work. *Management Learning*, 45(3), 289–316.

Contu, A. & Girei, E. (2016) NGOs management and the value of "partnerships" for equality in international development: What's in a name? *Human Relations*, 67(2), 205–232.

Contu, A. & Willmott, H. (2003) Re-embedding situatedness: The importance of power relations in learning theory. *Organization Science*, 14(3), 283–296.

Cook, S.D.N. & Yanow, D. (1993) Culture and organizational learning. *Journal of Management Inquiry*, 2(4), 373–390 373–390.

Cooke, B. (2008) Participatory management as colonial administration. In: Dar, S. & Cooke, B. (eds), *The New Development Management*. London: Zed Books, 111–128.

Cooke, B & Dar, S. (2008) Introduction: The new development management. In: Dar, S. & Cooke, B. (eds), *The New Development Management*. London: Zed Books, 1–17.

Cornwall, A. (2007) Buzzwords and fuzzwords: Deconstructing development discourse. *Development in Practice*, 17(4/5), 471–484.

Crewe, E. & Harrison, E. (1998) *Whose Development? An Ethnography of Aid.* London: Zed Books.

Dar, S. (2014) Hybrid accountabilities: When western and non-western accountabilities collide. *Human Relations*, 67(2), 131–151.

Dar, S. & Cooke, B. (eds) (2008) *The New Development Management*. London: Zed Books.

David, R., Mancini, A. & Guijt, I. (2006) Bringing systems in line with values: The practice of the accountability, learning and planning system (ALPS). In: Eyben, R. (ed.) *Relationships for Aid.* London: Earthscan, 133–153.

DFID – Department for International Development (2010) *The Politics of Poverty: Elites, Citizens, and States. Findings from 10-year of DFID funded research on governance and fragile states*. A synthesis paper. https://www.gov.uk/government/case-studies/dfid-research-the-politics-of-poverty. Accessed 13.12.2016.

DiMaggio, P.J. & Powell, W.W. (1983) The iron cage revisited: Institutional isomorphism and collective rationality in institutional fields. *Annual Review of Sociology*, 16, 137–159.

Ebrahim, A. (2003) *NGOs and Organizational Change. Discourse, Reporting, and Learning.* Cambridge: Cambridge University Press.

Edwards, M. (1997) Organizational learning in non-governmental organizations: What have we learned? *Public Administration and Development*, 17(2), 235–250.

Edwards, M. (2004) *Civil Society*. Cornwall: Polity.

Edwards, M. & Fowler, A. (2002) *NGO Management*. London: Earthscan.

Edwards, M. & Hulme, D. (eds) (1995) *Non-Governmental Organisations – Performance and Accountability. Beyond the Magic Bullet*. London: Earthscan.

Englund, H. (2006) *Prisoners of Freedom. Human Rights and the African Poor*. Berkeley, CA: The University of California Press.

Eriksson Baaz, M. (2005) *The Paternalism of Partnership: A Postcolonial Reading of Identity in Development Aid.* London: Zed Books.

Escobar, A. (1995) *Encountering Development. The Making and Unmaking of the Third World.* Princeton, NJ: Princeton University Press.

Eyben, R. (2006) *Relationships for Aid.* London: Earthscan.

Fejerskov, M.A. (2016) Understanding the nature of change: How institutional perspectives can inform contemporary studies of development cooperation. *Third World Quarterly*, 37(12), 2176–2191.

Feldman, M.S. & Orlikowski, W.J. (2011) Theorizing practice and practicing theory. *Organization Science*, 22(5), 1240–1253.

Ferguson, J. (1994) *The Anti-Politics Machine. Development, Depoliticization, and Bureaucratic power in Lesotho*. Minneapolis: University of Minneapolis Press.

Ferguson, J., Huysman, M. & Soekijad, M (2010) Knowledge management in practice: Pitfalls and potentials for development. *World Development*, 38(12), 1797–1810.

Foucault, M. (1991) *Discipline and Punish: The Birth of a Prison*. London: Penguin.

Fowler, A. (1997) *Striking a Balance: A Guide to Enhancing the Effectiveness of Non-Governmental Organisations in Development*. London: Earthscan.

Fowler, A. (1998) Authentic NGDO partnership in the new policy agenda for international aid: Dead end or light ahead? *Development and Change*, 29(1), 137–159.

Fowler, A. (2000) *The Virtuous Spiral. A Guide to Sustainability for NGOs in International Development.* London: Earthscan.

Fowler, A. & Malunga, C.V. (eds) (2010) *NGO Management: The Earthscan Companion.* London: Earthscan.

Gherardi, S. (2000) Practice-based theorizing on learning and knowing in organisations. *Organization*, 7(2), 211–223.

Gherardi, S., Nicoloni, D. & Odella, F. (1998) Towards social understanding of how people learn in organisations: The notion of situated curriculum. *Management Learning*, 29(3), 273–297.

Girei, E. (2016) NGOs, management and development: Harnessing counter-hegemonic possibilities, *Organization Studies*, 37(2), 193–212.

Gramsci, A. (1971) *Selection from the Prison Notebooks.* Edited and translated by Hoare Q. & Smith, G.N. London: Lawrence and Wishart.

Green, M. (2012) Framing and Escaping. Contrasting aspects of knowledge work in international development and anthropology. In: Venkatesan, S. & Yarrow, T. (eds) *Differentiating Development. Beyond and Anthropology of Critique.* New York: Bergham Books.

Greenwood, R., Oliver, C., Lawrence, T.B. & Meyer, R.E. (eds) (2017) *The Sage Handbook of Organizational Institutionalism.* Los Angeles, CA: SAGE.

Greenwood, R., Oliver, C., Sahlin, K. & Suddaby, R. (eds) (2008) *The Sage Handbook of Organizational Institutionalism.* Los Angeles, CA: SAGE.

Groves, L. & Hinton, R. (eds) (2004). *Inclusive Aid: Changing Power and Relationships in International Development.* London, UK: Earthscan.

Guijt, I. & Roche, C. (2014) Does impact evaluation in development matter? Well, it depends what it's for! *The European Journal of Development Research*, 26(1), 46–54.

Guljarani, N. (2010) New vistas for development management: Examining radical-reformist possibilities and potential. *Public Administration and Development*, 30(2), 136–148.

Hailey, J. & James, R. (2002) Learning leaders: The key to learning organizations. *Development in Practice*, 12 (3–4), 398–405.

Hayman, R., King, S., Kontinen, T. & Narayanaswamy, L. (eds) (2016) *Negotiating Knowledge: Evidence and Experience in Development NGOs.* Rugby: Practical Action Publishing.

Hickey, S. (2009) The return of politics in development studies (II): Capturing the political? *Progress in Development Studies*, 9(2), 141–152.

Hillhorst, D. (2003) *The Real World of NGOs. Discourse, Diversity and Development.* London: Zed Books.

Horton, K. (2010) The epistemic problem: potential solutions. In: Horton, K. and Roche, C. (eds) *Ethical Questions and International NGOs. An Exchange between Philosophers and NGOs.* Dordrecht: Springer.

Howell, J. & Pearce, J. (2002) *Civil Society and Development.* Boulder, CO/London: Lynne Rienner.

Hulme, D. & Edwards, M. (eds) (1997) *NGOs, States and Donors. Too Close for Comfort?* New York: Save the Children and MacMillan Press.

Igoe, J. (2003) Scaling up civil society: Donor, money, NGOs and the pastoralist land rights movement in Tanzania. *Development and Change*, 34(5), 863–885.

Johnson, H. & Wilson, G. (2009) *Learning for Development.* London: Zed Books.

Kabeer, N. (1999) Resources, agency, achievements: Reflections on the measurement of women's empowerment. *Development and Change*, 30(3), 435–464.

King, K. & McGrath, S. (2004) *Knowledge for Development. Comparing British, Japanese, Swedish and World Bank aid.* Cape Town/London: HSRC Press and Zed Books.

Kontinen, T. (2007) *Learning Challenges of NGOs in Development: Co-operation of Finnish NGOs in Morogoro, Tanzania*. Helsinki: Helsinki University Press.

Kontinen, T. (2012) *Towards Evaluation for Everyday Use. Helsinki: Service Center for Development Co-Operation KEPA*, KEPA's report series 117.

Kontinen, T. & Onali, A. (2017) Strengthening institutional isomorphism in development NGOs? Program mechanisms in an organisational intervention. *Sage Open*, 7 (1).

Kontinen, T. & Robinson-Moncada, S. (2014). *Towards New Practices of Monitoring in World Vision Finland: Pathways Of Empowerment.* Helsinki: Publications of World Vision Finland 1.

Kühl, S. (2009) Capacity development as the model for development. Aid organizations. *Development and Change*, 40(3), 551–577.

Lazar, S. (2012) Citizenship quality: A new agenda for development? *Journal of Civil Society*, 8(4), 333–350.

Lewis, D. (2002) Civil society in African contexts: Reflections on the usefulness of a Concept. *Development and Change*, 33(4), 596–586.

Lewis, D. (2003) Theorizing the organisation and management of non-governmental development organisations. Towards a composite approach. *Public Management Review*, 5(3), 325–344.

Lewis, D. (2007) The future of NGO research in development studies. In Opuku-Mensah, P., Lewis, D. & Tvedt, T. (eds) *Reconceptualising NGOs and their Roles in Development: NGOs, Civil Society and the International Aid System*. Aalborg: Aalborg University Press, 363–381.

Lewis, D. (2008) Nongovernmentalism and the reorganisation of public action. In: Dar, S. & Cooke, B. (eds) *The New Development Management*. London: Zed Books, 41–55.

Lewis, D. (2009) International development and the "perpetual present": Anthropological approaches to the rehistoricisation of policy. *European Journal of Development Research*, 21(1), 32–46.

Lewis, D. (2014) *Non-Governmental Organisations, Management and Development.* Third edition. London: Routledge.

Lewis, D. (2016) Abandoned pasts, disappearing futures: Further reflections on multiple temporalities in studying non-governmental organisation worlds. *Critique of Anthropology*, 36(1), 84–92.

Lewis, D. & Schuller, M. (2017) Engagements with a productively unstable category. Anthropologists and nongovernmental organisations. *Current Anthropology*, 58(5), 634–651.

Lister, S. (2000) Power in partnerships? An analysis of NGO's relationship with its partners. *Journal of International Development*, 12(2), 227–239.

Lister, S. (2003) NGO legitimacy: Technical issue or social construct? *Critique of Anthropology*, 23(2), 175–192.

Martin de Holan, P. & Phillips, N. (2011) Organizational forgetting. In: Easterby-Smith, M. & Lyles, M.A. (eds) *Handbook of Organizational Learning and Knowledge Management*. Chichester: John Wiley and Sons, 433–452.

Matturi, K. (2016) Progress towards knowledge sharing in an NGO. In Hayman, R., King, S. Kontinen, T. & Narayanaswamy, L. (eds) *Negotiating Knowledge: Evidence and Experience in Development NGOs.* Rugby: Practical Action, 93–110.

McFarlane, C. (2006) Knowledge, learning and development: A post-rationalist approach. *Progress in Development Studies*, 6(4), 287–305.

Mercer, C. (2002) The discourse of *maendeleo* and the politics of women's participation on Mount Kilimanjaro. *Development and Change*, 33(1), 101–127.

Meyer, J.W. & Rowan, B. (1977) Institutional organizations: formal structure as myth and ceremony. *American Journal of Sociology*, 83, 340–63.

Meyer, J.W., Drori, G.S. & Hwang, H. (2006) World society and the proliferation of formal organisation. In: Drori, G.S., Meyer, J.W. & Hwang, H. (2006) *Globalization and Organization: World Society and Organizational Change.* Oxford: Oxford University Press, 25–49.

Mitlin, D., Hickey, S. & Bebbington, A. (2007). Reclaiming development? NGOs and the challenge of alternatives. *World Development*, 35(10), 1699–1720.

Morgan, G. (1986) *Images of Organization*. Thousand Oaks, CA: SAGE.

Mosse, D. (ed.) (2011) *Adventures in Aidland: The Anthropology of Professionals in International Development.* New York: Berghahn Books.

Mougeout, L.J.A. (ed.) (2017) *Putting Knowledge to Work: Collaborating, Influencing and Learning for International Development*. Rugby: Practical Action Publishing.

Mueller-Hirth, N. (2012) If you don't count, you don't count: Monitoring and evaluation in South African NGOs. *Development and Change*, 43(3), 649–670.

Olivier de Sardan, J.-P. (1995) *Anthropology and Development. Understanding Contemporary Social Change.* London: Zed Books.

Orlikowski, W.J. (2002) Knowing in practice: Enacting a collective capability in distributed organizing. *Organization Science*, 13(3), 249–273.

Pfeffer, J. & Salancik, G.R. (1978) *The External Control of Organization. A Resource Dependence Perspective.* New York: Harper & Row.

Powell, M. (2006) Which knowledge? Whose reality? An overview of knowledge used in development sector. *Development in Practice*, 16(6), 518–32.

Powell, W.W. & Colyvas, J.A. (2008). Microfoundations of institutional theory. In: Greenwood, R., Oliver, C., Suddaby, R. & Sahlin-Andersson, K. (eds) (2008). *The Sage Handbook of Organizational Institutionalism.* London: SAGE.

Powell, W.W. & Rerup, C. (2017) Opening the black box: The microfoundations of institutions. In: Greenwood, R., Oliver, C., Lawrence, T.B. & Meyer, R.E. (eds) *The Sage Handbook of Organizational Institutionalism.* Los Angeles, CA: SAGE.

Riles, A. (2001) *The Network Inside Out*. Ann Arbor, MI: The University of Michigan Press.

Roberts, J. (2012) Organisational ignorance: Towards a managerial perspective on the unknown. *Management Learning*, 44(3), 215–236.

Roberts, S.M. Jones, J.P. & Fröling, O. (2005) NGOs and the globalization of managerialism: A research framework. *World Development*, 33(11), 1845–1864.

Ronalds, P.D. (2010) *The Change Imperative. Creating the Next Generation of NGOs.* Sterling: Kumarian Press.

Roper, L. & Pettit, J. (2002) Development and the learning organisation: An introduction. *Development in Practice*, 12(3–4), 258–271.

Schein, E.H. (1999) Empowerment, coercive persuasion and organizational learning: Do they connect? *The Learning Organization*, 6(4), 163–172.

Scott, R.W. (2008) Approaching adulthood: The maturing of institutional theory. *Theory and Society*, 37(5), 427–442.
Scott, R.W. (2014) *Institutions and Organizations*. Thousand Oaks, CA: SAGE.
Seirafi, K. (2012) *Organizational Epistemology. Understanding Knowledge in Organizations*. Berlin: Springer.
Senge, P. (1990) *The Fifth Discipline: The Art and Practice of the Learning Organisation*. New York: Doubleday.
Smillie, I. (1995) *The Alms Bazaar. Altruism Under Fire – Non-profit Organisations and International Development*. London: Intermediate Technology Publications.
Thomas, A. (1996) What is development management? *Journal of International Development*, 8(1), 95–110.
Thomas, A. (2000) What makes good development management? In T. Wallace (ed.) *Development and Management*. Oxford: Oxfam, 40–52.
Tsoukas, H. (2005) *Complex Knowledge: Studies in Organizational Epistemology*. Oxford: Oxford University.
Tsoukas, H. & Vladimirou, E. (2001) What is organizational knowledge? *Journal of Management Studies*, 38 (7), 973–993.
Tvedt, T. (1998) *Angels of Mercy or Development Diplomats? NGDOs and Foreign Aid*. Oxford: Africa World Press.
Tvedt, T. (2002) Development NGOs: Actors in a global civil society or in a new international social system. *Voluntas: International Journal of Voluntary and Nonprofit Organizations*, 13(4), 363–375.
Tvedt, T. (2006) The international aid system and the non-governmental organizations: A new research agenda. *Journal of International Development*, 18(5), 677–690.
Wallace, T. with Bornstein, L. & Chapman, J. (2006) *The Aid Chain. Coercion and Commitment in Development NGOs*. London: Intermediate Technology Publications.
Watkins, S.C., Swidler, A. & Hannan, T. (2012) Outsourcing social transformation: Development NGOs as organizations. *Annual Review of Sociology*, 38(1), 285–315.
Weick, K.E. (2001) *Making Sense of the Organization*. Oxford: Blackwell.
Weick, K.E. (2009) *Making Sense of the Organization. Volume 2*. Chichester: Wiley.
Weick, K.E. & Quinn, R.E. (1999). Organizational change and development. *Annual Review of Psychology*, 50(1), 361–386.
Yanow, D. (2000) Seeing organizational learning: A "Cultural view". *Organization*, 7(2), 247–268.

2 Categorising learning in development

Towards organisational institutionalism

There is a lot of talk about learning among development practitioners, and a great number of learning theories circulating in academic literature of different disciplines. Commissioned reviews and guidelines promote dialogue between these two. The main question is: How to conceptualise learning in development NGOs? In this chapter, I will tease out a variety of answers to this question as discussed in development in general, and development NGOs in particular. First, I will develop a categorisation of learning in development, and second, I will further discuss the organisational and institutional learning perspectives that are the overall theoretical focus of this book.

In order to produce categorisation, I ask two questions: How does learning take place; and who is supposed to learn? In order to be able to reflect on the *how* question, I use heuristics from the classical categorisation of learning provided by Gregory Bateson (1987/1962). He distinguishes different levels (zero, I, II and III) of learning on the basis of qualitative difference in the learning processes. The *who* question is answered on the basis of a review of literature on learning in development. I identify different agents of learning including individual, project, partnership, organisation and institution. I then combine the proposed levels of learning with the identified agents of learning into a categorisation and provide illustrative examples of practice of learning in different categories. Since it is impossible to examine learning from all suggested perspectives, I further elaborate upon the debates focusing on organisational and institutional learning that form the overall theoretical background for the following chapters.

Levels of learning: how does learning take place?

The notion of levels of learning in this context means qualitatively different forms of learning. It is, thus, distinct from the levels typically associated with spaces such as "local" or "global". The levels of learning, therefore, are different answers to the question of how learning takes place. This categorisation is drawn from the classical theory of logical types of the concept of learning proposed by Gregory Bateson (1987/1962), which has been further developed, for example, in the organisational learning literature (Argyris & Schön 1978). Bateson (ibid.) reminds us that the logical categories differ from the world of phenomena; that is learning in practice. Therefore, none of the proposed levels of learning take place as a "pure form" in real-life situations. However, the logical categories can be used heuristically to analyse learning. Bateson argues that learning always implies some kind of change and thus, the logical categories of learning can be distinguished on the basis of the kinds of change they denote. Moreover, he suggests that each type of learning implies reacting to some kind of error. Thus, qualitatively different types of learning can also be distinguished on the basis of what kinds of errors they address. Overall, on the basis of the nature of change implied and the characteristics of errors addressed, Bateson categorises learning into zero learning, learning I, learning II and learning III. Bateson's categorisation is based on a view of a system or organism responding to its environment in qualitatively different ways. Such an idea of learning being an organism's reaction to its environment is restricted in a way, but still provides a basis for reflecting on different categories of learning.

The lowest level, *zero learning*, refers to a minimal change, like a routine reaction to a certain stimulus (Bateson, ibid.). In everyday life, zero learning can be understood to take place in instances, where same information is continuously received from a similar external event, and it evokes every time quite stereotyped responses with no need reflection for. Bateson provides an example from his era; a factory whistle at the end of a working day. Today we could think of the relation between pushing the stop button and the illumination of the stop sign on the bus, or the ping sound from our laptop informing us of an email received. We react to these events in a routine way. As long as the sign is turned on and the bus stops after pushing the button, or new email is found in our inbox after the ping sound, no specific attention is given to the event. Consequently, not much learning takes place. When the usual response follows to a specific stimulus, there is no need to correct any mistakes, or change our behaviour. However, when the routine way of acting is disturbed, when the bus does not stop despite pushing a button, or there is no new email in the inbox after the sound, a new kind of learning might start. Often, we tend to dismiss learning zero as something undesirable and as a sign of stagnation. However, when analysing empirical realities, we should also recognise the importance of not changing, and the significance of the unconscious skills, routines, and performances (Tosey et al. 2011, 298). Without these continuous flows of routine action, the everyday life of individuals (or organisations, for that matter) would be impossible.

While zero learning implies no need for correction, as there has not been an error in choice or reaction, the level of *learning I* refers to change in the "specificity of the response by correction of errors of choice within a set of alternatives" (Bateson, ibid.). In other words, the notion of learning I means learning in which a learner has to make a choice between an unchanged set of alternatives. Through learning, a learner revises the choice between these alternatives. In organisational learning literature, the notion of learning I has inspired the idea of single-loop learning (Argyson & Schön 1978), or first-level learning that implies learning to perform a given task better through making better choices, for example, concerning the means and tools of task performance. Thus, single-loop learning in organisations is primarily concerned with effectiveness. It addresses the challenges of how to best achieve the existing goals, and its results are evaluated vis-á-vis existing norms and measures of performance (Argyris and Schön 1978, 22). Most activities, either individual or organisational, entail single-loop learning as it helps to get the work done, in a better and more effective way. Learning I is also encouraged when complex tasks or goals are decomposed into simpler tasks. The correct way of carrying out the individual, simple tasks and their results can be easily identified, notwithstanding the complexity of the entire task (Argyris 1999, 69).

Consequently, *learning II* refers to revision, not of the choice, but the set of alternatives from which the choice is made (Bateson, ibid.). Learning II can also be called *learning to learn*, as it refers to the "change in the process of learning I". Bateson (ibid.) argues that while learning II includes a change in the set of alternatives, it can also refer to "changes in the manner in which the stream of action and experience is segmented or punctuated into contexts together with changes in the use of context markers". In practice, this kind of punctuation can refer to the ways in which events, interaction, and relationships are understood on the basis of a kind of tacit agreement between the persons involved. This agreement includes shared, although implicit, understanding of the situation, the expected roles and the contextual frame. When these understandings are changed, learning II takes place. In organisational learning literature, learning II has been the basis for the notion of double-loop learning (Argyris & Schön 1978). Double-loop learning refers to learning where organisations do not only learn to do things better, but learn to do "better" things. In practice, learning II in an organisation includes reflection on organisational values, assumptions and goals, and the consequent change in them. The outcomes of learning II cannot be measured by the existing norms and measures of performance, as these are questioned and changed within the same process.

In the same vein, *learning III* refers to change in the process of learning II. Learning III includes a "corrective change in the system of set of alternatives from which the choice is made". Bateson (ibid.) argues that learning III is rare. At the individual level, such learning can occur in psychotherapy, or religious conversion. Learning III includes confrontation with old premises. Such confrontation can be made through exaggerating or making caricatures of the old premises in a process of changing these fundamental elements of identity. According to Bateson (ibid.), learning III requires receiving freedom from the bondage of habits, and implies a profound redefinition of the self. As selfhood develops throughout a lifetime, it can be seen as a product or aggregate of learning II that has taken place over an extended time-span. Therefore, in learning III this established "self" will become almost irrelevant, and that makes learning III challenging. (Bateson, ibid.).

Even if in the original account of Bateson, learning III is rare, in organisational learning literature the notion of triple-loop learning has gained currency. This idea builds on Argyris and Schön's single- and double-loop learning, and refers to change in entire organisational paradigms and epistemologies. Especially in some consultancy approaches, triple-loop learning is considered a desired goal for any organisation. However, this prioritisation has been criticised for providing "utopian solutions" (Tosey et al. 2011, 298–301), as in many organisational situations, zero learning and learning I would actually suffice to enable greater use of existing competencies (ibid. 303). Bateson's category of learning III, taken seriously, involves high risks since individual selves and organisational identities should be abandoned and totally transformed in the process of learning (Tosey et al. 2011, 298–304).

The above categorisation provides conceptual tools for understanding types of learning that are qualitatively different from each other. Moreover, each type of learning can be undertaken by different actors. Next, I will discuss the different ideas of who these actors could be, and thus, seek answers to the question of *who* is learning in development.

Agents of learning in development

In his classical article, Bateson (1987/1964) discussed both animals and human beings as agents of learning in both laboratory and real-life contexts. In this book, my focus is on human beings and organisations in real life. Much learning literature focuses on the learning of individuals or organisations. In development literature, learning projects and partnerships have also been discussed. Furthermore, I suggest that there is a need to discuss institutional learning. In what follows, I will depict in more detail the different agents of learning relevant to learning theories and development literature.

Most psychological learning theories address individual learning. Learning in psychology and the educational sciences revolves around issues such as individual cognition, attitudes, world views and reflection. As illustrative examples, learning in classical theories can refer to change in cognitive schemata (Piaget & Cook 1952), or to change in action on the basis of reflection on experience (Kolb 1984). Moreover, the theories of expertise have emphasised a change in the learning practices of individuals from reflection-on-action to reflection-in-action. The latter refers to a competence of an expert to use knowledge flexibly, to learn while doing and to adjust it to different situations in their professional conduct (Schön 1987). Some learning theories that focus on human cognition subscribe to a methodological individualism, while others are preoccupied with distributed cognition and situated learning (Brown et al. 1989; Salomon 1997). Social learning theories emphasise how individual learning always takes place in interaction with social and material environments (John-Steiner & Mahn 1996; Vygostky 1978) or through trajectories of participation in communities (Lave & Wenger 1991) or activity systems (Engeström 2001).

Social theories of learning are relevant for the purposes of this book as they locate individual learning within a certain institutional practice – in this case international development – rather than provide an abstract and universal theory of individual learning. For example, the theory of learning as a process of legitimate peripheral participation in communities is useful (Lave & Wenger 1991). It argues that individual learning takes place in the course of participation in communities of practice. An individual who enters international development for the first time – for instance, a volunteer in an NGO – gradually learns the meanings and practices relevant to the development community through taking part in the practices. Although in many communities of practice learning the "tricks of the trade" are seen to increase individual competence and help one move from the status of a novice to that of an expert, in development this kind of learning creates contradictory reactions. While individuals willing to work in development often have strong commitment, values and worldviews in regard to participating in doing good, after entering the field of international development their learning tends to be geared towards management systems and use of expected buzzwords, which might be in contradiction to their overall value commitments to fight for global equality and solidarity (Edwards 1997; Fowler 2000). Interestingly, while many of the practitioners in NGOs consider learning about project management tools and approaches to be desired learning outcomes, many accounts in development literature would rather consider individual learning as a potential trigger for change of these same practices. For example, the "self-reflexivity" of practitioners (Eyben 2006), and a change in "personal practices of individual actors" have been proposed in order to improve the complex system of development with its mainstream management practices and the power relations typical to development (Groves and Hinton 2004, 14–16).

Therefore, in development literature, individual learning is often discussed in relation to the wider contexts. Agency has on occasions been attributed to projects; the main form of action in international development. Projects do not possess agency, but the long-lasting debate between development projects as rigid blueprints or as learning processes often speaks of "learning projects" and, thus, construct them as some kind of agents of learning (Upphoff 1996). A learning project includes flexibility, collection of feedback from stakeholders, and modification of project goals and activities accordingly. The learning projects are experiments and adaptive processes, and kind of antidotes to rigid rationalistic planning and implementation (Rondinelli 1993). While the discussion critical of project blueprints and rational planning started almost three decades ago, surprisingly little has happened to the project formats used. Many learning elements have been included in project plans, and project cycles are depicted as learning processes.

However, at the outset, many development institutions and organisations still tend to use project tools and models that are variations of the logical framework approach. These approaches and their attached accountability rules tend to guide implementation of the designed plan rather than flexible experimentation.

Closely related to learning projects is the idea of learning partnerships. A particular kind of collaboration relationship labelled as a partnership between actors from the global south and north involved in development has been part of the development vocabulary for a long time (Brinkerhoff 2002; Fowler 1998). One of its characteristics has been that mutual learning should challenge the traditional idea of knowledge and expertise transferred from the "developed" northern actors to the "developing" recipients. Moreover, development literature discussing learning in relationships emphasises how the traditional power relations embedded in development should especially be subject to reflection and change (Eyben 2006). Development partnerships include negotiations between actors that have different interests, values and goals (Long 2001), and cooperative relationships in development always have to deal with the historically formed asymmetries related to funding relationships (Wallace 2006). Therefore, real learning partnerships are those in which these differences are acknowledged rather than those based on a superficial assumption of joint objectives and shared meanings. In learning partnerships, the differences are valued and deliberated upon rather than being hidden (Johnson & Wilson 2009, 130). Reflection and reflexivity, performed by the professionals or organisations involved, have been considered as essential for learning partnerships (Pasteur 2006, 21). Reflection aims to promote profound dialogues and identification of new collaborative ways of working. Critical reflection should address, for example, the power relations, changes in the rules and procedures leading to a more equal partnership, and the need to use new words and meanings to facilitate real dialogue (Chambers & Pettit 2004, 138).

Obviously, organisations, both in the global north and south have been considered central agents of learning. In the late 1990s, OD and organisational capacity building became central approaches in NGO development cooperation (Ubels et al. 2010). These approaches stressed that in addition to learning from the beneficiaries about their ideas and needs, learning in development should also entail the goal of becoming a better organisation. The general literature on organisational learning and learning organisation has informed the analysis and promotion of learning in development NGOs. (Britton 1998, 2002, 2005; Chambers & Pettit 2004; Ebrahim 2003; Edwards 1997; Krohwinkel-Karlsson 2007; Pasteur 2006). Organisational learning in development has been attached to both increasing effectiveness and undertaking self-reflection. It has also referred to both increased flexibility, including learning with the beneficiaries, and learning of different fashions and fads due to external pressures and funding requirements (Britton 2005; Edwards

1997). The theoretical approaches to organisational learning in development research have included, among others, experiential learning (Fowler 2000; Kolb 1984), learning as deliberation inspired by Habermasian notion of communicative action (Johnson & Wilson 2009), and single- and double-loop learning (Argyris & Schön 1978; Ebrahim 2003).

Organisational and institutional learning have sometimes been used as synonyms in development literature (Edwards 1997, 235; Whatley 2013). For the purposes of this book, however, I distinguish between an organisation and an institution as agents of learning. Institution refers to a larger, historically evolved constellation of organisations, practices, funding systems and rules. In international development this constellation has been named, for instance, the aid industry (De Haan 2009), the developmentalist configuration (Oliver de Sardan 2005), the development discourse (Escobar 1995) or the international system or organisational field (Tvedt 1998, 2002, 2006). The proposals for learning and change concerning these constellations have been articulated from at least two perspectives. On the one hand, development has taken pride in being a knowledge-based institution that uses knowledge to draw lessons from its experiences in order to carry out better development in future (King & McGrath 2004; Powell 2006). On the other hand, the critical literature that seeks to have alternative development or alternatives to development, would like to see development as a "collective learning experience" in order to change existing norms, ideologies and institutions (Nederveen Pieterse 2001, 159–163). In this book, I refer to this wider constellation as an institution as defined in organisational institutionalism (Greenwood et al. 2017). Development NGOs are understood as members of the international organisational field characterised by particular flows of money and certain terminologies and practices (Tvedt 1998), including institutionalised learning practices.

Institutional learning mechanisms include those embedded in the project management cycle such as monitoring and evaluation, and knowledge-management systems used by institutions in general. Learning can also refer to changes in the institutional goals and approaches. The pace of institutional learning is slow, and it is not necessarily very clear or well-defined. For development NGOs the institutional shifts from service-delivery to more advocacy-oriented, or from needs-based to rights-based approaches, have been influential. Additionally, in the institutional constellation of international development, the policy shift in 2015 from the Millennium Development Goals to Sustainable Development Goals, represented a change in the institutional thinking – or at least rhetoric – towards addressing the root causes of poverty and equality everywhere in the world, and not just in the so-called southern hemisphere. This shift was depicted as a turn towards transformative development, and the Agenda2030 with a subtitle of "Transforming our World" articulates ambitious goals for sustainable transformations

Learning and transformation

How could we, then, connect the notions of learning and transformation? In the Agenda2030, transformative development refers to addressing the root causes of economic, social, political and environmental inequalities. Transformation is, thus, related to alteration in a more fundamental way than a simple change. The debates on differences between change and transformation are many. For example, in civil society and development literature, a distinction between incremental and transformative change is common (Hickey & Mohan 2004; Mitlin et al. 2007). The normative suggestion is for civil society to be an agent of transformative rather than incremental change. In this argument, transformative change refers to shifts in societal power relations, and is therefore considered a more fundamental exercise than incremental improvements within the existing social orders.

Thus, transformative development should require specific kinds of learning by individuals, organisations and institutions. In reference to Bateson's levels of learning, transformative learning resonates with learning III. For example, in the context of learning sustainable development, Sterling (2010, 23) proposes that while leaning I is about doing things better and is concerned with efficiency and effectiveness, and learning II is concerned with doing better things and to question existing purposes, values assumptions, learning III is learning that "facilitates a fundamental recognition of a paradigm or world view and enables paradigmatic reconstruction". He (ibid. 25) labels different learning levels as related to conformative change (doing things better), reformative change (doing better things), and transformative change (seeing things differently). Transformative learning is often difficult, lengthy, uncomfortable, and even traumatic, as it requires a change in the overall world view. Accordingly, transformative learning that would lead to transformative development should require changes in current worldviews that include, among others, existing social orders.

Transformative learning has several meanings that are not directly related to Bateson's distinction between levels of learning. When it comes to individual, one of the most prominent theories of transformative learning of adults has been proposed by Jack Mezirow (1991, 2000). According to his theory, in the course of learning, individual meaning perspectives are transformed through critical self-reflection. Meaning perspectives consist of sets of beliefs, values and assumptions through which individuals give meaning to their experiences. Through critical reflection, the meaning-making structures can be changed, and, as a result, a more inclusive and open perspective can be achieved. Mezirow distinguishes between instrumental and transformative learning, and between transmissional, transactional and transformative education. While transmissional education focuses on delivering information, and transactional education embeds learning into experiences, transformative education includes critical interaction with others. One of his examples is from a women's group where the participants experienced empowerment when they learned to change their self-image as a result of their joint inquiry into their existing meaning perspectives.

While Mezirow's theory of transformative learning focuses on individuals, other critical learning theories consider merely societal structures (English & Mayo 2012; Freire 1970). Learning in these approaches refers to becoming aware of prevailing power relations or achieving critical consciousness of oppressive relationships. Further, critical learning not only refers to increased awareness, but also to action in an attempt to change the power relations integrated into learning. Action is often associated with collective mobilisation for emancipation. Antonio Gramsci's (1971) distinction between reformation (*tranformismo*) and transformation when it comes to the cultural and economic hegemonies in societies, provides a useful background for the distinction between incremental change and the transformational one. For Gramsci, learning and education of what he called subaltern groups, in reference to workers and peasants of his era in Italy, facilitated by so-called organic intellectuals, was essential for counter-hegemonic struggles and societal transformation (Gramsci 1971; Holma & Kontinen 2015).

In organisational change literature, the notion of transformation has been quite different from those inspired by critical theory and discussing societal power relations. In management literature of the 1990s, the term transformation became so commonly used that it no longer "necessarily meant anything" (Tosey & Robinson 2002, 101). In this literature, transformation is distinct from incremental change and is used in reference to qualitative change in organisations' fundamental assumptions or paradigms (ibid. 101–103). In consideration of organisational learning in development NGOs, Fowler (2000, 156–157) defines organisational transformation as "reappraisal and organisational reorientation, but not necessarily a shift in purpose or mission". In her account on donor–recipient relationships, Eyben (2006, 51–52) equates transformative learning with double-loop learning and defines it as "seeing the world in a new way". She makes a distinction between transformative and regressive learning, where transformative learning refers to genuine mutual learning between donors and recipients and consequent changes in the fundamental assumptions behind relationships that tend to take the power relations for granted.

While power is central in several accounts concerning transformative learning, organisational and management literature rarely includes a change of organisational power structures in its definition of transformation (Tosey & Robinson 2002, 107). In the same vein, organisational learning theories have little to say about power which is essential for development (Chambers & Pettit 2004, 151). Even if the transformative organisational learning argues for paradigms shifts in organisations, the existing organisational control and power relationships are often supposed to remain intact. While this is the case with mainstream management, critical management and organisation theory has discussed power in organisations in many ways (Clegg 2011/1979; Dovey 1997). Vis-á-vis that literature, transformation in power relations can refer to change in power division inside organisations as well as analysis of the effects of the larger and more powerful societal phenomena such as capitalism, neoliberalism, managerialism and Foucauldian technologies of governmentality. In the context of learning in development, Johnson and Wilson (2009, 36) argue that notwithstanding its imprecise nature, the concept of transformation captures well the process whereby current practices and approaches, embedded in institutions or organisations, are reframed, rethought and recast. In my categorisation, I locate transformative learning on the Batesonian level of learning III, while it can, in the above-mentioned forms, also be understood as part of learning II. The transformative learning, in this instance, refers to learning in which organisational world views and paradigms, including those concerning power relations, are reflected and changed in a way that shows in new meanings, routines and practices.

Towards a categorisation of learning in development

All in all, while different levels and agents of learning can be analytically distinguished, in practice individual, organisational, and institutional learning in development are intertwined. When it comes to learning in this specific context, individuals learn through participation in organisations that are affected by their institutional environments. At the same time, the action of individuals and organisations construct institutions. The sociological notions of social construction (Berger & Luckmann 1966) and structuration (Giddens 1986) that are behind the kind of organisational institutionalism utilised here, stress the interaction between micro-level action and larger social structures, and the constant co-construction of actors and institutions in this interaction (Greenwood et al. 2017). Therefore, in this view, also the phenomenon of learning moves between local and social, and takes place in interaction with actors and structures. However, arguing that learning is everywhere, and everything relates to everything, is not a very fruitful starting point for an analysis. Therefore, I suggest the following categorisation of learning in development on the basis of levels of learning inspired by Bateson and the review of literature (see Table 2.1). Naturally, this categorisation is one among many possibilities, and provides one potential heuristic to understanding learning in development.

On the basis of the above categorisation, we could discuss learning in development in 20 qualitatively different ways with varying understanding of agents and levels of their learning. For instance, individuals working in development, on rare occasions, can be socialised in such a way that their daily practices are mainly repetitive routines and, thus, examples of zero learning. It can be assumed, however, that most individuals in development continuously learn at level I in order to perform their tasks better and thus to achieve their objectives in a more efficient and qualitatively better way. At times, they might also learn at level II and critically reflect on their own assumptions and values, and as a result, undertake learning as transformation of individual

Table 2.1 Suggestion for categories of learning in development

Levels of learning agents	*Zero learning*	*Level 1/First-order Conformative*	*Level 2/Second-order Reformative*	*Level 3/Third-order Transformative*
Individual	Habitual, routine behaviour as a result of socialisation	Reflection on better ways to act within the existing meaning perspective	Reframing meaning perspective and redefine what it means to be a "development practitioner"	Reformulation of self and identity
Project	Non-reflective technical implementation of blueprints	Adaptive project implementation in such a way that planned outcomes can be achieved in the best possible way and can be measured with existing tools	Project implementation that includes changes in project objectives, approaches and means of performance measurement resulting from questioning and analysis	Questioning and abandoning existing project approach and innovate new collaborative arrangements
Partnership	Taken-for-granted donor –recipient relationships	Improving collaboration and communication within existing relationships	Reflection and reframing relationships on the basis of acknowledging difference	Reformulation of the power relationships in partnerships
Organisation	Taken-for-granted conduct of organisational routines and practices	Changing practices in order to better implement organisational goals and strategies	Questioning the existing organisational goals, strategies and their underlying assumptions and values	Fundamental change in organisational identity, epistemology and paradigm
Institution	Institutionalised routines, practices and logics of development	Improving institutional practices, meanings and logics of development in order to reach existing goals	Change in the institutional goals, practices, meanings, relationships and the overall logic behind them; alternative development	Questioning and abandoning the ideas, norms, roles, and practices related to "development" as currently known; post-development

meaning perspectives and refine what is means to be a development practitioner A few might go through fundamental reformulation of the self through learning III, and perhaps abandon the profession all together.

Projects, of course, have no agency by themselves, but their learning characteristics are constructed by the individuals included and the material aspects such as funding and tools. The combination of individual actors, their interaction, project management tools, and funding that provides resources for the project constructs the kind of learning that takes place in the projects. In extreme cases, a rigid implementation of a blueprint with well-defined resources can be an example of zero learning where well-defined activities are implemented as a routine by those involved notwithstanding any feedback and contributions from stakeholders and beneficiaries. Most often, however, projects include plenty of learning in interaction at stages of design and implementation at level I and sometimes at level II. Learning I could include identification of better ways to implement the existing project activities in order to better reach the goals, measured by the existing performance indicators. Learning II might occur when the project goals and assumptions are critically reflected upon and changed, along with the measures of performance and the power relationships inherent in project implementation. While possibilities for learning I are already quite well-established in the project management cycles and practices, the opportunities for learning II are rarer and are often hindered by the existing funding structures that assume implementation, with some adjustments, of the plan attached to the funding application. However, sometimes the feedback from beneficiaries, or sudden changes in working environments might lead to drastic changes in project assumptions, and consequently, in the objectives and activities of a project. The entire redefinition or abandonment of a project approach, as an example of learning III would require critical reflection on the assumption that a "project" and "project cycle" are appropriate ways to structure collaboration or relevant contributions to development. There is a wealth of discussion critical of project approach in development literature, but it is not likely that the approach would be abandoned in the course of learning during implementation of an ongoing project.

However, such learning might be possible in partnerships, where partners might reconsider the project form, and identify different, novel forms of collaboration. The discussion on learning in partnerships has focused on the critical reflection of the nature of the power relationships involved, and learning in order to change those. In learning I, the traditional relationship based on the taken-for-granted donor-recipient model with routine accountability systems can be improved, while in learning II, the inherent power relations, their implications, and principles behind them are critically reflected upon and changed. Institutionally, much debate on development partnerships and a lot of learning in relation to power relationship has taken place over the years. The notions of partnership, participation and ownership have not remained only rhetoric, but assumptions about the relationships and collaboration practices have changed. Nowadays, equal collaboration and mutual learning are often explicit goals in development partnerships, but continuous reflection of and change in both structures and taken-for-granted attitudes are still needed for these goals to be achieved.

In organisations, learning I is probably the most common form, whereas learning zero embedded in the taken-for-granted meanings and routines forms a backdrop to any organisational existence. Without routines and shared meanings, no joint action, nor its change and reflection, would be possible. In the framework of learning I, NGOs continuously receive feedback from their beneficiaries, donors and government representatives, and also conduct internal meetings and workshops to discuss their goals, practices and their performance – thus, engaging in learning I. While NGOs tend to develop new strategies at three- to five-year intervals, this change rarely includes learning II, a change in their overall values and assumptions behind their action. However, at times organisations' identities are rethought, and new positions learned. For example, one of the case organisations of this study recently changed its identity from a "donor" to a self-implementing agency. As a result of rethinking its identity, it designed its own development programme and established field offices. Even more rarely do NGOs change their overall worldview; for example, faith-based organisations turning into secular ones, or those valuing global solidarity turning into nationalistic organisations. Even less common would be the total abandonment of organisational identities based on the very idea of development.

The notion of development with its belief in the possibilities of bringing about positive change through interventionist practices is also at the heart of the development institution. International development has changed its policy priorities and approaches in instances that could be identified as learning I and occasionally II; however, the basic developmentalist background has remained. Additionally, while the Sustainable Development Goals represented a kind of shift in thinking in terms of binaries of developed-developing, or north and south, the institutionalised funding structures and practices often still maintain these binaries. The international policies and practices of development constitute much of the cultural-cognitive pillar of development institution that interacts with individual NGOs (Scott 2014). Next, and in the following chapters of the book, I will focus on learning as it takes place in this interaction between NGOs and their institutional environments, in the context of socially constructed institutionalisation.

Organisational and institutional learning

A common reaction to an idea of organisational learning is: "But only individuals can really learn, not organisations!" Answers to the question whether organisations or institutions can learn, obviously, depend on the definitions of learning. It is widely acknowledged that human beings have unique cognitive and affective capacities, and thus, particular abilities to learn (Cook

& Yanow 1993). Organisations are not analogous to individuals, and so organisational learning is not equal to learning of individual human beings (Shepherd & Sutcliffe 2015). However, it is also widely agreed that organisational learning is not the same as a group of individuals learning. Individual learning is necessary, but not sufficient for organisational learning to take place (Argyris & Schön 1978). We all are familiar with situations where organisational learning does not take place despite a number of individuals having learned. A common example comes from training courses and workshops where new approaches or tools such as the human rights-based approach or outcome mapping are learned by individuals coming from different NGOs. After the training these specific individuals might be very conversant with the approach, but their new knowledge and skills do not necessarily lead to any change in organisational practices. Turning individual experience, knowledge and skills into organisational learning needs them to be embedded in organisational memory, specific organisational vocabularies, and routines (Argote & Miron-Spektor 2011, 1126; Argyris & Schön 1978, 19). Similar challenges apply to situations where an external change agent, for instance an OD consultant, facilitates a process of adaptation of new approaches. During the change process and immediately after it, members of the organisation might be really enthusiastic about the new ways, but gradually go back to the old routines if the new ideas and practices are not really embedded in the organisation.

Moreover, organisations are not any kinds of entities or groups, but are constellations of people, material artefacts and structures gathered together to do something. Therefore, organisational learning focuses on acquiring and preserving understandings and abilities relevant to what the organisation is doing (Cook & Yanow 1993, 386). It is also clear that organisations do not exist in a vacuum. They are situated in varying societal contexts and different organisational environments. The wealth of organisational learning literature emphasises interaction between an organisation and its environment as the main source of learning and change. For development NGOs, however, defining organisational environment is a tricky task. Besides the societal contexts, such as Zambia, Peru, Germany, Sweden or Bangladesh, development NGOs, at least those enjoying funding from the system, are situated in a particular institutional environment of international development.

In development literature, this international environment has often been conceptualised as a Foucauldian inspired discourse (Ebrahim 2003; Escobar 1995; Johnson & Wilson 2009). The discoursive approach has shown how the knowledge/power constellations in international development affect the production of "truths" that guide directions of learning (ibid.). It has also pointed out the ways in which certain definitions of expert knowledge and reporting practices tend to have more influence on learning than the knowledge received from those who are supposed to benefit from the organisation (Ebrahim 2003). Additionally, development discourse constructs certain groups of people as "those to be developed" (Escobar 1995), and guides development practices towards becoming depoliticised practices (Ferguson 1994). Both discourse and institutional approaches have valuable insights into development (Lister 2003). In this book, I mainly draw from the latter in analysing the dynamics between organisations and institutional environments.

While institutionalisms are numerous (Scott 2014, 1–20), I focus on organisational institutionalism, and especially its strands that draw from the general idea of social constructivism in social sciences (Berger & Luckmann 1966; Greenwood et al. 2008, 2017). Institutions, in this tradition, do not have a single definition. Generally, they are understood as comprising "regulative, normative, and cultural-cognitive elements that, together with associated activities and resources, provide stability and meaning to social life", and thus, are durable social structures constituted by symbolic, social and material aspects (Scott 2014, 56–57). Regulative elements of institutions include rules, laws and sanctions. The normative aspect concerns social obligation, certification and accreditation, while the cultural-cognitive aspect is based on taken-for-grantedness and shared understandings. Consequently, institutional legitimacy can be legally sanctioned, morally governed, and based on comprehensibility, recognisability and cultural support (Ibid.). In regard to learning as investigated in this book, the cultural-cognitive elements are central. These taken-for-granted parts of organisational lives are perceived from the constructionist point of view, where institutional rules, norms and meanings arise in interaction, and they are preserved and modified by human action.

Thus, the underlying theme of this book is interaction between organisational learning and cultural-cognitive aspects of institutions. While theories of organisational learning deal with organisational practices, goals and values, they do not always address the question of where these are derived from. In development, institutional aspects, such as the pervasive power relations and related perceptual frames, can be regarded as part of the taken-for-granted governing factors that either hinder or enable organisational learning (Ebrahim 2003, 11; Argyris & Schön 1978, 68). This institutional taken-for-grantedness applies to the very model of an NGO as well. Much of organisational learning in development is geared towards being a better-functioning organisation, with improved capacities to conduct strategic planning, to implement and to measure activities. That resonates with the overall model of an organisation as a rational actor spread globally in fields far beyond international development (Driori et al. 2006).

Selected concepts for bridging between organisations and institutions

All in all, organisational institutionalism provides a conceptual framework for setting organisational learning in a wider context. In what follows I briefly discuss some selected concepts that bridge between organisations and institutions in the context of learning. These include the intertwining notions of learning for legitimacy, experience, knowledge, memory, routines and meanings. On the basis of these notions, it becomes possible to analyse how organisations have a tendency to change in order to be legitimate, how they learn from both their own experience and that of others, and how the learning can be of adaptation or change of organisational memory, routines and meanings.

In resonance with the difference between organisational learning at levels I and II, organisations are often assumed to change for two reasons: in order to be more effective in reaching their existing goals; or to create space for reflection and redefinition of their goals, values and relationships. Organisational institutionalism suggests a third perspective: learning for legitimacy. According to this view, organisations learn and change in order to gain legitimacy, that is, to be appropriate and accepted by their organisational environments. Therefore, learning for legitimacy means that NGOs seek to be in alignment with practices, perception and actions assumed to be desirable with the socially constructed institution of development (Suchman 1995, 574). For organisations, legitimacy is worth pursuing. When an organisation has legitimacy, it is not continuously questioned either by its internal or external audiences (Deephouse & Suchman 2008, 51).

Two notions are central for the learning in order to be legitimate: isomorphism and decoupling. Isomorphism means that organisations that seek legitimacy in the same institutional environment become increasingly similar to each other. For example, development NGOs all over the world tend to have similar structures, goals and management practices (Claeyé & Jackson 2012; Tvedt 1998). There are coercive, normative and mimetic mechanisms of institutional isomorphism (DiMaggio & Powell 1983). Thus, the similarity can results from regulative frameworks, professional norms and imitation of others that are perceived successful. Organisational decoupling can be a result from isomorphic pressures (Meyer & Rowan 1977). An organisation can adopt structures and rules considered appropriate, but the actual practices of its members might be "decoupled" from these formal structures (Scott 2014, 185). This means that the actual behaviour of organisational members does not conform to official prescriptions, and therefore there is institutional isomorphism only on the surface. In development, similar phenomena are often discussed in terms of difference between rhetoric and practice.

However, organisations can exercise different adoption strategies, and their organisational responses to these isomorphic pressures vary (Chandler & Hwang 2015; Haunschild & Chandler 2008, 624; Powell & Colyvas 2008, 278). The variety of responses can be understood in terms of different types of learning. Strategies that resonate with learning I include adopting directly experiences and practices of other organisations (Chandler & Hwang 2015, 1449). This kind of replication of prior actions of others that are considered successful has been called low-intelligent learning (March 2010, 15). In contrast, in the process of high-intelligent learning, organisations do not directly replicate actions, or "best practices", but reflect the causal structures behind them and their success in other organisations (ibid.). In such instances, learning resonates with learning II, and includes reconfiguration and translation of others' experiences and actions according to organisations own situation and context (Chandler & Hwang 2015, 1449; Sahlin-Andersson 1996; Sahlin & Wedlin 2008).

Experience is commonly seen as a source of organisational learning. Organisational learning can be defined as a change that "occurs as the organisation acquires experience" (Argote & Miron-Spektor 2011, 1124). The question is what is meant by experience. It can be an organisation's own or that of others. In the instances of organisational decoupling and learning as direct replication, organisational learning is not necessary based on an organisation's own experiences, but is vicarious learning; learning from the experiences of others (Chandler & Hwang 2015, 1454). Moreover, the range of organisational experience varies. It can be quite specific experience of performance of a certain task (Argote & Miron-Spektor 2011, 1124) or refer to wider, historically accumulated information gathered from past events relevant to an organisation (March 2010). Whatever the specific definition of organisational experience is, learning from experience is often described as a cyclical process; experience affects both the actors and organisational contexts, which in turn, affect the future experiences, and the cycle continues. The model of experiential learning (Kolb 1984) used in the context of organisations also focuses on the cyclical process in which experience is reflected and conceptualised, after which new practice is experimented resulting into a new experience.

Furthermore, not all experience leads to learning. Learning occurs only when experience is turned into new knowledge, action or routines. Knowledge is in the heart of organisational learning debates. The definitions of the concept of knowledge in organisational literature range from wide epistemological debates to more focused ideas in knowledge management. For example, Argote and Miron-Spektor (2011, 1128) argue that organisational learning has three sub-processes: creating, retaining, and transferring knowledge, which can be more or less mindful or more or less routine. Typical distinctions in organisational contexts are between explicit and tacit knowledge (Nonaka & Takeuchi 1995) or propositional and narrative knowledge (Seirafi 2012). Explicit and propositional knowledge is easier to store and retrieve in knowledge-management systems, while tacit and narrative knowledge is merely embedded in practices. Organisational knowledge is connected with organisational goals and action. From the point of view of practice, it refers to distinctions that members of an organisation make in particular concrete contexts in the process of carrying out their work (Tsoukas 2005; Tsoukas & Vladimirou 2001, 983). In this view, organisational knowledge is thus a product of historical, evolved and collective understandings and experiences about what the organisation does and how, rather than a "thing" that can be stored, retrieved and transferred.

Learning is not organisational before new knowledge, skills and routines are embedded in organisational memory. The fact that these do not reside only in the heads and bodies of individual members of an organisation implies that organisational knowledge will not disappear when individual persons in the organisation change (Martin de Holan & Phillips 2004, 1605). There are different ways to understand the notion of organisational memory. It can refer, for instance, to digital knowledge-management systems, rules, routines or practices. In the early accounts, organisational memory was conceptualised as "retention bins". These retention bins referred to individuals, organisational structures and external archives in which the information was stored (Walsh & Ungson 1991, 61). In later works, the idea of organisational memory as stored in retention bins has been challenged. Rather, organisational memory is seen as a dynamic process, something that is continuously constructed by human interaction (Casey & Olivera 2011). According to this view, knowledge can be stored, but it is modified and reconstructed when used for different purposes, including learning. Therefore, for example, M&E information stored in digital systems is selected and re-interpreted when it is later retrieved and used to satisfy different knowledge needs. Organisational memory also plays a central role in organisational forgetting, which can range from rapid dismissal of new knowledge to slow decay of already established one (Martin de Holan & Phillip 2004, 2011). Organisational remembering and forgetting are also shaped by power dynamics in a way that some things become hegemonic and worth remembering, while others are silenced and forgotten (Casey & Olivera 2011, 308). Additionally, organisational memory can be guided by institutional effects; institutions encourage remembering events and issues that complement its "right" image and forgetting irrelevant issues (Douglas 1986, 112).

Finally, organisational learning is related to organisational meanings and routines. Meanings and routines are constructed in interaction between institutional structures and organisational practices (Zilber 2017). They are among the "taken-for-granted" carriers of the cultural-cognitive elements of institutions (Becker 2008, 3–6; Scott 2014). For the members of same institution, it is hard to identify such taken-for-granted elements before they are confronted with different meanings in other institutions. For example, the word "development" carries one meaning to NGO practitioners of development and quite another for a child psychologist. In organisations, meanings are embedded in language, artefacts and routines. Organisational learning can be defined as acquiring, sustaining and changing these meanings. (Cook & Yanow 1993; Yanow 2000). In resonance with the learning I, much organisational learning is about acquiring and sustaining organisational meanings. Changing them would require a type of learning comparable with learning II, or even III. Routines, the habituated behaviours and typical ways the organisation accomplishes its task embody meanings that are not necessary explicated through language. Organisations rely on routines for their capability to act. Routines provide stability in organisational behaviour (Powell & Rerup 2017, 216; Scott 2014, 102).

Both meanings and routines are important for organisational identity and its ability to do what it does. Organisational meanings and routines provide a basis for the ways organisations make sense of events and situations. Thus, learning as a change in organisational meanings would indicate a change in its identity.

Conclusion

In this chapter, I discussed different ways of conceptualising learning in development and set the theoretical agenda to examine the interaction between organisations and institutions. In order to understand different conceptualisations, I proposed a categorisation of learning. The categorisation showed a wide variety of perspectives to learning in development ranging from adoption to radical reformulation. Often we tend to think of different types of learning in normative terms; we prefer certain kinds of learning over others (Argyris 1999, 11). Usually, the types of learning resonating with the learning in categories II or III are seen as more desirable, while those of zero and learning I are perceived as not so valuable. However, when we look at the empirical realities of organisations, and development NGOs as well, the majority of learning that takes place does not fall into a category of fundamentally transformative learning by any agent, but more mundane change in meanings, routines and practices; learning that keeps the organisational life going. These types of learning are essential to build coherence, to coordinate, and to have the capability to do things. It is impossible for any individual or organisation to continuously change values and assumptions, not to mention worldviews or paradigms, and thus frequently engage in learning II or III.

Moreover, when we look at the institution of development we do not see much radical learning. While assumptions of the main locus of development – whether state, civil society, entrepreneurial citizens – have changed over decades, the underlying paradigm of intentional development has remained. The consistent paradigm relates to the urge to address issues such as global poverty and global inequalities under the umbrella of "development" and through intentional interventions (Cowen & Shenton 1996). Development NGOs that have a wide variety of organisational values, goals and tools share this underlying paradigm. While the institutional learning at level III would indicate critical reformulation of the paradigm, as suggested by post-development scholars, the empirical reality shows more learning taking place within it, and in constant interaction between NGOs and their institutional environment. In this context, parallel to the ideal of transformative learning, the notions of learning for legitimacy, organisational experience, knowledge, memory, routines and meanings are of importance in analysis of the current phenomena of learning.

References

Argote, L. & Miron-Spektor, E. (2011) Organizational learning: From experience to knowledge. *Organization Science*, 22(5), 1123–1137.

Argyris, C. (1999) *On Organizational Learning*. Second edition. Malden, MA: Blackwell.

Argyris, C. & Schön, D.A. (1978) *Organizational Learning: A Theory of Action Perspective*. Reading, MA: Addison-Weasley.
Bateson, G. (1987/1964) The logical categories of learning and communication. In: Bateson, G. *Steps to an Ecology of Mind*. New Jersey: Jason Aronson Inc.
Becker, M.C. (2008) The past, present and future of organisational routines: Introduction to the handbook of organisational routines. In: Becker, M.C. (ed.) *Handbook of Organisational Routines*. Cheltenham: Edward Elgar.
Berger, P.L. & Luckmann, T. (1966) *The Social Construction of Reality. A Treatise in the Sociology of Knowledge*. London: Penguin.
Brinkerhoff, J.F. (2002) *Partnership for International Development*. Rhetoric or Results? Boulder, CO: Lynne Rienner.
Britton, B. (1998) *The Learning NGO*. Occasional papers series no 17. UK: INTRAC.
Britton, B. (2002) *Learning for Change! Principles and Practices of Learning Organisations*. Sweden: Swedish Mission Council.
Britton, B. (2005) *Organisational Learning in NGOs: Creating the Motive, Means, and Opportunity*. Praxis Paper No 3. UK: INTRAC.
Brown, J.S., Collins, A. & Duguid, P. (1989) Cognition and the culture of learning. *Educational Researcher*, 18(1), 32–42.
Casey, A.J. & Olivera, F. (2011) Reflections on organisational memory and forgetting. *Journal of Management Inquiry*, 20(3), 305–310.
Chambers, R. & Pettit, J. (2004) Shifting power to make a difference. In: Groves, L. & Hinton, R. (eds) (2004). *Inclusive Aid: Changing Power and Relationships in International Development*. London: Earthscan, 137–162.
Chandler, D. & Hwang, H. (2015) Learning from learning theory: A model of organisational adoption strategies and microfoundations of institutional theory. *Journal of Management*, 41(5), 1446–1476.
Claeyé, F. & Jackson, T. (2012) The iron cage re-revisited: Institutional isomorphism in nonprofit organisations in South. *Journal of International Development*, 24(5), 602–622.
Clegg, S. (2011/1979) *The Theory of Power and Organisation*. Oxford: Routledge.
Cook, S.D.N. & Yanow, D. (1993) Culture and organisational learning. *Journal of Management Inquiry*, 2(4), 373–390.
Cowen, M. & Shenton, R. (1996) *Doctrines of Development*. London: Routledge.
Deephouse, D.L. & Suchman, M. (2008) Legitimacy and organisational institutionalism. In: Greenwood, R., Oliver, C., Sahlin, K. & Suddaby, R. (eds) *The Sage Handbook of Organisational Institutionalism*. Los Angeles, CA: SAGE, 49–77.
De Haan, A. (2009) *How the Aid Industry Works*. Sterling: Kumarian Press.
DiMaggio, P.J. & Powell, W.W. (1983) The iron cage revisited: Institutional isomorphism and collective rationality in institutional fields. *Annual Review of Sociology*, 16, 137–159.
Douglas, M. (1986) *How Institutions Think*. Syracuse, NY: Syracuse University Press.
Dovey, K. (1997) The learning organisation and the organisation of learning: Power, transformation and the search for form in learning organisations. *Management Learning*, 28(3), 331–349.
Drori, G.S., Meyer, J.W. & Hwang, H. (eds) (2006) *Globalization and Organization. World Society and Organizational Change*. Oxford: Oxford University Press,
Ebrahim, A. (2003) *NGOs and Organisational Change. Discourse, Reporting and Change.* Cambridge: Cambridge University Press.
Edwards, M. (1997) Organisational learning in non-governmental organisations: What have we learned? *Public Administration and Development*, 17(2), 235–250.

Engeström, Y. (2001) Expansive learning at work: Toward an activity theoretical reconceptualisation. *Journal of Education and Work*, 14(1), 133–156.

English, L.M. & Mayo, P. (2012) *Learning with Adults. A Critical Pedagogic Introduction*. Rotterdam: Sense.

Escobar, A. (1995) *Encountering Development. The Making and Unmaking of the Third World*. Princeton, NJ: Princeton University Press.

Eyben, R. (2006) *Relationships for Aid*. London: Earthscan.

Ferguson, J. (1994) *The Anti-Politics Machine. Development, Depoliticization, and Bureaucratic Power in Lesotho*. Minneapolis: University of Minneapolis Press.

Fowler, A. (1998) Authentic NGDO partnership in new policy agenda for international aid: Dead end or light ahead? *Development and Change*, 29(1), 137–159.

Fowler, A. (2000) *The Virtuous Spiral. A Guide to Sustainability for NGOs in International Development*. London: Earthscan.

Freire, P. (1970). *Pedagogy of the Oppressed*. New York: Continuum.

Giddens, A. (1986) *The Constitution of Society*. Berkeley, CA: University of California Press.

Gramsci, A. (1971) *Selection from the Prison Notebooks*. Edited and translated by Hoare, Q & Smith, G.N. London: Lawrence and Wishart.

Greenwood, R., Oliver, C., Lawrence, T.B. & Meyer, R.E. (eds) (2017) *The Sage Handbook of Organizational Institutionalism*. Los Angeles, CA: SAGE.

Greenwood, R., Oliver, C., Sahlin, K. & Suddaby, R. (eds) (2008) *The Sage Handbook of Organizational Institutionalism*. Los Angeles, CA: SAGE

Groves, L. & Hinton, R. (eds) (2004). *Inclusive Aid: Changing Power and Relationships in International Development*. London: Earthscan.

Haunschild P. & Chandler, D. (2008) Institutional-level learning: Learning as a source of institutional change. In: Greenwood, R., Oliver, C., Sahlin, K. & Suddaby, R. (eds) *Organizational Institutionalism*. Los Angeles, CA: SAGE, 624–649.

Hickey, S. & Mohan, G. (eds) (2004). *Participation: From Tyranny to Transformation: Exploring New Approaches to Participation in Development*. London: Zed Books.

Hinton, R. & Groves, L. (2004) The complexity of inclusive aid. In: Groves, L. & Hinton, R. (eds) Inclusive aid. *Changing Power Relationships in International Development*. London: Earthscan, 3–20.

Hodgson, G.M. (2008) The concept of a routine. In: Becker, M.C. (ed.) *Handbook of Organizational Routines*. Cheltenham: Edward Elgar.

Holma, K. & Kontinen, T. (2015) The rocky road of growth into contemporary citizenship: Dewey, Gramsci, and the method of democracy. *Studier i Pædagogisk Filosofi*, 4(2), 24–37.

Johnson, H. & Wilson, G. (2009) *Learning for Development*. London: Zed Books.

John-Steiner, V. & Mahn, H. (1996) Sociocultural approach to learning and development: Vygotskian framework. *Educational Psychology*, 31(3–4), 191–206.

King, K. & McGrath, S. (2004) *Knowledge for Development. Comparing British, Japanese, Swedish and World Bank Aid*. Cape Town/London: HSRC and Zed Books.

Kolb, D. (1984) *Experiential Learning. Experience and the Source of Learning and Development*. Englewood Cliffs, NJ: Prentice Hall.

Krohwinkel-Karlsson, A. (2007) *Knowledge and Learning in Aid Organisations. A literature review with suggestions for further studies*. Swedish Agency for Development Evaluation. Working paper 2007:1.

Lave, J. & Wenger, E. (1991) *Situated Learning: Legitimate Peripheral Participation*. Cambridge: Cambridge University Press.

Lewis, D. & Madon, S. (2004) Information systems and non-governmental organisations: Advocacy, organisational learning, and accountability. *The Information Society*, 20(2), 117–126.

Lister, S. (2003) NGO legitimacy: Technical issue or social construct? *Critique of Anthropology*, 23(2), 175–192.

Long, N. (2001) *Development Sociology. Actor Perspectives*. London: Routledge.

March, J.G. (2010) *The Ambiguities of Experience*. Ithaca, NY: Cornell University Press.

Martin de Holan, P. & Phillips, N. (2004) Remembrance of things past? The dynamics of organizational forgetting. *Management Science*, 50(11) 1603–1613.

Martin de Holan, P. & Phillips, N. (2011) Organizational forgetting. In: Easterby-Smith, M. & Lyles, M.A. (eds) *Handbook of Organizational Learning and Knowledge Management*. Chichester: John Wiley & Sons, 433–452.

McFarlane, C. (2006) Knowledge, learning and development: A post-rationalist approach. *Progress in Development Studies*, 6(4), 287–305.

Meyer, J.W. & Rowan, B. (1977) Institutional organisations: Formal structure as myth and ceremony. *American Journal of Sociology*, 83(2), 340–63.

Mezirow, J. (1991) *Transformative Dimensions of Adult Learning*. San Francisco, CA: Jossey Bass.

Mezirow, J. (2000) *Learning as Transformation: Critical Perspectives on a Theory in Progress*. San Francisco, CA: Jossey Bass.

Mitlin, D., Hickey, S. & Bebbington, A. (2007). Reclaiming development? NGOs and the challenge of alternatives. *World Development*, 35(10), 1699–1720.

Mueller-Hirth, N. (2012) If you don't count, you don't count: Monitoring and evaluation in South African NGOs. *Development and Change*, 43(3), 649–670.

Nederveen Pieterse, J. (2001) *Development Theory. Deconstructions/reconstructions*. London: SAGE.

Nonaka, I. & Takeuchi, H. (1995) *The Knowledge-Creating Company: How Japanese Companies Create the Dynamics of Innovation*. New York: Oxford University Press.

Olivier de Sardan, J.-P. (2005) *Anthropology and Development. Understanding Contemporary Social Change*. London: Zed Books.

Pasteur, K. (2006) Learning for development. In: Eyben, R. (ed.) *Relationships for Aid*. London: Earthscan, 21–42.

Piaget, J. & Cook, M.T. (1952). *The Origins of Intelligence in Children*. New York, NY: International University Press.

Powell, M. (2006) Which knowledge? Whose reality? An overview of knowledge used in development sector. *Development in Practice*, 16(6), 518–32.

Powell, W.W. & Colyvas, J.A. (2008). Microfoundations of institutional theory. In Greenwood, R., Oliver, C., Suddaby, R. & Sahlin-Andersson, K. (2008). *The Sage Handbook of Organizational Institutionalism*. London: SAGE.

Powell, W.W. & Rerup, C. (2017) Opening the black box: The microfoundations of institutions. In: Greenwood, R., Oliver, C., Lawrence, T.B. & Meyer, R.E. (eds) *The Sage Handbook of Organizational Institutionalism*. Los Angeles, CA: SAGE.

Rondinelli, D.A. (1993) *Development Projects and Policy Experiments. An Adaptive Approach to Development Administration*. London: Routledge.

Sahlin-Andersson, K. (1996) Imitating by editing success: the construction of organisational fields. In: Czarniawska, B., Joerges, B. & Sevón, G. (eds), *Translating Organisational Change*. Berlin: De Gruyter.

Sahlin, K. & Wedlin, L. (2008) Circulating ideas: Imitation, translation, and editing. In: Greenwood, R., Oliver, C., Sahlin, K. & Suddaby, R. (eds) *The Sage Handbook of Organizational Institutionalism*. Los Angeles, CA: SAGE, 218–242.

Salomon, G. (1997). *Distributed Cognitions: Psychological and Educational Considerations*. Cambridge: Cambridge University Press.

Schön, D. (1987) *Educating the Reflective Practitioner*. San Francisco, CA: Josey-Bass.

Scott, R. (2014) *Institutions and Organizations. Ideas, Interests, and Identities*. Fourth edition. Los Angeles, CA: SAGE.

Seirafi, K. (2012) *Organizational Epistemology. Understanding Knowledge in Organizations*. Berlin: Springer.

Shepherd, D.A. & Sutcliffe, K.M. (2015) The use of anthropomorphizing as tool for generating organisational knowledge. *The Academy of Management Annals*, 9(1), 97–142.

Sterling. S. (2010) Transformative learning and sustainability: Sketching the conceptual ground. *Learning and Teaching in Higher Education*, 5(5), 17–33.

Suchman, M.C. (1995) Managing legitimacy: Strategic and institutional approaches. *Academy of Management Review*, 20(3), 571–610.

Tosey, P., Visser, M. & Saunders, M.N.K. (2011) The origins and conceptualizations of "triple-loop" learning: A critical review. *Management Learning*, 43(3), 291–307.

Tosey, P. & Robinson, G. (2002) When change is no longer enough: what do we mean by "transformation" in organisational change work? *The TQM Magazine*, 1(2), 100–109.

Tsoukas, H. (2005) *Complex Knowledge: Studies in Organizational Epistemology*. Oxford: Oxford University Press.

Tsoukas, H. & Vladimirou, E. (2001) What is organisational knowledge? *Journal of Management Studies*, 38(7), 973–993.

Tvedt, T. (1998) *Angels of Mercy or Development Diplomats? NGDOs and Foreign Aid*. Oxford: Africa World Press.

Tvedt, T. (2002) Development NGOs: Actors in a global civil society or in a new international social system. *Voluntas: International Journal of Voluntary and Nonprofit Organizations*, 13(4), 363–375.

Tvedt, T. (2005) The international aid system and the non-governmental organisations: a new research agenda. *Journal of International Development*, 18(5), 677–690.

Ubels, J., Acquaye-Baddoo, N.-A. & Fowler, A. (2010) *Capacity Development in Practice*. London: Earthscan.

Upphoff, N. (1996) *Learning from Gal Oya. Possibilities for Participatory Development and Post-Newtonian Social Science*. London: Intermediate Technology Publications.

Vygotsky, L.S. (1978) *Mind in Society. The Development of Higher Psychological Processes*. Cambridge, MA: Harvard University Press.

Wallace, T. with Bornstein, L. & Chapman, J. (2006) *The Aid Chain. Coercion and Commitment in Development NGOs*. London: Intermediate Technology Publications.

Walsh, J.P. & Ungson, G.R. (1991) Organisational memory. *The Academy of Management Review*, 16(1), 57–91.

Whatley, B. (2013) Improved learning for greater effectiveness in development NGOs. *Development in Practice*, 23(8), 963–976.

Yanow, D. (2000) Seeing organisational learning: A "Cultural view". *Organization*, 7(2), 247–268.

Zilber, T.B. (2017) The evolving role of meaning in theorizing institutions. In: Greenwood, R., Oliver, C., Lawrence, T.B. & Meyer, R.E. (eds) (2017) *The Sage Handbook of Organizational Institutionalism*. Los Angeles, CA: SAGE, 418–445.

3 Learning as a search for a shared meaning for empowerment

What do we do when we empower? How do we know when empowerment takes place? These are questions NGO staff all over the world ask during the course of their work. It is hard to find any development NGO that would not, in one way or another, speak of empowerment as its goal. "Empowerment not disempowerment" is among the good programming practices in the HRBA. The empowerment approach is also associated with principles such as ownership over one's own development, in which external change agents such as NGOs are given the role of facilitator. Therefore, empowerment typically indicates both practical and moral organisational commitment to self-reliant and participatory development (Atack 1999, 862).

The notion of empowerment has appeared in development literature for a long time. In the 1970s and 1980s, it was, along with that of emancipation, within the vocabulary of alternative development. It was part of the critique of existing development paradigms where development was more about bringing about modernisation by means of knowledge and technology transfer. (Friedmann 1992; Nederveen Pieterse 2001, 80–87). With support from the human development paradigm, empowerment was gradually mainstreamed in development policies of influential institutions such as the World Bank (Narayan 2002; 2005). Human development paradigm and capability approach to development (Sen 1999) emphasised empowerment. In this instance, international donors appraised NGOs for their exceptional ability to empower and exercise participatory development (Salamon 1994). The empowerment of women was particularly high on the political agenda, and continues to be at the heart of the development discussion (Cornwall & Edwards 2016; Cornwall 2017).

In contemporary development policies and practices, empowerment is perceived as both a valuable and an ambiguous objective. It is valuable, as it is normatively desirable to provide human beings with a decent life and agency over making their life decisions, rather than leave large parts of populations in marginalised and disempowered positions. It is ambiguous, as empowerment as a generic term functions as an acceptable umbrella over a variety of social, economic and cultural objectives. Yet, it is hard to define empowerment in a specific way, and thus, quite challenging to measure it (Rahnema 1993, 122;

Alsop & Heinsohn 2005). Moreover, in the English language, empowerment can have both transitive and intransitive interpretations; it can refer to the act of somebody who empowers others, as well as to a process of empowerment, a change that takes place within an individual or community. Consequently, empowerment is among the buzzwords circulating in development, and can be used in many fora to refer to a range of things (Cornwall 2007). Critical research has argued that in the course of mainstreaming, empowerment has lost its once radical association with power and change in societal power structures (Batliwala 2007), and despite the inherent ideals of appreciating local knowledge and capacities, the practice of empowerment tends to appreciate Western values and education at the cost of existing knowledge systems: to be empowered is to be a schooled through Western education, and to hold values that, for instance, prioritise the individual over the community (Swai 2010). Moreover, literature critical of empowerment in general, suggests that it functions as a technology of governance in order to create a citizenry that consents to neoliberal governance through programmes of "helping people to help themselves" (Cruickshank 1999). Empowerment, thus, has seen as part of a process of so-called "responsibilisation" (Hansson 2015) in which individuals are given increasing agency to make choices that they can be responsible for, while at the same time, these choices are constrained through mechanisms of neoliberal governance. Ultimately, individuals can be held responsible for making "bad choices" even if the range of choices was restricted.

In this chapter, however, I do not aim to review the extensive debate on empowerment in research literature in different fields. Rather, I scrutinise the conceptions and perceptions of empowerment held by those who *do empowerment* as part of their role as members of NGO staff. More precisely, the analytical focus is not primarily on the individual employees, but on the organisational meanings attributed to the notion of empowerment in the course of organisational interaction. Organisational learning, in this chapter, is examined from the point of view of a search for shared organisational meanings. These meanings are important for both organisational functioning and organisational identity (Cook & Yanow 1992, 348). While there is little doubt that empowerment belongs to the core vocabulary of development institutions, each organisation and partnership has to achieve a shared meaning of it in order to be able to pursue shared goals. I analyse how World Vision Finland negotiated a shared understanding of empowerment with its partners in two partner seminars organised in Iten, Kenya in March 2012, and in Indore, India, in November 2012. Additionally, I draw from the individual interviews of staff of World Vision Finland and their partners conducted before and during the seminars.

The partner organisations, in this case Word Visions in Kenya, Uganda, India and Sri Lanka, are members of the same international federative international World Vision network. Therefore, they already share some objectives related to children's well-being, and have a collection of shared tools for programme management. Within the network, World Vision Finland occupies an institutional role as a donor, or support office, while the others are so-called recipients, or implementation offices. World Vision Finland is not the only support office that provides funding for these particular partners as they receive support from many World Vision offices over the global north. World Vision Finland also has its own donor-recipient relationship with the Ministry for Foreign Affairs of Finland and the individual private sponsors. In general, all the World Vision (WV) organisations are committed to empowerment, but WV Finland wanted especially emphasise empowerment, and hence, discussed it explicitly with its existing partners. Therefore, the chapter deals with organisational meanings of empowerment. By using the analytical concepts of scripts, roles and schemata I ask how the shared meaning of empowerment was negotiated within this particular organisational relationship and what kinds of perceptions about empowerment practitioners brought into the discussion.

Organisational learning as negotiating meanings

The definition of learning as a search for a shared meaning for empowerment illustrates well the interconnections between individuals, organisations, and institutions. From individual perspective, each member of staff interprets the words used in organisational language based on their prior life experience and educational background. In this case of empowerment, such individual frames ranged from one's own personal life-experience of empowerment from progressing from an impoverished child in a remote Kenyan village to an esteemed member of staff of World Vision, to having concluded an entire PhD dissertation on the concept, as was the case of the programme director of World Vision Finland. Partly due to his personal zeal for empowerment, in 2012–2013 World Vision Finland collaborated with our research team in order to search for an organisational definition for empowerment and to design an approach to monitor empowerment in a way that could capture its qualitative and processual nature. In the course of the research collaboration, we conducted interviews and a series of workshops both in Finland and in selected partner countries. The outcome of the collaboration was an approach entitled "Pathways of empowerment" that provided a platform to identify different, often quite circuitous rather than straightforward processes of empowerment among people the NGO was working with in implementing its programmes. It did not provide one definition of empowerment, but took its contextual and relational nature seriously and identified a variety of pathways relevant to various specific contexts, and paid attention to important turning points and impasses of empowerment along the way (Kontinen & Robinson-Moncada 2014).

The two seminars, accompanied by 36 individual interviews, used in this chapter are events from our research collaboration in which the aim was to facilitate a search for shared meanings of empowerment for organisations and organisational partnerships. In order to coordinate their actions, organisations need shared meanings; the members of organisations have to share understandings of certain events and words so that the coordination becomes possible. Thus, shared meanings create a shared symbolic space essential for organisational practices and cultures. In creating such symbolic spaces, organisations have a tendency to develop their own "esoteric language and particular practices" that have to be learned by any newcomer in order to be able to communicate (Tsoukas 2005, 24). Development cooperation in general and development NGOs in particular are famous for producing buzzwords, acronyms, and terminologies that outsiders and newcomers find difficult to comprehend (Cornwall 2007; Tvedt 1998; 2002; 2006). However, organisational meaning-making not only means assigning acronyms for activities or programme approaches distinct from the approaches of other NGOs, or from one's old ones as in the case of World Vision when shifting from "IDPs to ADPs (integrated development programmes to area development programmes)"; it also refers to a more profound organisational characteristic, an essential practice that holds an organisation together. Through their everyday meaning-making, organisations continuously form both their identity and their "ability to do what they do" (Cook & Yanow 1993, 385). The official missions and visions, the annual plans and reports are all artefactual representations of organisational meanings. However, no matter how much they are used in the accomplishment of everyday tasks, much of the meaning-making happens through interaction and action in everyday work, in situations where people talks, write, and act. Obviously, words choice and language use are important means of meaning-making, but meaning can also be embedded in bodily routines, and artefacts (Zilber 2017).

Organisational learning, in this context, refers to "acquiring, sustaining and changing" the meanings embedded in organisational language and practices (Cook & Yanow 1993, 384). Both identities and abilities can be either maintained or modified in the course of interaction (ibid. 386). For an NGO, it is vital to use words and practices that construct its specific identity as a development organisation; its language and practices show its abilities in doing development and promoting positive change in people's lives, and demonstrate it is a proper organisation with well-functioning organisational systems. From a more cognitive stance, learning as generating organisational meanings can be defined as a change in organisational schemata (Bartunek & Moch 1987). The concept of schema as a cognitive framework originates from psychology, but it has also been used in reference to organisations, and furthermore, it has been suggested that organisations can draw from institutionalised schemata (Scott 2008).

Thus, in an organisational context, schemata refer to "generalised cognitive frameworks that give form and meaning to an experience and contain a specific knowledge about the domain" (Labianca et al. 2000). In NGOs, the idea of empowerment can be perceived from different schemata, drawing from the members' experiences, prior organisational meanings, and existing institutional definitions familiar to them. Schemata often become explicit in the course of negotiation where members of organisations explicate their taken-for-granted perceptions. Different levels of learning in Bateson's account (see Chapter 2) resonate with first-, second-, and third-order change in schemata (Bartunek & Moch 1987). First-order change refers to tacit reinforcement of present understandings, second-order change to a conscious modification of present schemata in a particular direction, and the third-order change to awareness of present schemata and therefore, the ability to change these schemata.

In this case, the first-order change would be articulating and agreeing on the present idea of what empowerment is, the second-order change would actively search for changes in the present schemata, and the third-order change would reveal a number of different taken-for-granted perceptions of empowerment, and thus, facilitate explicit reflection, not only on one "right" organisational idea, but also on the co-existing schemata and their pros and cons. As different schemata can co-exist, certain ones can be consolidated and institutionalised through organisational negotiation (McKinley et al. 2000). This idea is based on the general account of institutionalisation in social constructionism (Berger & Luckmann 1966) that suggests that institutionalisation includes an objectification and reification process where agreements negotiated through social interaction transform into external social reality. Thus, multiple schemata can be consolidated into one through negotiation, and gradually, can evolve into taken-for-granted institutionalised reality. In concrete interaction situations, the members of staff of World Vision articulated, and thus, negotiated their different schemata on empowerment.

Some of the schemata articulated were drawn from the institutional environment of international development. Meanings are carriers of institutions in organisations (Scott 2014 Zilber; 2017) and institutional frameworks shape how organisations give meaning to events and ideas, such as empowerment in this case (Douglas 1986). Institutional meanings are taken-for-granted as they are already part of the institutionalised order. In NGOs, holding empowerment to be a good, desirable and natural part of "what we do" is a powerful example of an institutionalised schema supported both by the symbolic and normative carriers of institutions, and played out through certain roles and routines, "the way we do these things" (Scott 2014, 68). However, organisations do not just passively adopt and repeat institutionalised talk of empowerment; they actively reproduce and modify it in their everyday activities while they make sense of empowerment (Weick 2009).

Therefore, the focus of organisational analysis here is on the cognitive and cultural aspects of "everyday processes rather than momentous events" (Powell & Colyvas 2008, 277). The continuous enactment and, often retrospective, sense-making is needed, as life is uncertain and does not smoothly fit into existing categories (Weick 2009). In addition to symbolic meanings and institutional repertoires, scripted interaction and role expectations are important means of constructing institutional orders and making sense of organisational life. Therefore, it is interesting to see what kinds of actions are situated under the category of "empowerment", from which kinds of institutional repertoires the practitioners' definitions of empowerment draw, and how the institutionalised scripts and roles constitute the very process of learning.

In examining negotiations about organisational meanings on empowerment, the question of power relations becomes relevant. While the cultural and practice-based perspectives on organisations emphasise the social construction of meanings, the critics have pointed out the tendency of having a "blind spot concerning power and politics", the strategies, tactics and processes of privileging certain views in negotiations and constructions of meanings (Marshall & Rollinson 2004). Therefore, any analysis of meaning-making should acknowledge power relations and the ways in which power relates to both the construction of identities in negotiating situations, and to the constitution of the entire practice under study, including broader asymmetries (Contu 2014, 290). Organisational learning as an everyday practice is enabled and constrained by relations of power, and the negotiations over meanings can include conflicts as well as consensus (Contu & Willmott 2003, 283). The organisation power relations, thus, can refer to more explicit hierarchies and dynamics of participation, more implicit discursively created positions and related knowledge claims, and either explicit or implicit knowledge needs of the organisational centre and periphery (Bunderson & Reagans 2011; Heizmann 2011). In development NGOs, struggles between knowledge needs and the priorities of headquarters and field offices are among the most typical ones, especially when it comes to knowledge production for monitoring and reporting purposes (see Chapter 3). In the same vein, in the partnerships analysed in this chapter, the need for a shared definition for empowerment was introduced by World Vision Finland who had explicitly emphasised empowerment in its new development programme.

Scripts for discussing empowerment in a learning event

The two events analysed in this chapter are so-called *impact seminars.* When we started our research collaboration, the impact seminar was a concept recently introduced in World Vision Finland. The organisation has started to arrange such annual seminars with its partner World Visions, in order to bring together staff from Finland and partner countries to jointly reflect on issues related to the impact of their work. The idea of seminars was introduced because much of the interaction between World Vision and its partners, often conducted by email, focused on solving daily problems and financial management details, and left no room for broader joint discussions. Both seminars, one conducted in Iten, Kenya in March 2012 and the other in Indore, India in November 2012, lasted for five days. A number of organisational issues, such as World Vision Finland's new programme, and mainstreaming disability and gender were discussed. One day was dedicated to a "field visit" to one of the programme areas; a village in Kenya and an urban slum area in India. The programme director of the World Vision Finland attended both seminars for part of the time, while the Finnish project coordinators responsible for the ongoing projects attended for the entire week. Empowerment was allocated slots during one day in both seminars. While all the World Vision offices shared certain meanings explicated in their international goals and indicators related to the children's well-being, the World Vision Finland wanted to put even more emphasis on the idea of empowerment as an impact.

In this section, I analyse the scripts and roles on the basis of recorded and transcribed seminar slots with the topic of empowerment in order to see how the negotiation about its shared meanings was conducted. We are all familiar with the scenes and scripts of an NGO seminar or workshop. Most of us are very competent in playing our roles in seminars, or we are fluent in "workshopping" with the following scenario. Participants stay in a hotel. The main material environment includes conference rooms, name badges, nicely set tables with notebooks, pencils, water bottles, maybe a plate or two of candy. The necessary artefacts include flipcharts, marker pens, masking tape, Post-its, copied programmes placed in folders, and nowadays also data projectors and laptops. Presentations and group work are conducted in turns, and many flipcharts are filled with analysis and ideas. Coffee and tea is served for breaks and there is a generous buffet for lunches. There is some free time during the evenings. At some point in a seminar, a group photo is taken, and perhaps certificates of participation are distributed at the end. This was more or less the scenario of the two seminars under analysis.

The arrangements of a "seminar" are so familiar that we often just take them for granted. But exactly because of the familiarity of the scenario, it is beneficial to have a look at how the seminar arrangements, the institutionalised scripts and role expectations are enacted in the practical conduct of a NGO seminar (cf. Weick 2009). A script can be defined as a routinised procedure of any organisational action; for example, meetings usually have certain scripts that everyone is familiar with. Roles, for their part, are institutionalised positions individuals play out in certain settings, and thus, are part of the scripts. Roles and scripts are enacted in communication styles, and interaction patterns. Scripts can be explicit, such as workshop programmes and training schedules, or more mundane institutionalised scripts. Therefore, deviations from scripts, such as changing topics or planned time allocations, can reveal something about the institutionalised relationships. In more profound cases, totally surprising topics can be introduced or explicit action against the routinised roles and patterns of action undertaken.

The discussions on empowerment within the particular slots reserved for it in Kenya and India followed quite standard scripts with no fundamental deviations. The scripts followed a pattern of presentations, group work and general discussion, with little variation in the sequence of the topics discussed, scheduled around lunch and coffee breaks (see Table 3.1). The typical ritual for starting a workshop, making introductions and discussing expectations, had already been conducted on the first day, so this was not repeated when empowerment was discussed. Our research project, however, was a new issue for the participants and was introduced. In Kenya, I started the empowerment sessions with a short introduction to the research project, and a presentation of the general challenges that NGOs struggle with in their M&E. This was followed by a group assignment where the participants were asked to list all the tools they were already using in their M&E, and reflect on whether these were used at levels of activity, outcome, or impact. The results were then presented to everyone, discussed, and then we proceeded to the issue of empowerment with an open question: What is empowerment? The answers were first written down individually then taken to groups with an assignment to reflect on how empowerment was defined and how the process of empowerment took place. After the group work, the results were presented group by group, and then a general discussion took place until lunch time when the session allocated to empowerment was supposed to end. However, it was decided to continue the discussion after lunch when the presentation of the programme director was supposed to begin. The lively debate on empowerment continued for over one hour after lunch, until the coffee and tea break, after which the new programme approach, Development Programme Approach introduced in WV, was discussed after being introduced by the Finnish programme director.

In India, the structure was slightly different. The day started by morning devotion and prayers conducted by the programme director. He then continued with an introduction to the funding structure of World Vision Finland and the related reporting requirements, and stressed two issues that are at the centre of WV Finland's new programme: the rights-based approach and youth employment. After a short discussion, he introduced the "next subject", empowerment, and asked the participants to take a piece of paper and write their definitions of empowerment on it, after which the definitions were shared. Then, the director showed a video of a man from Latin America who had succeeded in his life despite having a severe disability, followed by a discussion of what was learned from it, and then the programme director's presentation of his own ideas concerning empowerment. After a coffee break, I started my section on empowerment with a longish introduction to the research project, including a review of general academic debates on the concept of empowerment, the challenges in measuring empowerment, and the results from the discussions in Kenya. Then, a group assignment was conducted to identify the factors that enable and hinder empowerment. These were reported, and I continued by presenting the idea of "pathways of empowerment" that had been developed after the seminar in Kenya in collaboration with researchers and World Vision Finland. Then I provided groups an assignment to experiment the approach and describe pathways of empowerment in their own programme areas. The task was experienced as challenging, and the presentations of the results included a lively discussion about the participants' strong tendency to use "project" language.

All in all, scripts aligned with a typical *workshop* that includes both presentations and assignments in groups. Explicit scripts for these days were

Table 3.1 Structure of workshop sections on empowerment in Kenya and India 2012. "Researcher" refers to the author

Structure of empowerment section in Kenya	*Structure of empowerment section in India*
Researcher introduces research project and general challenges of M&E, and provides a group assignment	Programme director presents the new programme of World Vision Finland
Participants conduct a group assignment about different M&E tools they currently use	Programme Director facilitates a discussion on the question: What is empowerment?
Participants present the results of group assignments written in a flipchart accompanied by a general discussion chaired by the researcher	Researcher provides a general introduction to the research project, challenges in M&E, empowerment and the results of the discussions in the seminar in Kenya
Researcher provides a short assignment to discuss in pairs about what empowerment is	Researcher facilitates a short group discussion on the factors that hinder and enable empowerment
Participants conduct a group assignment about the stepping stones of empowerment, writing their results in a flipchart	Participants conduct a group assignment on the pathways of empowerment, drawing their results on a flipchart
Participants report the results followed by a general discussion chaired by the researcher	Participants present the results of their group assignment by flipchart
Participants conduct a short group discussion about what kinds of factors facilitate and hinder empowerment	Researcher chairs a general discussion that ends with participants enquiring about when the new tool would be ready, and a coffee break
Participants report the results, and the section ends with a coffee break	
Programme director facilitates a section on ADP – approach to development programmes	

planned by me and the programme director, and there were few spontaneous deviations from the plans, except the decision to extend the discussion about empowerment by an extra one and half hours in Kenya. This decision was related to the typical seminar scripts where keeping to a planned timetable is usually a challenge; the monologue presentations are longish, and it is often the dialogue between participants that is cut when being time-conscious. This privileging of presentation over dialogue is typically supported by the artefact of Power Points, as the one who presents has to be allowed to proceed *until the end of the slide show*, no matter how long it takes. The taken-for-granted role expectations in seminars include that those who are facilitators, also control time allocation and cut short topics, if needed. In these seminars, those who presented – me and the programme director – simultaneously chaired. In the workshop in India, in the conclusion after sharing his ideas about empowerment, the programme director said: "so that was a lot of preaching today, I think you have earned your coffee". This revealed a lot of the institutionalised interaction patterns that included amounts of preaching, lecturing and teaching on our part. In this script, the main role of the NGO participants was to listen, to perform the group assignments, and to actively converse on the topics within the time allocated; a role that was not openly resisted and the role expectations were played out smoothly.

At the same time, roles realised through interaction patterns of me, an academic researcher, and the programme director varied from those who *tell how things are* to those who would like *to know what the participants think about the issues.* At the same time, the roles of the participants varied from those who *should be able to give the right answers* to those who were welcome to *express different points of view and opinions.* My approaches varied between *lecturing* and *inquiring about* participants' opinions. In an academic role, while lecturing, I presented different general debates with a lot of "on the one hand – on the other hand" dilemmas on M&E and empowerment. However, in the course of the debates I often presented my own opinion on "how things are", and the participants also expressed expectations of me to know and to "answer their many questions". In contrast, the communication style of the programme director was more to present what he thought about empowerment, and how things were concerning the WV programme; a position very much expected from someone high in the organisational hierarchy. In Kenya, while presenting the new programming approach, an additional "schoolmaster" style was adopted when participants were asked to repeat together in a choir the mission and vision of the organisation and then remember and list the existing new programming principles.

From the outset, the discussions proceeded smoothly, more or less according to the ready-made plans. In India, an interesting small deviation from the ready-made script occurred during the experimentation on the pathways of empowerment in the groups. While the group presentations were supposed to describe the content of empowerment in different locations, the main topic of discussion became the difficulty of speaking without *development jargon*. After I had prompted one group to describe more precisely the realities in the community they were talking about, one of the participants commented: "There is a lot of jargon, she is asking to take away our jargon; the world is full of that jargon!" This comment was followed by laughter, but it explicated the challenges well. The assignment given was to describe different pathways of empowerment that take place in communities. When groups started to draw their pathways, they actually replicated their project logical frameworks (LFAs). I prompted one group to consider what would happen in the communities as a consequence of these activities, and everyone burst into laughter while one of the participants commented: "One problem I see is how they write in the log frame". The group agreed and reported that they had discussed whether some of the changes they had identified in the community could be defined as "result" or "impact", a distinction prevalent in LFA –logic. Another group, at one point of the group work, focused on the status of leadership in their project: "That's not an activity; It's a goal maybe; That's an objective; It's an output". These debates illustrated the power of LFA as an institutionalised interpretive framework. Moreover, within the LFA logic, the emphasis was on activities. For example, one of the groups described the process of empowerment as "gap assessment, sharing knowledge, training, providing resources…", and explained: "We can see the activities, we can define to a certain extent the impact, but we found it difficult to know how to contribute to the empowerment". The participants found it hard to distinguish between the linear intervention logic depicted in LFA and the idea of multiple, at times backwards-going pathways taking place within communities. After the concluding discussions, one of the members commented on the pathways approach: "This is a beautiful one! If you get that right, I am sure we will eventually reach sustainability!"

All in all, the discussion about meanings of empowerment followed quite standard and institutionalised scripts and role expectations typical of an NGO seminar. The negotiations, by no means, were about coercion to adopt a certain kind of definition of empowerment, but were characterised by curiosity about participants' perceptions and some room for dialogue. However, one may ask whether empowerment was discussed in a particularly empowering way when the role expectations, including the power of a "director" and a "researcher", were certainly prevalent. The practitioners were given some more room to reflect on empowerment in my individual interviews, the content of which will be used in the analysis of schemata in the following section.

Schemata of empowerment

> "empowerment, hope, choices, agency … they are all in the same package, within the same cube, no matter from which angle you look into it"
>
> (WVFi6)

After discussing the script and structure of the learning event, I proceed to describe the contents of the discussions on the meaning of empowerment. During the five seminar days I was able to conduct individual interviews with the participants during breakfast, lunch and in the evenings. In the course of the interviews, questions related to practitioners' definitions of empowerment and practical examples of empowerment were asked. In this section, I analyse the schemata, the generalised cognitive frameworks, of empowerment articulated in the workshop discussions and interviews. These draw from particular experiences, but at the same time, are carriers of institutions in organisations (Scott 2014). Therefore, when the members of World Vision searched for a shared organisational meaning for *empowerment* they simultaneously drew from meanings and discourses circulating in development cooperation in general. In quotes, WVfi refers to an interviewee in WV Finland and

WVField to an interviewee in partner WVs; interviewees in each group are identified with a running number.

Not surprisingly, an overall schema articulated was empowerment as a certain kind of development. In empowerment, "communities participate in identifying their development problems", or it is a learning process of equipping people with the necessary skills and knowledge so that "they are able to identify their own problems and come up with strategies for addressing their own problems, through utilising available resources and potentials", as repeated in many of the definitions given in the workshops. These definitions drew from a prevalent institutionalised idea of development as a process that includes the steps of identification of problems, potential solutions, and mobilising resources in order to realise these solutions. Additionally, in the seminar in Indore, some groups offered a definition of empowerment as "the power to make a right choice and an informed decision", which echoes the idea of empowerment as an increase of capability to makes choices based on the influential work of Sen (1999). This perspective is widely used, and occurs, for instance, in some of the World Bank's definitions such as "the process of enhancing the capacity of individuals or groups to make choices and to transform those choices into desired actions and outcomes" (Narayan 2002).

In organisational literature, a schema of "employee participation and shared responsibility for decisions leading to more effective organisational functioning" is one example of the highly institutionalised schemata (Bartunek & Moch 1987). In the same vein, an overall schema of "empowerment leads to good and sustainable development" is very prevalent in development. Empowerment as something good and desirable was a taken-for-granted, institutionalised schema that was reproduced in seminar discussions and interviews without being questioned. Only in one interview in Finland did a project coordinator challenge the usage of empowerment:

> I do not like the word "empowerment". For me it seems like a top-down idea in which the members of the community are some kind of objects, kind of weaklings in need of empowerment. I do not speak of empowerment in my daily life, why should I speak of it in the context of the everyday life of others?
>
> (WVFi5)

Even this account was not exactly a criticism of the inherent idea of empowerment, but spoke against the tendency to use certain institutionalised vocabularies rather than everyday language.

Thus, the basic normative schema according to which empowerment is desirable was well consolidated. However, more variation occurred when it came to the cognitive frameworks from which the actual meaning of empowerment was interpreted. In many instances, the definition of empowerment was clearly connected to the organisational terminologies used in World Vision. For example, both in the group discussions and interviews, empowerment was related to "identification of resources in order to improve well-being and to transform lives". Additionally, many definitions included vocabulary of "igniting the hidden potentialities". These frequently used terminologies of well-being, igniting and transforming lives were part of World Vision's established organisational language. World Vision speaks of transforming lives. A theory of change of World Vision's international network at the time of our research (World Vision 2013, 1) defined development as "transforming communities to improve the well-being of children and reduce poverty". It had three elements that formed the integrated focus of the organisation: it is a Christian, child-focused and community-based.

However, there were differences in regard to the articulations of transformation within the international World Vision network. Most importantly, the "Theology of Change" included in the Theory of Change was part of the organisational vocabulary for some offices, while others, including World Vision Finland, maintained a distance to it. The Theology of Change (World Vision 2013, 3) articulates that any change is "ultimately a work of God" in achieving fullness of life in loving relationships with God, with other people, and the environment. This echoes a definition of transformational and holistic development that includes spiritual, physical, mental and social dimensions (Myers 1999; 2014). Accordingly, the ultimate goal in the Theory of Change is "Life in all its fullness through God as the agent of change", while the Ministry Goal is "Sustained well-being of Children within Families and Communities, especially the most Vulnerable" (World Vision 2013, 11). The latter was the basis for the development cooperation programme for the World Vision Finland.

In other contexts, research has shown that in the practice of empowerment, the biblical and secular notions of increased agency can be intertwined. For instance, a member of staff in WV Tanzania explained (Hasu, forthcoming), how prayer can be seen as a form of agency through which a person can be empowered by an action plan delivered by God. While in the interviews and discussions in World Vision Finland, the faith-based interpretation of empowerment was not prevalent, in the interviews of the staff of the partner organisations, empowerment was also related to a "gift of God regardless of the vulnerabilities". In a number of interviews, the idea that everyone has God-given potentialities, and there is a moral urge to empower and work with the marginalised, was articulated through a religious language in which empowerment was part of following the example of the conduct of Jesus Christ. These accounts illustrated organisational, but more importantly, also personal world views and consequent schemata for empowerment. Such personal schemata were applied outside the organisational contexts as well; for example, some of the members of staff considered empowerment as their "passion", or part of their identity and a principle they realised in all areas of their lives.

When the schemata on empowerment drew from personal experiences, organisational vocabularies, and institutional definitions, multiple, even conflicting schemata were articulated, some of them being quite similar to those identified in World Vision Tanzania in early 2000s (Kelsall & Mercer 2003). In what follows, I will discuss three pairs of intertwining schemata that emerged in the discussions: (a) empowerment is an intervention approach vs empowerment is an indigenous process; (b) empowerment primarily refers to change in structures vs empowerment is primarily a change in agency; and (c) empowerment means an increase in power vs empowerment refers to growth in inner strength. These competing schemata coexisted, and in the course of negotiation did not consolidate into one dominant one. (cf. McKinley et al. 2000).

Empowerment is an intervention approach or an indigenous process

A general dilemma concerning development is that it entails changes that are simultaneously something that can be planned and realised through "powerful outsiders assisting powerless insiders" and an "indigenous process in no need of outside intervention" (Long 2001, 89). In their study of empowerment in WV Tanzania, Kelsall & Mercer (2003) identified a paradox in the implementation of empowerment initiatives. Paradoxical situations occured when external agencies are needed to somehow install desires internal to community, and in the way the NGO represented community members as "passive" and in need of active empowerment. Similar dilemmas apply to the cognitive frameworks from which empowerment was interpreted in the case discussions and interviews. The schema "empowerment is an NGO-intervention approach" was prevalent to the extent that the participants struggled to think of an alternative of empowerment being a process experienced by individuals or communities. In both seminars, one of the group assignments dealt with "stepping stones" or "pathways" of empowerment from the point of view of communities. In the instructions, I emphasised that the groups should try to think from the perspective of the communities; to describe "what happens, *not what we do*; not that we conduct training or do this and that, but what happens to the people who feel empowerment". However, the reported outcomes of the group discussions aligned very much with the schema of empowerment as an intervention, and described a process of "doing empowerment". The processes of empowerment presented included phases such as *involving communities in capacity assessment*, *resource mapping*, *identifying partners*, *capacity building* and *delegation of responsibilities*, *following up* and *evaluating* and, finally *ensuring ownership* that all depict clearly empowerment as intervention. In India, the groups not only described empowerment as an intervention with certain phases, but they also replicated the overall LFA logic as presented in the project documents. Empowerment was equated with project activities and stages of interventions rather than the processes or changes taking place in communities as a result of these activities. Therefore, the schema not only took intervention as a taken-for-granted starting point, but also depicted it very much with the institutionalised vocabularies of development management.

While the schema of empowerment as an intervention was the main framework, not all kinds of interventions were categorised as empowerment. On the contrary, especially in the interviews, the participants gave plenty of examples of development initiatives they considered not empowering. These included initiatives that were labelled in terms of "helping" and "charity" which were especially described as schemata held by some communities:

> We have the programming approach, you know, igniting the communities to take the lead in their own development; but in some previous projects in the area there have been disempowering approaches, so these communities were used to receiving things, and this created a kind of dependency syndrome.
>
> (WVField18)

Thus, empowerment as an intervention approach included the idea of *igniting hidden potential*. This combined the activities and resources provided by the outsider NGOs with those already residing in the communities. Some of the interviewees described empowerment as "a process of igniting human potential, to be able to utilise the local resources to help them reach where they want to reach" (WVField20), or "an act of igniting, tapping, enabling, put up that talent and seeing the potential these people have and helping them to put it into use" (WVField23). The terminology of igniting the potential, drawing much from the Christian principles, were repeatedly used in describing how there are some "dormant" or "hidden" resources in the communities, and with facilitation of the NGO these can be discovered and put into an active use. Therefore, a prevalent schema of empowerment being an intervention approach was combined with an expectation of empowerment being an indigenous process, but in need of some kind of intervention to be triggered at the first place.

Critical literature has argued against the schema of empowerment as an intervention approach, and suggested that empowerment should get rid of its interventionist connotations. On the contrary, empowerment should be looked at from the framework of self-reliant "empowering ourselves" rather than intentional, aid-funded projects where empowerment is supported by others (Mosedale 2005, 244). This view did not emerge in the seminar discussions or interviews which articulated quite strong belief in the need of outside contributions for empowerment to take place. Empowerment as an outsider intervention that could trigger an indigenous process was perceived as a sustainable strategy. As one of the Indian participants stated: "If we do not empower them properly, whatever we ignite may not continue when we withdraw" (WVField8). Similar thoughts were provided by a Kenyan participant: "WV goes to a place and it does not stay there for life but moves on; so if you do not leave an empowered community behind, then you've done nothing in the 15 years you spent there" (WVField12). The 15-year programme approach employed by the NGO was expected to result into sustainable, indigenous, empowerment that would continue without further inputs from the World Vision.

Within the schema of empowerment as an intervention, one of the main strategies was to form and support groups. Groups were perceived as typical spaces where indigenous empowerment, with little facilitation from outsiders, could take place and flourish. The rationale was that when people are brought together and they are provided with spaces to interact and do things together, a process of empowerment will be triggered. In India, most of the interviewees mentioned self-help groups (SHGs) as the main means of empowerment: "We have formed 72 groups; that is from zero to 72, a great achievement for our area context" (WVField4). In Finnish interviews, rewarding examples of groups coming together and "innovating new things" were cited, as well as better possibilities to discuss legislation or future plans. Also an Indian interviewee said: "When you are a group of people, it is not one person's issue, so you can better go to the decision-makers" (WVField6). Peer groups were also seen as effective in changing group members' own attitudes towards themselves and their possibilities to act, but also as spaces for shared responsibility. The strategy of supporting groups aligned directly with the schema of empowerment as an intervention, but it also had the option of moving towards the schema of empowerment as an indigenous process. This was exemplified by arguments that the NGO should support existing groups rather than establish new ones. As one of the Kenyan workshop participants commented:

> There should be something that had brought them together, not your organisation … it is much easier to sustain this kind of group, as they know that it is not only WV that brought them together; WV just found them on the way.

Supporting groups has been among the institutionalised strategies in NGO development cooperation for a long time. Micro-loans are provided for groups, different peer groups have been established, the latter involving the WVs strategy of establishing children's clubs. Additionally, supporting more established constellations of community-based organisations, and even local NGOs, has been a central strategy. However, literature has pointed out how the groups established are often formed by the local elites and power holders and might strengthen the marginalisation of those not included (Kelsall & Mercer 2003). The Indian interviewees often cited examples in which SHGs were established by those belonging to higher castes. Moreover, the critical literature has argued that "establishing organisations under the label of empowering interventions" does not necessarily bring about development, and that the donor strategies should rather be geared towards influencing the creation of supportive political environments (Batliwala, 2007; Moore, 2001). This leads us to the next pair of schemata concerning the question of the extent to which enabling environments and societal structures were at the heart of empowerment.

Empowerment as a change in individuals, communities or structures

In the workshop discussions and interviews, a tentative schema of empowerment as influencing change in societal structures was not very prevalent. Rather, the taken-for-granted ideas of the locus of empowerment were connected to the agency of individuals and community. Especially, but not exclusively, in the interviews with Finnish staff, the schema of empowerment resonated with educational and psychological theories of empowerment that revolve around concepts such as individual self-awareness, motivation and confidence (Zimmerman 1995, 574). In this schema, empowerment was mainly seen as a psychological process that takes place inside human beings, and results in better "knowledge of self". The experience of individuals was seen as central in empowerment, to the extent to that the "courage to say something" could be a sign of empowerment, no matter whether the consequences of the saying would be non-existent.

Change in self-confidence is needed before the potential change in structures occurs, as people have to "change their low self-esteem and the habits of being the government's subordinates" (WVFi2). Moreover, one of the Kenyan interviewees said: "Empowerment is self-confidence and independence, self-driven; you do not necessary need external pressure to propel, get moving" (VWField13), and another described an empowered person as "someone who knows what to do. When something happens to you, you do not remain there vulnerable and waiting for help, waiting for someone to be told, to tell you what to do" (WVField12). Success stories on empowerment also often concentrated on a change in individuals. For example, one of the Finnish interviewees narrated a story of an Indian girl who came from a very poor family. Her brother had run away, leaving debts to be paid by the girl and her mother. The girl had been offered a chance through World Vision sponsorship to attend training to be a hairdresser, and after receiving the necessary equipment from the NGO she established a beauty salon. Now "she has a lot of customers and is very self-reliant" and has successfully paid the debts (WVFi4).

In development literature, Kabeer's (1999) influential definition combines subjective and structural aspects of empowerment. Her definition of empowerment integrates elements of structure, agency and outcomes, and defines empowerment as a process where "those who have been denied the ability to make choices acquire such an ability" (ibid.137). This was echoed in a schema according to which empowerment refers to demanding the realisation of rights articulated in the interviews and discussions: "Empowerment is that people know about their rights". Dissemination of knowledge and information about the existing rights is a central strategy through which passive recipients will learn to be active citizens (Robins et al. 2008). Practical strategies include, for example, translating legislation into local language, conducting awareness-raising sessions, and establishing clubs and groups. As one of the Finnish members of staff said: "You might have whatever rights, but you do not know about them; when you receive information, you became more capable, some kind of mental change takes place, you can change from being a passive spectator to an active participant" (WVFi3). An example from a Ugandan respondent adds: "Having a voice, a say in decision making; when you are empowered there is no way you can keep quiet on some issue that's affecting you whether positively or negatively, you know you must participate" (WVField15).

Community development and empowerment of communities rather than individuals has been a prevalent strategy in NGO development cooperation, and community development programmes have been central to World Vision as well. The connection between individual and community empowerment was particularly focused upon in the seminar discussions in Kenya, where most of the arguments followed the line, "community is empowered but it is a result of individual empowerment" or "we are targeting individuals but through groups as a strategy". However, counter arguments pointed out that within vulnerable groups many "individuals, especially women and youth, might have a potential, but they are suppressed by the cultural barriers". This should be taken into account, for example, in the strategy of forming groups, as they are easily formed by the powerful men or local elite women. In the same vein, when discussing the hindrances to empowerment, these could be found in individuals' "lack of will" or "personality" which sometimes led to frustration since "once you ignite, you cannot continue igniting and igniting". The identified hindrances at community level included lack of knowledge, negative cultural values, illiteracy and ignorance, educational disparities, lack of exposure, and rigidness to change.

Therefore, the cultural habits and knowledge-related characteristics in communities were perceived to be in need of change. While the main schemata located empowerment to actors' agency at individual or community level, very few accounts mentioned societal structures. On the basis of the material at hand, one could argue that change in societal structures did not have primacy in the organisational schemata when it came to development programmes. For example, when the hindrances to empowerment were discussed in the Kenyan workshop, local power struggles including powerful local politicians were mentioned only once. Interestingly, in the same conversation, social structures were mentioned, but in reference to countries *other* than Kenya or Uganda, those that have structures such as "socialism" or a "caste system". On the contrary, the local caste system was frequently mentioned in India as the main structural barrier to empowerment. For example, a member of staff said in an interview:

> Caste is there; sometimes when we are organising a programme the low caste and the high caste women will not sit together, they do not want

> their food to be cooked together; we are struggling to convince them to accept each other.
>
> (WVField8)

Additionally, in India, the role and duties of government, and the barriers related to relationships with local political and religious elites were discussed a little more extensively. There were some references to elite-related hindrances to NGOs' activities, for example, in Sri Lanka: "Sometimes the political authorities join the Buddhist monks and convince them that World Vision is trying to convert people into Christians, and then everything is impossible" (WVField 2). However, as in Kenya, the Indian interviewees also often cited "cultural barriers" such as powerful role of mother-in-law in the family as the main hindrances of empowerment. In order to draw connections between individuals, communities and societal structures, WV has implemented the Citizen Voice and Action approach since 2009 in some of the programme areas, but not in those programmes included in this research. Citizen Voice and Action is based on Freirean pedagogical principles to enhance community empowerment for social accountability where communities are enabled by reducing fear and mutual blaming, and encourage community gatherings (Walker 2017). Moreover, the Theory of Change situates addressing the structural and systemic causes of poverty under the category of advocacy, not development (World Vision 2013, 7). The structures therefore did not play an important role in the vocabularies of those who worked in community development projects.

Empowerment is change in the power balance or in people's inner strength

The weakness of an organisational schema of empowerment as a structural change is related to the question about the role of the phenomenon of power in empowerment. Some critics have pointed out that the idea of political power has disappeared from the notion of empowerment in development cooperation (Batliwala 2007), others have pointed out how power can be understood in many different ways (Rowlands 1997). All in all, in the practitioners' schemata the place of power was ambiguous. One of the Finnish interviewees strongly argued, "we are not looking for power but strength; strength with which a human being can change her environment" (WVFi4). She also reflected that "power is often a zero-sum-game; strength is more essential". The kind of putting power aside echoed a view that searching for power is something negative. However, for example Kabeer (1999, 438) has reminded us about the centrality of power in empowerment. Not all increase of choice is empowerment, but of "those previously being disempowered through deep-seated constraints on the ability to choose".

The complicated questions of empowerment as a zero-sum-game in regard to power balance, and whether empowerment of some requires simultaneous disempowerment of others was discussed at length in the seminar in

Kenya. At the outset, the discussion echoed a schema where empowerment of one group meant disempowerment of another. Examples were given from different project experiences. When children were empowered, parents have "felt they have been weakened", and therefore the NGO should be careful not to "teach children their rights but forget the responsibilities". Similarly, changes in power balances between genders were reflected. One of the participants argued that sometimes the programmes were "empowering the girl child while disempowering the boy; we can find at the end of the day that, according our indicators we empowered girls, but in regard to boys, it turned out terrible". A story from Uganda illustrated violent and quarrelsome reactions by husbands to the relative economic empowerment of their wives brought about by piglets donated by World Vision. This extended to a harsh criticism towards the NGO itself: "whenever they see me or our vehicle they become aggressive; they say we only facilitate breakage of families" (WVField 22). A female participant referred to another kind of negative impact of the economic empowerment of women: "Now some men have delegated their responsibility to these empowered women, because now women are able to bring in income, so now the man does not pay for school fees, or buy food". Another participant contested the idea that change in gender relations would mean the disempowerment of men: "Empowerment, of course, influences the power relations dictated by the traditions, but influence is not the same as disempowerment". In this regard, a Finnish project coordinator also shared examples of a project in Kenya where at the beginning, men had been "very suspicious about women's empowerment", but in the end, "they were so proud of their wives who had been so successful".

Additionally, awareness-raising about policies and rights had been perceived as disempowerment on the part of local power holders. They were concerned about losing their authority and power if people knew more about their existing rights. As a consequence, "those holding power can create a lot of problems" for the projects. Such reactions could, according to the participants, be avoided if "you bring them on board at an earlier stage". A Finnish participant challenged the overall idea, and asked, "How can you disempower government as you are the government, you are the ones that give the authority to the government; there might be feeling of losing authority, feeling of being checked, but that is not disempowerment". He also suggested that there should be an *ethical* aspect to empowerment. Empowerment does not refer to any increase in one's power, but it has to be something that is ethically used: "Dictatorship is not empowerment". Some of the interviewees also referred to the importance of the ethical content of empowerment, as "empowerment is for the benefit for others, for goodness" and "we have to include moral values; empowerment can be used to so many ends".

Increase in hope and expanding future perspectives were important elements of empowerment. For example, one of the Finnish interviewees argued that empowerment is a "kind of realisation of the difference between your own stage and that of someone else, and a desire to reach the other's stage"

(WVFi2). All in all, in workshop discussions it was agreed that empowerment is relational, as "a person on an island cannot be empowered". In the workshop in Kenya, a Finnish participant also introduced the notion of "over-empowerment". He provided an example of a Finnish factory worker in the food industry: "If you over-empower that person, there is no way to manage that person anymore". So, the goals of empowerment should be different in different levels as well, and he explained that the NGO should be careful about what kinds of "images we paint for people about what is possible and what is not possible".

In conclusion, it became evident on the basis of the articulated understandings of the members of staff, that in NGOs it is hard to define one prevalent organisational schema for empowerment. However, drawing on the data available, one can argue that those who "do empowerment" hold a general schema that "empowerment is desirable and leads to sustainable development", and that "empowerment is a certain kind of intervention approach"; a kind of intervention that supports existing processes. Moreover, the prevalent schemata mostly understood empowerment, when ignited, as a process taking place in individuals and communities, while changes in political and societal structures remained more peripheral issues within practitioners' interpretations.

Conclusion

In conclusion, I will return to the idea of organisational learning as acquiring, sustaining, and changing meanings embedded in organisational practices, related to either preserving or changing organisational identity and ability to do what the organisation does (Cook & Yanow 1993), and learning as first-, second- and third-order change in schemata that offer frameworks for meaning (Bartunek & Moch 1987). The shared meanings of empowerment were searched for in the institutionalised setting of an NGO seminar where everyone – including myself as a researcher – acted according to their roles and the institutionalised scripts. The presentations were given according to the plans; participants took part in group work and discussions in a committed way. Nobody refused to participate, or contested the agenda, nor introduced totally new items to the agenda.

Both seminars in their entirety can be seen as learning as acquiring, and as sustaining the organisational meanings in regard to the programme approaches and cross-cutting issues that form an important part of the organisational vocabulary. The workshops enhanced the ability of World Vision Finland and its partners to define what it does; community empowerment programmes with the ultimate goal of supporting the well-being of children. The learning revolved around first the vocabularies and approaches shared by the entire World Vision network; and second, around World Vision Finland's new programme. In the latter, learning emerged more as the acquiring or adapting of terminologies and approaches developed either by World Vision International or World Vision Finland. However, discussions on empowerment were not clearly about transferring or adapting its already existing organisational definition, but more about revealing the different interpretations and schemata of empowerment that already circulated among the staff. While there were multiple schemata the organisation schema of empowerment as desirable and a right way to do development provided an overall shared meaning.

On occasions, my aspiration to be a researcher who merely would like to know what the participants think did not fit the role expectations towards an outsider academic to tell and advise "how things should be done". This was explicated not only in requests to teach how to monitor empowerment but also in participants' occasional worries about whether they "had it right" when reporting the group works. The need to align with the "right definitions" was apparent in seminar discussions and interviews in which the respondents tended first to provide a definition of empowerment with organisational terminology before narrating examples of empowerment in a more everyday language. The need to succeed and to know the right answers reflects the more general institutional setting of development cooperation where reporting success in partnerships is central. A small step towards an alternative direction was taken in Kenya, where the negative effects of women's empowerment projects were discussed. These were welcomed by the Finnish participants who reminded how important it would be to include also the negative impacts in the reports: "We never hear about the negative parts; here I can hear some coming up, and that is a good point for learning, to focus sometimes on the negative parts."

Seminars provided instances of learning as building awareness of existing perceptions to enable their reflection. In relation to the notion of empowerment, the group assignments and discussions revealed some ideas of coexisting perceptions that were jointly reflected in the discussions. These ideas included trying to change the empowerment perspective from an intervention approach – what we do when we empower – to identifying a process that takes place in individuals and communities – what happens to them in the process of their own empowerment. Moreover, the discussions on whether empowerment is geared mainly towards individuals or communities, or different understandings of power and disempowerment in the processes of empowerment all explicated various schemata and introduced them into explicit discussion.

In the Indian workshop, the participants' realisation of their extended use of development jargon opened a space for reflection about the vocabularies through which NGO practices are typically described and their implications for meanings and relationships with the people they work with. Applying occasionally a schema different from the project management and the NGO's point of view provides opportunities for learning about the rationalities and dynamics prevalent in the communities. Without doubt, as became evident in the interviews, in their everyday work, the members of staff continuously engage with so-called beneficiary logics in addition to their organisational intervention logics (Olivier de Sardan 2005). According to the World Vision principle, some members of staff stay in the communities and are thus very familiar with the contexts, and the ways the beneficiaries perceive and talk about their lives. However, the institutional settings of an NGO seminar with partners seemed to strengthen the tendency to speak in "dev-speak" (Tvedt 2002) rather than encourage them to bring the beneficiary discourses into the organisational discussions.

In conclusion, the answer to the general question of whether learning in this case was about preserving or changing World Vision's identity as a development organisation and its ability to do what it does is that the seminar functioned to preserve and strengthen that identity. In its own modest way, it also provided reflective spaces for enhancing World Vision's ability to do better what it does – to implement community development programmes in an empowering way. The analysis showed the strength of institutionalised meanings in development NGOs, and indicated how institutionalised power relationships in partnerships are reconstructed in everyday practices such as arranging NGO seminars.

References

Alsop, R & Heinsohn, N. (2005) *Measuring Empowerment in Practice: Structuring Analysis and Framing Indicators*. World Bank Policy Research Working Paper 3510. Washington: World Bank.

Atack, I. (1999) Four criteria of development NGO legitimacy. *World Development*, 27(5), 855–864.

Banks, N., Hulme, D. & Edwards, M. (2015) NGOs, states, and donors revisited: Still too close for comfort? *World Development*, 66, 707–718.

Bartunek, J.M. & Moch, M.K. (1987) First order, second order, and third order change and organisation development interventions. A cognitive approach. *Journal of Applied Behavioral Science*, 23(4), 483–500.

Batliwala, S. (2007) Taking the power out of empowerment – an experiential account. In Cornwall, A. & Eade, D. (eds) *Deconstructing Development Discourse Buzzwords and Fuzzwords*. Rugby: Practical Action Publishing, 111–122.

Brown, H. & Green, M. (2015) At the service of community development: The professionalization of volunteer work in Kenya and Tanzania. *African Studies Review*, 58(2), 63–84.

Contu, A. (2014) On boundaries and difference: Communities of practice and power relations in creative work. *Management Learning*, 45(3), 289–316.

Contu, A. & Willmott, H. (2003) Re-embedding situatedness: The importance of power relations in learning theory. *Organization Science*, 14(3), 283–296.

Cook, S.D.N. & Yanow, D. (1993) Culture and organisational learning. *Journal of Management Inquiry*, 2(4), 373–390 373–390.

Cornwall, A. (2017) *The Role of Social and Political Action in Advancing Women's Rights, Empowerment, and Accountability to Women*. IDS Working Paper no. 488. London: Institute of Development Studies.

Cornwall, A. (2007) Buzzwords and fuzzwords: Deconstructing development discourse. *Development in Practice*, 17(4/5): 471–484.

Cornwall, A. (2016) Women's empowerment: What works? *Journal of International Development*, 28(3), 342–59.

Cornwall, A. & Edwards, J. (2014) (eds) *Feminism, Empowerment and Development: Changing Women's Lives*. London: Zed Books.

Cruikshank, B. (1999) *The Will to Empower. Democratic Citizens and Other Subjects*. Ithica, NY: Cornell University Press.

Dar, S. (2014) Hybrid accountabilities: When western and non-western accountabilities Collide. *Human Relations*, 67(2), 131–151.

Deephouse, D.L. & Suchman, M. (2008) Legitimacy and Organisational Institutionalism. In: Greenwood, R., Oliver, C. & Sahlin, K. & Suddaby, R. (eds) *The Sage Handbook of Organizational Institutionalism*. Los Angeles: SAGE, 49–77.

DiMaggio, P.J. & Powell, W.W. (1983). The iron cage revisited: Institutional isomorphism and collective rationality in institutional fields. *Annual Review of Sociology*, 16, 137–159.

Douglas, M. (1986) *How Institutions Think*. Syracuse, NY: Syracuse University Press.

Friedmann, J. (1992) *Empowerment. The Politics of Alternative Development*. Cambridge: Blackwell.

Hansson, S. (2015) Analysing responsibilization in the context of development cooperation. In: Hansson, S. & Hellberg, S. with Stern, M. (eds) *Studying the Agency of being Governed. Methodological Reflections*. London: Routledge.

Hasu, P. (forthcoming) Faith-based Development of World Vision Tanzania. *Journal of Contemporary Religion*. Accepted for publication.

Heizmann, H. (2011) Knowledge sharing in a dispersed network of HR practice: Zooming in on power/knowledge struggles. *Management Learning*, 42(4), 379–393.

Kabeer N (1999) Resources, agency, achievements: Reflections on the measurement of women's empowerment. *Development and Change*, 30(3), 435–464.

Kelsall, T. & Mercer, C. (2003) Empowering people? World Vision & "transformatory development" in Tanzania. *Review of African Political Economy*, 30(96), 293–304.

Kontinen, T. & Robinson-Moncada, S. (2014) *Towards New Practices of Monitoring in World Vision Finland: Pathways of empowerment*. Helsinki: World Vision Finland, publications 1.

Labianca, G., Gray, B. & Brass, D.J. (2000) A grounded model of organisational schema change during empowerment. *Organization Science*, 11(2), 235–257.

Long, N. (2001) *Development Sociology. Actor Perspectives*. Routledge: London.

McKinley, N., Zhao, J. & Garnett Rust, K. (2000) A sociocognitive interpretation of organisational downsizing. *The Academy of Management Review*, 25(1), 227–243.

Marshall, N. & Rollinson, J. (2004) Maybe Bacon had a point: The politics of interpretation in collective sensemaking. *British Journal of Management*, 15 (51), 71–86.

Myers, B.L. (1999) *Walking With the Poor: Principles and Practice of Transformational Development*. Maryknoll, NY: Orbis Books and World Vision.

Myers, B.L. (2014) *Walking with the Poor. Principles and Practices of Transformational Development*. Revised and expanded edition. Maryknoll, NY: Orbis Books.

Moore, M. (2001) Empowerment at last? *Journal of International Development*, 13, 321–326.

Mosedale, S. (2005) Assessing women's empowerment: Towards a conceptual framework. *Journal of International Development*, 17, 243–257.

Narayan, D. (ed.) (2005) *Measuring Empowerment*. New York: The World Bank.

Narayan, D. (2002) *Empowerment and Poverty Reduction: A Sourcebook*. Washington, DC: World Bank. https://openknowledge.worldbank.org/handle/10986/15239

Nederveen Pieterse, J. (2001) *Development Theory. Deconstructions/reconstructions*. London: SAGE.

Olivier de Sardan, J.-P. (2005) *Anthropology and Development. Understanding Contemporary Social Change*. London: Zed Books.

Powell, W.W. & Colyvas, J.A. (2008). Microfoundations of institutional theory. In R. Greenwood et al. (eds) *Handbook of Organizational Institutionalism*. London: SAGE, 276–298.

Rahnema, M. (1993) Participation. In Sachs, W. (ed.) *The Development Dictionary: A Guide to Knowledge as Power*. London: Zed Books.

Robins, S., Cornwall, A. & von Lieres, B. (2008) Rethinking "citizenship" in the postcolony. *Third World Quarterly*, 29(6), 1069–1086.

Rowlands, J. (1997) *Questioning Empowerment: Working with Women in Honduras*. Oxford: Oxfam.

Salamon, L. (1994). The rise of the nonprofit sector. *Foreign Affairs*, 73(4), 109–122.

Scott, R.W. (2014). *Institutions and Organizations*. Thousand Oaks, CA: SAGE.

Sen, A. (1999) *Development as Freedom*. Oxford: Oxford University Press.

Suchman, M.C. (1995) Managing legitimacy: Strategic and institutional approaches. *Academy of Management Review*, 20(3), 571–610.

Swai, E.V. (2010) *Beyond Women's Empowerment in Africa: Exploring Dislocation and Agency*. New York: Palgrave Macmillan.

Tsoukas, H. (2005) *Complex Knowledge: Studies in Organizational Epistemology*. Oxford: Oxford University.

Tvedt, T. (1998) *Angels of Mercy or Development Diplomats? NGDOs and Foreign Aid*. Oxford: Africa World Press.

Tvedt, T. (2002) Development NGOs: Actors in a global civil society or in a new international social system. *Voluntas: International Journal of Voluntary and Nonprofit Organizations*, 13(4), 363–375.

Tvedt, T. (2006) The international aid system and the non-governmental organizations: A new research agenda. *Journal of International Development*, 18(5), 677–690.

Walker, D. (2017) Leveraging communities' capabilities to increase accountability for health rights: The case of Citizen Voice and Action. *Journal of Human Development and Capabilities*, published online before print. DOI: 10.1080/19452829.2017.1411894

Watkins, S.C., Swidler, A. & Hannan, T. (2012). Outsourcing social transformation: Development NGOs as organizations. *Annual Review of Sociology*, 38, 285–315.

Weick, K.E. (2009) *Making Sense of the Organisation. Volume 2*. Chichester: Wiley.

Weick, K.E. & Quinn, R.E. (1999) Organizational change and development. *Annual Review of Psychology*, 50(1), 361–386.

World Vision International (2013) *World Vision's Theory of Change*. Accessed 15.4.2013, www.wvi.org/international/publication/world-visions-theory-change

Zilber, T.B. (2017) The evolving role of meaning in theorizing institutions. In: Greenwood, R., Oliver, C., Lawrence, T.B. & Meyer, R.E. (eds) (2017) *The Sage Handbook of Organizational Institutionalism*. Los Angeles, CA: SAGE, 418–445.

Zimmerman, M.A. (1995) Psychological empowerment: Issues and illustrations. *American Journal of Community Psychology*, 23(5), 581–599.

4 Learning as a change in organisational epistemology

In this chapter, the analytical focus shifts from organisational meanings to organisational knowledge criteria. Like other organisations, development NGOs have profiled as knowledge-intensive organisations. They collect and restore increasing amounts of information concerning, for example, their beneficiaries, working environments, and the progress of their activities (Hayman et al. 2016). The potential wealth of knowledge is limitless; however, it is constrained by time, money and other resources, and the judged relevance is based on organisational knowledge criteria. This chapter scrutinises the concept of organisational knowledge and analyses the process of organisational learning as a change in the knowledge criteria – in other words, organisational epistemology. Most NGOs rarely engage with in-depth epistemological debates since they are busy fulfilling the managerial knowledge production needs to satisfy their donors (Horton & Roche 2010). However, some, often implicit, epistemological criteria are used in the everyday selection of relevant knowledge and the appropriate means of knowledge creation.

Research into *organisational epistemology* (Seirafi 2012) concentrates on analysing these criteria. Organisations tend to judge knowledge vis-á-vis their goals and structures rather than any philosophical epistemological criteria concerning knowledge production in general. Therefore, organisational epistemology is embedded in organisational practices, constructed in the processes of organisational meaning-making vis-á-vis the organisational goals and structure, and as such is flexible and subject to possible changes. In this chapter, I suggest organisational learning should be analysed as a change in organisational epistemology, and propose that organisational epistemologies should be understood as constructed in interaction with institutional environments.

A learning process as a change in organisational epistemology is illustrated by an analysis of an attempt to introduce a story-based M&E approach in International Solidarity Foundation (ISF), a Finnish development NGO focusing on themes of gender equality and decent work and livelihood and implementing projects in Nicaragua, Uganda, Somaliland and Kenya. The analysis is based on interviews, meetings and documents collected with the staff of the ISF in 2014–2015. At the time of starting our research project, the NGO had already developed the approach for a few years. Therefore, some of the research material consists of retrospective reflection on what has happened in the past, while some is about participant observation of ongoing discussions. The analysis will show how change in organisational epistemology requires time, experimentation and networking, and despite a series of innovative efforts, the tendency to align with the institutionalised epistemologies and the practical effects of institutional environments is strong, and sometimes even "lethal" to learning.

Organisational knowledge and epistemology

The organisational knowledge can be discussed along cognitive and constructionist lines (Rowland 2004, 34), or from cognitivist and embodied perspectives (von Krogh et al. 1994, 54). The cognitive view sees knowledge merely as static representations of the world that can be stored and retrieved from the knowledge structures of organisations, while the constructionist and embodied approaches understand knowledge as negotiated, practised and as a dynamic phenomenon. In the same vein, the structural view of organisations stresses organisation charts, and institutionalised roles and rules, while the practice-based approach used in this book, emphasises human interaction, meaning-making and negotiation within organisations (Feldman & Orlikowski 2011; Gherardi 2000; Tsoukas & Vladimirou 2001, 979). In this chapter, I draw from the notion of organisational knowledge as a phenomenon negotiated in organisational interaction and embedded in organisational practices, and argue that there is a constant movement between practices and structured forms of knowledge such as expertise positions, reports, guidelines and templates.

Knowledge is essential for an organisation to be able to function, coordinate its actions and achieve its goals. Intertwined with the shared organisational meanings, organisational knowledge allows shared distinctions made by the members of organisations in support of a joint understanding of "what we are doing here". While organisational life – and the life of development NGOs as well – might consist of rather similar events and activities, each organisation tends to name and categorise these events in a slightly different way (von Krogh et al. 1994, 59–60). Thus, organisational knowledge reflects members' capacities to draw distinctions in particular concrete situations where organisations' members carry on their work (Tsoukas & Vladimirou 2001, 983). This ability is developed in the course of interaction and the accomplishment of actual organisational tasks and, as such, is not easily transferred from one organisation to another that has different interactional habits, different tasks, and different organisational language. In a development NGO, the creation of organisational knowledge is challenging. While the large NGOs are famous for developing their own symbolic spaces articulated through different acronyms, creating shared meanings, categories and distinctions within one organisation does not suffice. In development NGOs, the tasks have to be accomplished and categories understood across organisational borders in partnerships. Therefore, the significance of the institutional categories and language, the "devspeak" (Tvedt 2002, 2006) increases as it provides some shared coordination points in regard to "what we are doing", as illustrated in Chapter 3.

Different types of organisational knowledge can be distinguished. For example, explicit and tacit knowledge (Nonaka & Takeuchi 1995), individual and collective knowledge (Spender 1998), and propositional and narrative knowledge (Tsoukas 2004; Seirafi 2012) have been identified. While these distinctions are useful to aid understanding, the focus here is more on the knowledge as part of practice, not as something possessed but as something emerging in action, that is, a focus on *knowing* (Cook & Brown 1999, 382–383). For the analysis presented in this chapter, also the distinction between propositional and narrative knowledge is relevant. The organisational M&E practices include both types of knowledge and movement between these two. The propositional view takes knowledge merely as possessed and stored in organisational structures and routines while the narrative view emphasises knowledge making, meaningful actions, and judgement.

Propositional knowledge is explicit and includes organisational rules that are necessary for coordinating organisational action. In NGOs, it is commonly expected that all members follow rules and procedures explicated in plans, guidelines, reporting templates, and knowledge-management systems. However, guidelines and templates are always applied and enacted by certain members in specific contexts (Tsoukas & Vladimirou 2001, 980). For example, in all the case organisations, there were plenty of guidelines and templates for monitoring, but monitoring as a term used by the staff could refer to anything from detailed indicator-based data collection and analysis to making a single phone call to a partner organisation. The context-specific description of concrete individual actors and events are often articulated in the form of narrative knowledge; knowledge that is embodied in practice and can be articulated through stories, anecdotes and experiences with certain cultural meanings (Tsoukas 2005, 71, 82). In development NGOs, the staff members tell stories about their prior visits to particular programme villages, the challenges with local leaders, their positive experiences on progress observed, and their struggles with indicator matrices; they share tips on how to negotiate with government officials in a certain country, and how to best mobilise community members in a certain place. These experiences constitute an important part of organisational knowledge on how to implement programmes and achieve the organisational goals in an effective and context-sensitive way, but are rarely included in any guidelines or other propositional forms of knowledge.

Organisations do not usually exist for the sake of knowing only. They have their goals to be met and tasks to be accomplished. Therefore, they do not collect, create and use knowledge for its own value, but for use in their conduct (Spender 1998, 237). This leads to a question of what counts as knowledge in any particular organisation and on what criteria. These criteria of knowledge are at the core of organisational epistemology (Tsoukas 2005, 5). Organisational epistemology differs from the philosophical search for criteria for knowledge as "justified true belief", and resonates with the philosophical notion of social epistemology. In social epistemology, production, validation and acceptance of scientific knowledge are understood as a social process within the scientific community (Longino 2002). The aims and standards prevalent in the community contribute to validation of knowledge; if the content of the knowledge claim is acceptable and complies with the aims of the community, the knowledge claim can be transformed into knowledge (Longino 2002, 145). In an organisational context, social epistemology implies that the criteria of organisational knowledge define knowledge as "distinction accepted by the organisational structure, and confirmed by the organisational goals" (Seirafi 2012, 168). These knowledge criteria also define what the appropriate knowledge production means are (Tsoukas 2005, 3). Consequently, NGOs judge the relevance of knowledge on the basis of their goals and structures. For instance, the lives of people in a certain community can provide different knowledge to different NGOs. A gender NGO searches for knowledge on distribution of property and labour between men and women or for cultural constructions of gender roles; an NGO working on agricultural extension focuses on knowledge about soil, yields and crops produced; while an education NGO scrutinises the enrolment rates and accounts of the quality of education. The methods used in baseline studies and M&E might differ and thus provide different kinds of knowledge. While some NGOs focus on measuring the characteristics of the material environment, others conduct surveys to measure social phenomena, and others focus on collecting experiences of the people living in the community.

Complexity in organisational environments and uncertainty in their objectives characterise development NGOs (Watkins et al. 2012). They also pose challenges to the definition of criteria for organisational knowledge. There are plenty of environments to take into account; goals such as empowerment are often both ambiguous and ambitious; and organisational knowledge claims need to be not only internally validated, but are geared towards a number of external audiences (Tsoukas 2005, 3). In development NGOs, what counts as knowledge is not only evaluated vis-á-vis organisational goals and structure, but also in relation to what is considered knowledge by donors, by the general public on whom the resources and political support for NGOs depends, and by the NGO beneficiaries.

Organisational epistemologies can be examined through looking at the kinds of distinctions made, for example, in organisations' mission statements (von Krogh et al. 1994, 62). However, mission statements and other documents show only the explicated forms of organisational epistemology. Therefore, attention should be paid also to the ways in which multiple knowers enact knowledge and the kinds of language used not only in documents but in everyday practice (King & Zeithaml, 2003). Organisational epistemology and organisational learning are connected by the occurrence of negotiation between different perspectives. Organisational knowledge creation should include critical interaction and inclusion of multiple perspectives, even if the inclusion of these new perspectives is constrained by the prevalent organisational epistemology, the organisational goals, structures and context (Seirafi 2012, 168). Organisations, thus, can learn by creating new knowledge within the existing organisational epistemology, or learn through critically reflecting, and then changing these constraints (ibid.). These different types of learning resonate with the levels of learning introduced in Chapter 2; the creation of better knowledge within existing epistemology would result from learning I, whereas attempts to create better knowledge criteria would be indicators of level II learning.

On the above basis, in this chapter organisational knowledge in development NGOs is defined as distinctions and categories accepted by organisational structure, confirmed by organisational goals, and aligned with institutional standards. Furthermore, organisational epistemology refers to the ways in which knowledge is judged in regard to these aspects, and organisational learning means both knowledge creation within existing organisational epistemology and attempts to critically reflect upon and change it. As the empirical investigation of organisational knowledge and organisational epistemology in general is a wide task, I focus on the criteria used to judge knowledge creation in M&E in the context of one NGO.

Learning trajectory: from scattered ideas to organisational epistemology

Recently, there has been a lively discussion about different M&E approaches in development and their appropriateness to different purposes (Guijt & Roche 2014; Horton & Roche 2010). Increased acknowledgement of the complexity of development has challenged the linear logics in LFA (Davies 2004, 2005), and initiated reflection of the pitfalls of indicator-based M&E used in measurement of social change (Horton & Roche 2010). The participatory approaches (Chambers 2008), life-histories (Davis 2011), and the most significant change (MSC) (Davies & Dart 2005) have all attempted to capture qualitative change processes and the experiences of beneficiaries.

The case of the ISF analysed in this chapter joins these general trends. Established in the year 1970 as a campaign organisation as part of the third world solidarity movement, and gradually transformed from the 1980s onwards into a professional development NGO, ISF implements development projects together with partner organisations in countries such as Uganda, Somaliland, Kenya and Nicaragua. It also conducts communication and advocacy work in Finland and has a significant number of individual sponsors from Finnish public. Its annual budget in 2015 was €3.5 million, of which development programme budget was €3.1 million. In 2015, ISF received €2.5 million funding from the Ministry for Foreign Affairs of Finland. The number of employees revolves around ten in Finland and six in the partner countries.

The ISF is an example of an experienced and competent development NGO. It has had a well-established LFA-based project model explicated in detailed guidelines since the early 1990s and has followed a programme approach since 2003. At the time of the data collection, its development programme was divided into two sub-programmes: gender equality, and decent work and livelihood. The programme was realised through a variety of projects addressing gender-based violence and livelihood support especially through producer cooperatives. Thus, the new idea of story-based M&E entered a solid organisational epistemology. Since the introduction of a programme framework, the knowledge focus had been on gender and livelihoods including decent work. Therefore, information about the level of income in cooperatives and producer groups had been relevant, along with the rates of domestic violence and female genital mutilation (FGM). Both programme and projects implemented under the programme conformed to the epistemological criteria of the LFA. The results of evaluation of the programme framework conducted in 2011 confirmed that the ISF had a well-established indicator-based M&E. The main donor, the Ministry for Foreign Affairs of Finland, was satisfied with the organisation's reporting and results.

Therefore, at the time the discussion of the story-based M&E started, there were no major challenges facing the organisational epistemology or the knowledge production practices. However, some of the partner organisations in Uganda and Somaliland had a habit of collecting success stories from the beneficiaries, and at the same time, the partner cooperatives in Nicaragua became interested in exploring not only economic but also experienced elements of poverty. The initiatives undertaken by partners, when communicated to the ISF headquarters, triggered a five-year learning process, the main events of which are depicted in Figure 4.1. The trajectory clearly illustrates how story-based M&E evolved from scattered ideas into a part of organisations' explicated epistemology; in the end, the story-based method was integrated into the ISF's official programme document submitted to the donor. The trajectory also shows how organisational learning is a long-term process that requires a wealth of events, interaction and joint experimentation, as well as the utilisation of available networks.

On the basis of their practices, between 2010 and 2012, partner organisations came up with questions of whether more qualitative M&E means could be used. In Nicaragua in 2012, partner cooperatives opted for designing contextual poverty indicators embracing "meanings people give to poverty". They came up with a questionnaire that included open questions on beneficiaries' perspectives on certain themes such as poverty, capacities and gender roles. The plan was that the questionnaire would be administered before and after project activities to capture possible change. In Uganda a partner

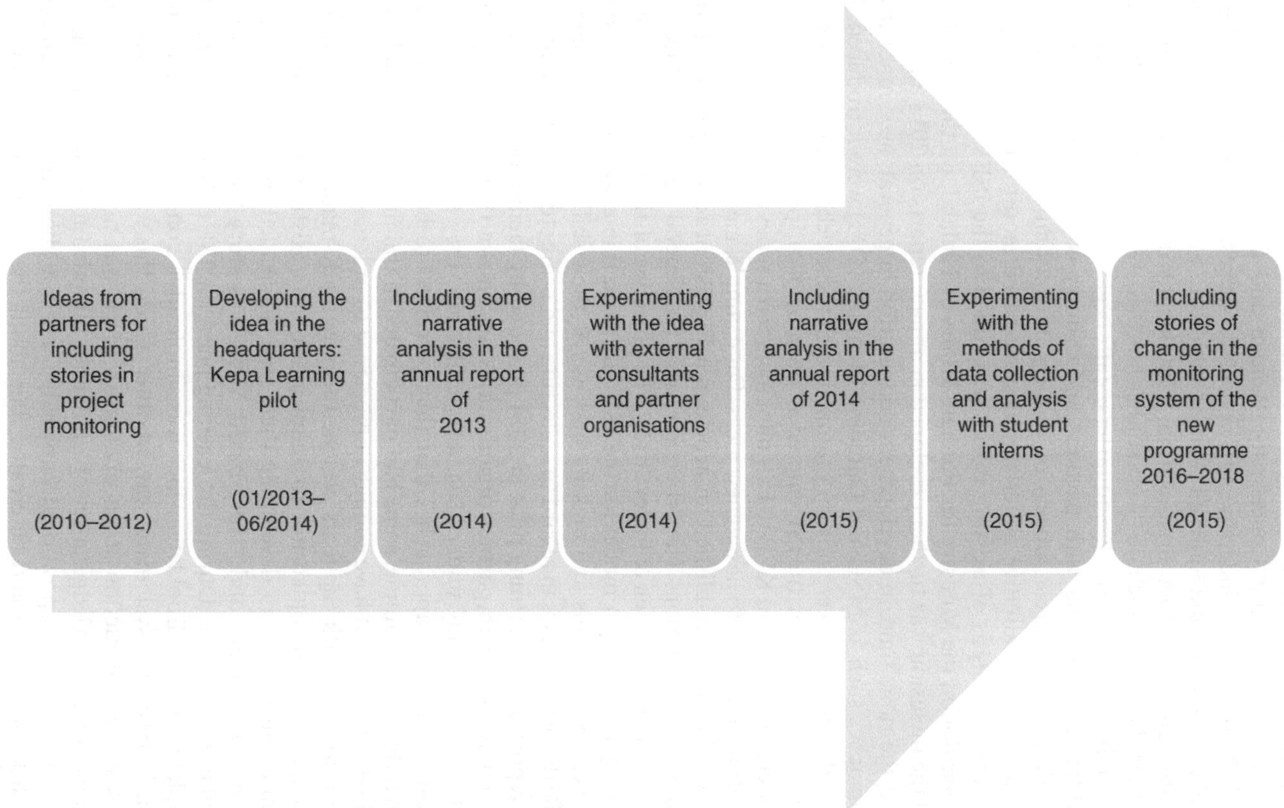

Figure 4.1 The organisational learning trajectory concerning story-based M&E in ISF

organisation, the Uganda Women Media Association (UMWA) had gradually collected a wealth of stories from the beneficiaries in their projects addressing domestic violence, and Concern for Women and Children Empowerment (COFINGOWE) had independently collected "success stories" from different beneficiary groups and annexed them in their 2012 annual report to the ISF. Additionally, a partner organisation, Candlelight in Somaliland, inquired whether they could include "case studies" in their reports. As a result of all these initiatives, in 2012 headquarters staff began discussing prospects of qualitative monitoring with partners and country coordinators. Gradually, they decided to start a process of inquiry into potentialities of more systematic use of qualitative material and story-based monitoring. A one-page annex with analysis of existing stories was added to the ISF's annual report to their donor, the Ministry for Foreign Affairs of Finland, on the year 2012, and the inclusion was further developed in annual reports on 2013 and 2014.

At the same time, in development cooperation in general, new, innovative approaches such as MSC and Outcome Mapping (OM) were introduced. In 2012, the ISF staff were not very familiar with these debates, and in order to get to grips with them, the ISF entered a "learning pilot" provided by a Finnish umbrella organisation KEPA. This pilot included a series of meetings, reading literature, and tasks to design new ideas. For example, members of KEPA and ISF staff together published an article in a Finnish academic journal in the field of administration. The article reviewed the general debates on M&E in development (Mäkinen & Lager 2015). The objective of the learning pilot was not only to develop a model for the ISF, but to do it in a way that "supports partner organisations and making best use of their skills and competencies while decreasing fears in regard to collecting and using stories" as reiterated in the report on the learning pilot in 2014 prepared by facilitators from KEPA. The interaction with partner organisations has shown that even though the partners had already undertaken story collection, they were simultaneously afraid of any new approaches that they perceived to be very complex and demanding. For example, some had participated in training sessions on MSC, and felt they did not have enough competence to practice it.

To do away with the fears attached to any ready-made "methodological package", the ISF opted not to adapt any of the existing ones, but to use them as inspiration in developing their own. It decided to simply speak of "stories of change" and "story-based M&E", as story-telling is something familiar to everyone. During the learning pilot, the ISF developed a concrete template, "A Story Booklet", which was simple advice on how to collect beneficiary stories in a systematic way. In other words, this was the first time that the scattered interaction about qualitative M&E was turned into a form of propositional knowledge; a set of guidelines intended to be used in number of contexts. The propositional knowledge was not about the issues around which knowledge should be created, but about the procedure of collecting information that could fit into the new and emerging organisational epistemology – not numbers or short answers to questionnaires, but stories told in a free manner. Thus, the tool attempted to combine the new universalistic ideas of narrative knowledge creation with the contextual emphasis of the content of knowledge.

While the Story Booklet was a first step in embedding story-based M&E in organisational routines and practices, the next challenge was to come up with an organisational practice of analysing the stories collected. Although a pile of stories are interesting and "nice to read", the question central to organisational epistemology is how to turn them into knowledge that fits the organisational knowledge needs. There were many experimentations of analysis that showed the difficulty of designing new analysis criteria on a basis of narrative analysis without collapsing into the existing indicator-based criteria. The programme coordinator said about the attempts to incorporate analysis of stories into the annual report on 2013: "It was really hard to think in qualitative ways; we always started to turn the stories into numbers, like how many stories addressed this theme, and how many addressed another theme." To address this challenge, the ISF hired an external Finnish consultant in summer 2014 to provide general "step-by-step guidelines and examples of effective ways of organising, managing and analysing stories" (Consultant report 11.6.2014). The guidelines were a further attempt to consolidate the story-based approach in organisational practices, and provide criteria for the knowledge production process. They included eight steps from data collection to revisions of programme objectives. For analysis, the consultant proposed a categorisation of narratives on the basis of themes; first on the basis of the contents of narratives, and second, grouped according to the existing programme indicators. In that way, the narrative knowledge received from the interviews would communicate with the numerical ones under the same indicators.

After the delivery of the report and guidelines from the consultant, the ISF was eager to systematically try out the story-based approach. In autumn 2014, the approach and guidelines were included in the Terms of Reference for a Kenyan consultant evaluating an ISF project in Somaliland. While the ISF's new criterion of story-based knowledge production was used in the evaluation, the partner organisations in Somaliland were not closely included, and according to the country coordinator, the experimentation was experienced as a top-down exercise. The inclusion of partners in designing the new approach was more successful in Uganda where the ISF programme coordinator facilitated two workshops: one with quite a small partner NGOs in northern Uganda, and one with the long-term partner UMWA in Kampala. The workshops not only introduced the approach and guidelines, but actually provided an opportunity to "live through" the method. In the beginning, the facilitator asked everyone to reflect on one change in their own life and the meanings they attached to this change. Then these stories were discussed, including a reflection of the impact of the workshop situation for the selection of the story, and potential categorisations of the stories were brainstormed. The small NGOs in northern Uganda were enthusiastic about the approach.

They did not have many established monitoring systems, and the story-based system seemed to be quite inviting and "easy to use". The workshop with the more experienced partner, UMWA in Kampala, included more in-depth methodological discussions, for example, about the analysis of the stories. The significance of these two workshops with Ugandan partner NGOs was that they offered spaces to reflect together on the logic and practical implications of the new approach, rather than providing training to adapt any ready-made system developed in the headquarters.

In 2015, the stories collected in Somaliland and some of the answers received to the open question in Nicaragua were included in the ISF's annual report on 2014. The stories were grouped according to the programme indicators, and a synopsis of their content was added to the monitoring matrix in parallel to the numeric indicators. During the same year, for the first time, a systematic story-based impact assessment was conducted by Finnish and Ugandan student interns with support from the partner organisation UMWA on their "Gender Education Programme on Prevention of Domestic Violence". The aim of the assessment was to learn what had taken place in the lives of the participants after training provided by the project, having involved an especially wide range of duty bearers. Duty bearers were also the majority among the respondents in a total of 60 narrative interviews collected in two districts. In the course of the impact assessment (Joro & Jascent 2015), some academic literature on narrative research was consulted with regard to both the collection and analysis of the material (Andrews et al. 2008; Atkinson 1998; Bold 2010; Mikkelsen 2005), and the material collected was further used in a Master's thesis (Joro 2016). Thus, epistemological criteria from academic narrative research were brought more explicitly into the picture. These criteria emphasised the theoretical contextualisation, and importance of a variety of narratives. All kinds of stories should be collected instead of just success stories, and a systematic analysis of the types of narratives in terms of processes – plot, actors, and outcomes – rather than themes included could be conducted.

Until 2015, story-based assessment occurred in annual reports as additional information. Towards the end of the year, it was time to prepare a new programme document for the Ministry for Foreign Affairs to ensure funding for the period 2016–2018. In this document, for the first time, the story-based approach was incorporated in the proposed monitoring framework, not as an addition but as integrated part of the system. The story-based approach was integrated into the monitoring matrix under two outcome indicators regarding change in attitudes. The main challenges encountered in this integration were whether the stories should depict the process or outcomes and whether in the monitoring matrix the "story" should appear as an issue to be followed, or the means of measurement in regard to certain indicators. During the drafting process some indicators were formulated as "a tendency in change of action shown in the stories of change", and it was debated whether this was an appropriate formulation of an indicator, or whether the "tendencies in the stories of change" should rather be included in the means of verification. In the final document, in the monitoring matrix, the stories of change and beneficiary interviews were located under means of verification, under the indicators focusing on beneficiaries' perceptions, understandings, and changes in attitudes or self-esteem, and the framework was accepted by the donor in the funding negotiations. The incorporation of the story-based approach in the existing logic of LFA-based monitoring matrices illustrated, again, the challenges of combining new emerging narrative and existing indicator-based organisational epistemologies.

The analysis of the learning trajectory showed how learning from scattered ideas to established organisational practice took time and multiple experimentations. In the ISF, it took over four years to proceed from initial ideas of using stories in M&E to the approach being established in the official documents. The need to embed the new way of knowledge production into the routines of both the ISF and its partner organisations continued after the integration. Changing organisational epistemology does not usually take place overnight, or as a result of a one-off training course but, as the process in the ISF indicates, it requires participation in developing the criteria and "living through" the new ways of thinking. In that way, the new criteria will be gradually accepted by the organisational structure, and confirmed by organisational goals, required for an establishment of a new organisational epistemology. These processes of acceptance and confirmation, however, did not happen without a number of challenges and debates, which I will describe in what follows.

Challenges in changing organisational epistemology

Developing a story-based method for M&E meant introducing new criteria for organisationally appropriate knowledge and the methods of its production. Therefore, from the point of view of organisational epistemology, the new criteria needed to be embedded in the organisational practices, accepted by the organisational structure, confirmed by the organisational goals and, further, aligned with the institutional pressures.

Story-based method and organisational structure

New kinds of M&E had to be accepted by the structure and division of labour in the ISF. New approaches and tasks needed to fit with existing organisational roles, task descriptions and the ways organisational action was structured. In the introduction of new knowledge criteria, the ISF discussed the roles concerning the leadership of new initiatives, division of labour in practical conduct of the new ways of knowledge production, and the programmatic structure of the ISF's work.

Who leads the process?

New ideas and organisational change are often initiated and led by some active staff members acting as change agents (Weick & Quinn 1999) or institutional entrepreneurs (Maguire et al. 2004). They might hold leadership positions, but often new initiatives are led by programme staff with the approval of those higher in the organisational hierarchy. In the case of story-based M&E, after the first initiatives from partner countries, the person in the position of programme director in the headquarters – even though the individual occupying this position changed during the process – took the lead in pushing it forward. However, the division of labour in leading the process was not clear-cut, as questions such as whose initiative it was and whose knowledge needs new practice should address, were frequently asked in the field coordinators' headquarters communication. In Nicaragua, the country coordinator together with the partner organisations led a process of developing poverty indicators, and did not actively experiment with the story-based approach in the form developed with the lead of the headquarters, as the indicators developed independently were considered best to meet the local knowledge needs. Similar tensions between the headquarters' attempts to coordinate and standardise, and partner country offices' needs to localise knowledge production emerged at different phases of the process. For instance, in relation to the consultant-led evaluation in Somaliland, it was reflected that: "The need was there, in Helsinki, to get this done, and the consultant came with a task of effectively collecting stories of change."

The change in organisational epistemology was, thus, related to the hierarchical relationships between the headquarters and country coordinators, and between the ISF and its partner organisations. The headquarters had a need to consolidate organisational epistemology that would embrace all the ISF programme countries and project locations, while both the country offices and partner organisations emphasised the need for contextualised knowledge production and their autonomy in deciding what knowledge was relevant. This need was well-acknowledged by the headquarters' staff, but did not, however, do away with the organisational aspiration to produce coherence from the point of view of the entire ISF.

Building bridges between projects and programmes

The tensions between headquarters' need to harmonise and country offices' and partner organisations' urge to localise, were closely related to the ways the organisational action was structured in the programmatic approach implemented by the ISF from 2003. Its Thematic Programme Framework assumed that all the implemented projects contributed to one of the two main thematic areas. Starting from 2010, the ISF had reported according to its programme indicators to the Ministry for Foreign Affairs, and one of the purposes in developing story-based evaluation was to include its results in the programme-based reporting system. However, the discussion about how the stories collected in particular projects could be connected with the programme goals revealed the general difficulties in programmatic approaches.

During the process, it was challenging to draw connections between the local stories, project indicators and programme indicators. As project indicators are specific to contexts and project objectives, programme indicators seek to address an overall change taking place as a result of all the projects supported by a particular NGO. Consequently, when thinking in programmatic terms is necessary in the headquarters, the country coordinators and partner organisations tended to perceive their activities primarily vis-á-vis the projects and immediate environments. In the headquarters attempt to embrace a wide range of projects, the programme goals and indicators unavoidably stayed at a quite general and abstract level. In the meeting with all the ISF country coordinators in Helsinki in June 2015, the gap between project and programmes was discussed. As one of the participants said in an interview in September 2015:

> All the country coordinators gave quite harsh feedback about the programme; the goals and indicators were far too high, as if there were a level missing in between the countries and programme; I understand it has to be in the donor's language but still the programme feels too abstract.

The struggle for successful combination of different levels also created ambiguity about the suitability of the contextual methods used. For example, in a memo concerning the new poverty indicators, the coordinator in Nicaragua pondered whether these could "meet the standards of ISF headquarters". In contrast to many other international organisations, the ISF did not strongly advocate its organisational programme or indicators to partner organisations, but encouraged them to realise their own goals. The programme coordinator explained:

> The ISF does not say much about what should be monitored; those who plan the projects, also plan project monitoring, and their own LFAs. They have their processes, and our job here in Helsinki is then to reflect on how these connect with our programme.

While this practice provided much autonomy for the partners and projects, it perhaps also contributed to the perception of partners and country coordinators of the organisational programme of the ISF to be somewhere "out there", and not very relevant to their own particular work.

Division of labour: who collects, who analyses?

Introducing story-based M&E in parallel to the already existing indicator-based approach with no additional staff implied that new tasks of collecting, analysing and reporting beneficiary narratives should be conducted by already existing staff. Furthermore, the new tasks also had implications for the staff of the partner organisations. How, then, were the new kinds of M&E approaches embedded in the existing practices and division of labour structured in the organisation? Concerning the task of story collection, it fell into the agenda of partner organisations in Uganda and Nicaragua who had already collected qualitative data as part of their frequent work, and actively engaged in the development of the method. In the case of Somaliland, the first experimentation of the story collection was done by an external consultant, and due to the objectivity requirements typical of external evaluation, the partner organisations were not trained in the use of the method nor included in the data collection. However, it was foreseen that in future the partner organisations would play a bigger role, as in the case of Kenya, where new projects included the story-based principle starting from the planning phase.

While the role of a "data collector" was quite smoothly embedded in the already existing structure of partner organisations being responsible for the implementation and monitoring of projects, the division of labour in the analysis of the stories was more challenging. At some point, it was decided that all the analysis would be conducted by partners and country coordinators in the south, and the Helsinki office would only receive the ready-made categorisations. However, later it was established that in order to be able to use stories in reporting at the programme level, it would also be necessary to receive the original stories. Looking at the categories did not make much sense without being familiar with the original stories. However, from the organisational point of view this meant a double addition to the workload, for both staff in the partner countries and in the headquarters. The general labour-intensive nature of analysis of qualitative material as well as the lack of clear organisational guidelines for conducting analysis implied a significant amount of additional work. Therefore, at times, some of the steps of developing the new approach were outsourced to external consultants and students who were able to provide extra labour for experimentation with the approach. All in all, it was assumed and accepted that additional work would be done within the existing structures.

Confirmation by organisational goals: attitudes, practices and empowerment

In addition to the acceptance by the organisational structure, the new organisational epistemology should be confirmed by organisational goals; the knowledge produced and the means of knowledge production should speak to what the organisation aspires to do in the first place. The ISF's main goals have revolved around two main themes, gender equality and decent work and income, even if the exact formulations of the programme goals have slightly changed over the years. The projects implemented under these two thematic areas have included, for example, support for producer cooperatives in Nicaragua and agricultural production in Uganda, youth employment in

Somaliland, addressing female genital mutilation in Uganda, Somaliland and Kenya, and reduction of domestic violence in Uganda. Goals have also included capacity building for civil society, and empowerment has been a guiding principle in all the work of the organisation.

Narrating attitude change

In the course of the introduction of the story-based M&E, it gradually became clear that new ways of knowledge production resonated especially with the programme theme of gender equality. This theme has a lot to do with changes in attitudes, whereas livelihood and income strengthening was easier to measure in numerical terms. The staff and partners experienced the numeric measurement of change as challenging, while the stories were perceived to provide a novel grasp of the processes of attitude change. For example, in the projects addressing domestic violence, the number of reported cases had been used as a proxy indicator. The challenge was that with the increased awareness of domestic violence the number of reported cases also increased – which did not mean that the occurrence of domestic violence itself would have increased. Therefore, the narratives on how thinking about domestic violence among project participants had changed, how they had informed others about their new insights, and practised their new ideas in everyday conflict resolution concerning domestic violence were considered to provide a more in-depth picture of the attitude change.

Problematizing organisational goals

The process of developing story-based M&E also revealed critical comments concerning the goals themselves. Development cooperation is often criticised for its tendency to promote Western values and models without being able to take into account the local knowledge and existing practices. This challenge had also been noticed in previous evaluations of the projects addressing domestic violence supported by the ISF in Uganda (Ndidde 2015). The challenge was again brought up in various interviews with staff. One of the country coordinators reflected on the challenge of Western models:

> We cannot bring our models here where things are handled differently; we speak always about individuals, their rights, and their cases. However, for example, the cases of rape or domestic violence are not issues between individuals, but rather issues between families. And when we promote this kind of individual-based approach it leads to some kinds of conflicts, and beneficiaries being critical towards the project in general.

As a result of these reflections, the existing resolution mechanism in communities had been taken into increased consideration; for example rather than searching for punishment for perpetrators, the persons with a mediator role in communities were supported, so that "the conflicts could be solved even before violence comes into the picture". While the approach working with existing practices had brought acceptance for the project in the eyes of beneficiaries, it had also partly worked against the rights-based model. For example, the impact assessment showed how in a few cases a strategy used in local conflict resolution was to encourage wives to return to their violent husbands: "While forgiveness is an important part of resolving disputes, some stories from respondents heavily focused upon counselling the wife. This type of counselling involved encouraging the wife to remain in the household and accept her husband's behaviour; keeping the family unity and harmony intact was the priority" (Joro & Jascent 2015, 25). In these instances, the cultural value of sustaining family became more important than the individual rights of a woman to live without a fear of domestic violence. In other examples, mobilising the local motorbike taxi drivers, *bodabodas*, and local healers to undertake messaging against domestic violence had effectively facilitated change in attitudes.

The new organisational epistemology that emphasised the diversity of experiences of the beneficiaries potentially enables knowledge production that shows a more realistic picture of the programme areas; at times a modest pace and a limited level of change, taking place in the everyday lives of people and embedded in their own existing practices and habits. Additionally, stories may reveal knowledge about the various mechanisms and events that potentially lead to more fundamental changes in attitudes and practices. In this sense, the organisational epistemology concerning M&E widens the mainstream purpose of knowledge production. It does not only search for evidence of change in alignment with the pre-defined organisational goals, but seeks also to identify a variety of changes taking place in beneficiaries' lives. In so doing, the knowledge produced might effect a change in the goals as well.

Empowerment as a guiding principle

For a long time, empowerment has been an explicit guiding principle in the ISF. Story-based M&E was considered to align with this organisational goal as it contributed to the empowerment of both partner organisations and beneficiaries. The programme director reflected:

> The whole idea behind this development was that M&E should contribute to the goal of empowerment, it should not be something that is experienced to be separate from the project activities, something that is perceived as very difficult and time-consuming by the partners. The ideal situation would be that the organisations collect information for their own use, and then take out some of it for the purposes of our collaborative projects, but in reality, it is still often though that they produce information mainly for us and for our needs..

In order to be an empowering effort, the involvement of partners in the process was seen important. The programme director continued: “We could have taken, for example the Most Significant Change method, hire a consultant to train ourselves and our partners, and then we could have just started to implement it, but this would have been against our principles.” Such an approach, however, would have strengthened the power positions in partnerships, and probably increased partners’ “fear of not doing the right thing”.

At the same time, experience from the experimentations of the story-based approach in Uganda supported the idea that participating in the story-based M&E could be an empowering experience in itself for the respondents. The programme director stated: “Story-based M&E is not only a means of knowledge production, but it is also a way to realise our organisational goals”, as it allows people to get their stories told and heard. Telling their story was seen as more familiar to the respondents than answering a questionnaire. Narrative can be considered as quite universal form of communication, which has been “present in every age, in every place, and in every society” (Barthes 1981, 251). Narratives are easily understood even by people from opposite cultural backgrounds. It is possible that narrating a significant life event can facilitate positive change in people’s lives, as everyone has a desire for others to hear their story and have their voice heard (Chase 2005). However, the method does not completely do away with the institutionalised power relations. Questions such as who decides what kind of stories will be collected, who is given a voice and who is silenced, and who has access to stories and how they feed the wider networks of routine power embedded in development partnerships, need still be answered (Plummer 1995, 26).

Aligned with the institutional environment: methodological and managerial questions

In knowledge production, NGOs have to deal with different methodological, managerial and ethical questions (Kontinen & Katsui 2015). The institutional environment of development cooperation set explicit criteria for managerial knowledge production in M&E. These criteria overlap to some extent but are not identical to criteria for knowledge production in academic methodological literature. In the process of introducing story-based M&E in the ISF, the staff and partner organisation negotiated about their organisational knowledge production criteria in resonance with both these discourses, when they reflected practical data collection, analysis and reporting, together with the more general dilemmas considering measurement of change and the sufficient alignment with the institutional criteria.

Distance or proximity in collecting stories

Epistemological criteria for collecting stories were related to practical data collection and considerations of who is in the best position to collect reliable narratives. Differences among questionnaires and narrative interviews were discussed. In an attempt to standardise the data into a comparable form, Nicaraguan partners opted for quite well-formulated open questions to be added to a questionnaire. In Uganda, the aim was merely to collect narratives in as open a way as possible. In the partner workshops in Uganda, the participants tried out telling a life story, and reflected on the best possible situation to encourage people to tell their stories. They also discussed the ways in which people could be helped to tell a story covering an extended period of their lives rather than reflect on their emotions and opinions at the very moment of the interview. In the opinion of the participants, the situation should encourage people to talk about their life rather than "answering interview questions", and opening questions such as "tell me about your journey" and prompting questions such as "what happened next", were brainstormed.

Both options, questionnaires and open interviews, echoed different ideas of "good knowledge"; the questionnaires looked for standardised data collection while open narratives aimed at capturing experience that was as personal as possible. The latter view resonates with the literature on narrative interviewing which emphasises that narrative data collection involves interaction and co-creation (Polkinghorne 2007), where the relationship should be that of a narrator and listener rather than that of interviewee and interviewer (Chase 2005, 663). In contrast to questionnaires, the listener should be careful not to "interview" in order to avoid receiving only the stories expected. For example, in collecting life stories in an impact assessment in Bangladesh, the idea was to receive stories that were as open as possible (Davis 2011). The stories were elicited through introducing some general historical events in the area and people were asked to draw their life trajectories and significant events in their lives inspired by these general historical events. The interviewers were careful not to guide attention to the intervention by questions asked on it. The idea was to assess whether the intervention would be mentioned as a significant event, in order to place interventions in a more realistic and wider perspective and to reduce interviewer-imposed bias in seeing development programmes as more important events in people's lives that they actually are (ibid. 278). However, in M&E or research situations, narratives are most likely short summaries compared with the narratives people tell each other in their everyday life, and thus, should be perceived as "answers" of some kind. Therefore, the narratives have a certain bias towards the aims of the interviewee, in the case of M&E towards the organisation and the project at hand (Cortazzi 1999, 230–231).

Especially in the context of Somaliland, ways to elicit stories about sensitive issues were discussed. The coordinator said that in Somaliland, many studies are continuously conducted with the help of the NGO. These studies use different questionnaires, the sensitivity of which has to be checked. Acknowledging that all issues, such as one's sexual life or level of income, are not easily discussed, alternative ways of asking, "narratives by proxy" were identified. For example, the level of income could be investigated by asking people to talk about how they prepared for the latest festivities; what kinds of clothes were bought and what kinds of food served. Additionally, the practice of FGM could be inferred on the basis of the increase in girls' absences from school and fathers' complaints about the amount of medical expenditure for girls of a certain age. When discussing sensitive issues, alternative means of data collection to individual narrative interviews were suggested. These included, for example, drama pieces about a general change in life in communities, and photos and drawings which would not necessarily connect with someone's personal experience but would depict the general patterns.

In addition, the question of who should collect the stories was much discussed. In all the partner countries, partner organisations had taken independent initiatives to collect stories from their beneficiaries, and thus felt they had ownership over the approach. When an external consultant conducted the evaluation in Somaliland, it was experienced as side-lining the partner organisation, and as losing some of the sensitivity needed to acquire relevant information. Therefore, the main question was how to ensure the best possible knowledge was gained by collecting stories. On one hand, there was an argument that people would talk about their lives more openly to the representatives of partner organisations, as they were already familiar figures in the communities and had the necessary background information. On the other hand, the argument that achieving the best possible knowledge through collecting stories should require objectivity and collection by an impartial outsider was supported. These debates resonate with the epistemological discussion about objectivity in data collection. In the so-called positivistic tradition, objectivity is related to impartiality and a distance between data collectors and respondents guarantees the best quality of data. In the qualitative tradition, some even argue that such objectivity "is a mythological creature that never existed" while knowing is always inseparable from the knower (Guba & Lincoln 2005, 208). The quality of qualitative data depends not on the number of interviews but on good, in-depth content. Moreover, a "prolonged engagement" rather than distance is seen as a means to increase the credibility that depends on trustful relationships and good understanding of the context (Lincoln & Guba 1999, 407). In the example of impact assessment in Bangladesh, the researcher spent two weeks in each research site and conducted two interviews per day, and was even able to go back to the communities with initial analysis (Davis 2011). Two weeks in each location sounds like luxury for any development consultant or member of NGO staff, but is far from the expectations of the duration of field presence in other research areas, for example, in anthropological research.

Trustworthiness and generalisability

Related debates considered the validity or, rather, the trustworthiness of the story-based methodology (Polkinghorne 2007). Additionally, whether the results of the analysis of the collected stories could be generalised. For example, the question of the truth value of stories was continuously revisited. In resonance with the methodological literature on qualitative research (Lincoln & Guba1999), the country coordinator in Nicaragua suggested that the information received through narratives should be triangulated and cross-checked with other possible sources before it could be accepted as knowledge to be reported under the programme indicators. On various occasions, it was noted that in articulating narratives, first, people can purposefully tell a story that is not true, and second, they naturally have their own, partial views of the events that have taken place in the past. In the same vein, traditions in narrative research hold different ideas about the need and ability of a narrative to correspond with "real" events. In the sociolinguistic perspective, Labov (1972, 359) defines narratives as "means of representing past experience by a sequence of ordered sentences that match the temporal sequence of events which, as inferred, actually occurred" whereas other approaches emphasise that narratives are retrospective "meaning-making of human experience", and as such, do not directly correspond to actual events (Chase 2005, 656). This does not, however, mean that stories are "false", but due to human characteristics, they present multiple constructions of the past. From this point of view, the task of the data collector is to acknowledge these multiple views and analyse them in a credible way as, after all, most of the qualitative traditions do not hold perspectives and experiences to be individual, but socially constructed interpretations (Lincoln & Guba 1999, 401). In his influential contribution to the structural analysis of narratives, Bruner (1986, 11–12) suggests that there are different criteria of well-formed knowledge for two modes of thought, the logico-scientific and narrative modes, which are complementary but cannot substitute each other. The former convinces with argument, the latter convinces with a good story – and they convince of different things – the former of truth, the latter of lifelikeness.

Moreover, stories are told in a socially situated interaction, from certain positions (Chase 2005, 657) and issues such as a motive to please the interviewer, or even an intention to lie, can possibly occur (Douglas 1986). As one of the coordinators reflected:

> Of course, on many occasions, respondents aim to please you; if we ask those who have benefitted from the project a lot, for example received a lot of allowances, they are not likely to say anything negative, as the idea is that when we say all these nice things, the project will just continue and continue.

Prolonged engagement and familiarity with the context helps a data collector to identify such issues. In contrast to some of the objectivity criteria that seek to neutralise contextual effects, narrative inquiry starts with the idea that multiple contexts – including a "monitoring context" – are always present. Therefore, the inquiry should exactly describe the ways people make sense of these contexts and experiences (Clandining & Rosiek 2007, 45).

The questions related to the credibility of collected information do not only apply to life stories, nor only to qualitative methods in general, but also to questionnaires and other forms of statistical data collection. Moreover, in the prevailing resource constraints, the choices NGOs are able to make are not usually methodological ones between robust statistical and rigorous qualitative research, but merely managerial and ethical ones; choices between collecting some information in numeric form or arranging a few qualitative interviews, focus group discussions or participatory exercises to capture people's perceptions and experiences (Kontinen & Katsui 2015). In managerial approaches, such as LFA, there is a tendency to consider numeric information as more trustworthy. An increase in reports on domestic violence by 20 per cent in two years in a certain community seems to be more reliable than the four different types of narratives concerning the attitude changes towards violence articulated by 20 project participants. However, as one of the coordinators said: "I gradually realised that it might not necessary to have a solid basis for the numbers and percentages. You know, if there are 63 it might as well be 54 or 72, and it is not because of any purposeful act, but the competence level when it comes to counting".

While numbers are good for describing general trends and averages, the varieties and nature of processes are often not well-captured. In a meeting in the ISF headquarters it was reflected: "a lot of information concerning attitude change remains invisible; somehow it should be made visible. I wonder why it is that the narratives are not accepted as sources of information, even if we know that there is also a lot of uncertainty behind the numbers, in situations where people do not even have the skill to use Excel". It was also noticed that in some institutions, qualitative and experiential evidence was valued. In addition to the qualitative traditions in social sciences, the use of people's accounts in institutional contexts was reflected upon: "It is amazing how, for example, in our legal system the evidence gathered by statements from witnesses is valued, and sometimes takes quite a significant role, while in evaluation and impact assessment we tend to be very critical about the truth value of narratives".

The debate between the priority of numbers and narratives is related to the criteria of generalisability. In the ISF's process, during data collection much effort was put into the sampling of the respondents, so that they would represent different locations, genders, groups, and so on. Accordingly, the Finnish consultant recommended counting frequencies of different themes that occurred in interviews in order to show their importance, but simultaneously, reminded that the themes identified in stories cannot be generalised. Therefore, there was continuous uncertainty about the epistemological criteria concerning the need for the knowledge produced to lend itself to general conclusions. This ambiguity benefitted from drawing from the academic literature, for example, in the impact assessment in Uganda. Qualitative inquiry, in general, cannot be generalised according to the methodological criteria typical of quantitative methods. The selection of respondents is not based on representation of a certain population but rather on their ability to shed light on the phenomenon under investigation. Accordingly, the analysis does not primarily focus on frequencies or averages, but on the qualitative diversity in an attempt to capture as many different types of experiences as possible. Chase (2005, 667) argues that narratives are not supposed to be generalisable to populations, but rather, their significance lies in the possibility to see what is possible in a certain context. Lincoln and Guba (1999, 404) suggest the idea of "transferability" instead; the analysis in one context can be transferred to others, depending on the similarity between contexts. It was however noted that in the individual stories collected, quite quickly similar patterns started to emerge, and certain typical change trajectories could be identified. This phenomenon is called "saturation" in qualitative research (Glaser & Strauss 1967) and it refers to a situation where conducting new interviews seems to bring no additional perspectives to certain themes or issues. In analysis of narratives, at certain point it becomes possible to identify repetition of general features of the processes, or a certain range of meanings given to events, rather than provision of additional, unique individual subjective experiences totally different from the previous ones. Therefore, the knowledge criterion is not that the knowledge can be generalised to certain population, for example to project participants, but that the phenomenon of attitude change in a particular location is described in depth and in as many of its socially located variations as possible.

Depicting change: from numbers to narratives and from percentages to change paths

Any M&E method in development cooperation should be able to somehow capture change. The methodological possibilities of how to measure change are many. For the randomised trials, proof of change might result from comparison between the intervention groups with counterfactuals, whereas in participatory approaches, changes are identified from participants' accounts and their own analysis. The mainstream management approach compares a situation at the beginning of the project with the situation at the end in reference to certain indicators. This kind of indicator-based measurement of change was also the prevalent practice in the ISF, while the story-based approach was expected to bring additional insights on the processes, perceptions and dynamics of change.

According to its project management guidelines, the ISF encouraged its partners to define indicators, to conduct baseline studies and to undertake frequent monitoring in each project. However, in practice, not all the projects always succeeded in conducting a baseline study. As reflected by one of the country coordinators: "we had quantitative indicators and we agreed to conduct a baseline study in which we would also develop qualitative indicators, but for many different reasons, this was delayed, and then there was no sense in conducting it anymore. And, then we decided that, since we did not have a baseline, we would try to establish change on the basis of stories". In this case, story-based monitoring was considered as a means to get retrospective evidence of change, as an alternative to the measurable difference between baseline and the end of project.

The question of ways to analyse and depict change came up continuously in the phase of analysing narratives. Plenty of different options were experimented with. For the annual report of 2014, stories were grouped on the basis of the question: "In the story, what indicates that an attitude, perspective or live skill has changed or is about to change?" and then these issues identified were grouped under the main goals of the programme. The excerpts from the stories were categorised under ten different kinds of change, for example: "Changes in the attitudes of female beneficiaries towards the physical inviolability of women and girls". Different stories going under this category were then merged together in a depiction of the situation; for example: "Women who participated in Somaliland in FGM training said that they had learned about the implications of FGM for health, social and women's rights, and had become sad and worried after receiving the information, and felt a need to spread the information further. Women said that people discuss FGM and its negative implications more openly; however, women are still in favour of conducting a *sunna*-form FGM."

In the workshop in Uganda in 2015, the participants wanted to differentiate between a typical "testimony", where beneficiaries talk about an achieved project outcome, and a story that depicts meaningful changes in respondents' life, not necessarily directly connected to project. They reflected that if the project goals were taken as a starting point, there would be a project bias and no information about significant issues taking place in beneficiaries' lives would be received. They tried out an analysis that would capture the process of change through using questions such as: "Who are the main actors in the story? What have been the main steps and turning points in the story? Has there been change in knowledge, attitude or behaviour?" Drawing from the literature of structural narrative methodology, these questions were based on a general assumption that a story, no matter how unstructured it might be, has some kind of plot, a beginning, some key events, actors, and an end state; that is, narrative contains events logically and chronologically linked to each other (Alasuutari 1998, 118). In order to connect the stories to the project, one suggestion was that a project activity, for example a "training", could be offered as a kind of starting point for the story.

All in all, throughout the entire process of developing story-based M&E, two different ideas of conceptualising change were constantly discussed; either as an ongoing trajectory or as a difference between baseline and end state. While some were of the opinion that the accounts of change were not appropriate if the change between the beginning and the end could not be measured, others perceived the prescription of chain of meaningful events as adequate knowledge about change. A related challenge was how to depict

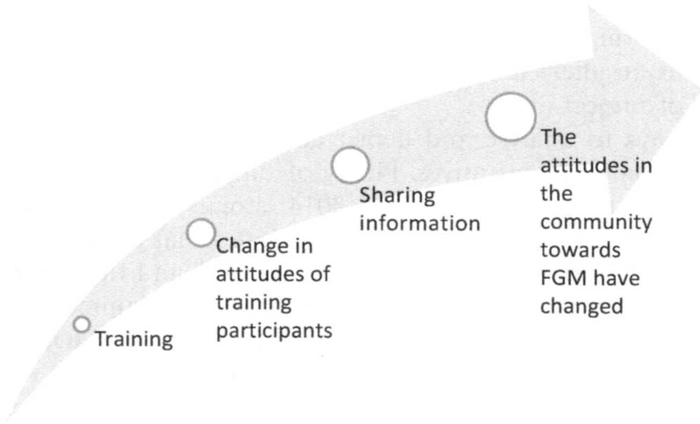

Figure 4.2 An example of a change path in regard to attitude change in an FGM project

change identified in the story-based M&E in reports. There was continuous negotiation between the existing criteria of representing change in the boxes of monitoring matrices, and the need to innovate new ways of depicting change. In the annual report on 2013, the ISF first included a one-page appendix with a visual representation of change, which was different from a monitoring matrix. The outcome was an arrow-shaped *trajectory of change* that led to multiple results. The main idea was to depict that one trajectory of activities, such as education on gender roles, could result in different kinds of outcomes, identified from the collected stories.

The idea of a trajectory as an arrow was further developed into descriptions of change paths (see Figure 4.2) used in the annual report of 2014. These paths were constructed on the basis of the stories collected in the evaluation in Somaliland, and the answers to the open questions in Nicaragua. The analysis was performed in the headquarters, where all the stories were read through and then grouped according to the programme indicators. Then, questions such as "what in the story indicates a change in a certain aspect" were used. These aspects included, according to the programme objectives, attitude, perception, or a life-skill. After drawing together the answers to these questions a synopsis was made on the basis of all the stories in one particular country and this information was added to the monitoring matrix along with the results of numeric indicators, and the change paths were attached as an annex to the report. The quotes from the narratives illustrated in what ways the participants experienced the training provided, how they spoke about signs of attitude changing, and what kinds of effort took place in an attempt to further share the new information and attitudes in the community.

Aligning with or challenging the institutional knowledge criteria

During the process, the story-based approach developed in the ISF was confronted in various instances with the general institutional trends. Monitoring and evaluation in development is often said to suffer from a tendency to focus on positive results and reporting success. This institutional habit of emphasising positive aspects was discussed on various occasions in the ISF as well. It was argued that for the sake of learning it would be important to collect stories of also not-so-successful examples of changes or no changes in peoples' lives, but at the end, as one of the Finnish participants said in a meeting: "We have to understand that we will never fully capture the failures". As reporting failures and challenges is perceived as risking further funding and collaboration, and the public image of organisations, the beneficiaries, partner NGOs and the ISF itself rather focus on successes, at least in their reports. Changing this basic tendency and the related power relations deep-rooted in the funding system was identified as something that is not possible for any individual NGO. To counteract the bias for success stories, however, collecting something explicitly called "stories we can learn from" or "stories on challenges" as part of monitoring and evaluation was suggested.

The tools and practices used in the ISF were very much in alignment with the institutional standards of development cooperation. The LFA- based project management system, programmatic approach and adoption of a human rights-based approach were all examples of institutional practices in this particular organisation. At the same time, the organisation was critical of some of the institutionalised practices. For example, in one of the meetings the ISF staff reflected: "somehow we have become stuck with the LFA thinking, we just wonder whether it is really so that in the last 50 years we have not come up with any alternative to this strategic tool; of course, now they have this result-chain approach which, to us, seems to be just a log frame in a horizontal position".

While the ISF considered it necessary to align with the institutionalised practices, it also understood the role of NGOs to be, in a sense, change agents: "We should show the donors that things can be done differently, if nobody suggests something new, the donors surely will not come and introduce alternatives, as we are the experts on how these approaches function in practice". To follow their agenda, the ISF started gradually to include story-based M&E and depictions of change trajectories in their annual reports to the Ministry. They experienced that these were welcomed by the donor, and at least individual donor officers had said in the funding negotiations that the narrative elements were "really good and interesting to read". The ISF explicitly included story-based M&E in their programme for 2016–2018 when they applied a new round of funding from the Ministry. In 2015, the Ministry for Foreign Affairs announced that it would conduct an overall assessment of the results frameworks in Finnish NGOs (Ministry for Foreign Affairs 2017), and the story-based approach was included in the ISFs own depiction of its framework, and it continued the systematisation of the approach.

More drastic institutional effects affected the ISF after the end of our research project. Towards the end of 2015, as a result of the parliamentary elections in Finland, the country's government changed its development cooperation policy priorities, and under the umbrella of general austerity measures decided to cut the development budget for 2016. As a consequence, the Ministry for Foreign Affairs of Finland announced a general cut of over 40 per cent in the aid allocations for NGOs for the following year. For the ISF, this meant cuts in the headquarters staff and thus difficulties in continuing organisational learning efforts. It also meant a quite sudden exit of the ISF from Uganda that had been a kind of "learning laboratory" for the story-based M&E approach in the ISF during 2010–2015. Therefore, the small NGOs in northern Uganda who had actively participated in the workshops on story-based M&E never had a chance to enter into actual collaboration with the ISF, and a long-term partnership with UMWA, one of the very initiators of the story-based approach, was phased out as new projects were not planned. Consequently, the post of ISF country coordinator in Uganda was also terminated. The announcement of the cuts created general turmoil in the Finnish NGOs, and put a stop to a number of already identified new collaboration initiatives. Therefore, while there are a plenty of discussions about evidence-based decision making, and the need to show results, in the end many of the institutionalised resource allocations depend on political climate and political decisions, rather than any evidence concerning outcomes, effectiveness, or learning.

Conclusions

The case of introducing a story-based M&E in the ISF illustrated a process of learning as a change in organisational epistemology. In the learning process, the organisation and its partners renegotiated their criteria for what counts as knowledge and how relevant knowledge can be produced. The idea of a more qualitative and narrative approach spoke to existing knowledge needs, especially in relation to how to understand change in attitudes. The new knowledge criteria were, thus, easily confirmed by organisational goals related to attitude change concerning gender equality, whereas they did not so smoothly fit those related to income and livelihoods. Additionally, new knowledge criteria had to be embedded in the existing organisational structure and division of labour, while the ways of knowledge production required new skills and additional activities concerning data collection and analysis. The division of labour in conducting story-based monitoring, even if at times contested, followed the already existing lines; the partner organisations were those that collected the stories, and the headquarters those that participated in the analysis and led the process in an attempt to harmonise actions from the point of view of the ISF as an entire organisation.

The process analysed showed that organisational learning is long-term rather than a one-time effort. The consolidation of story-based M&E from scattered ideas into an institutionalised practice took at least three years. While we could judge the ISF as a slow learner or as incapable of leading effective learning processes, we should rather understand the time-consuming learning process as an indicator of the pace of organisational learning processes in general. The learning process illustrated how new knowledge criteria need to be embedded in existing practices in order for those practices to change. In the course of learning new practices, the old ones do not cease to exist. For example, the ISF continuously compared and combined the story-based approach with its well-established indicator-based approach, and at times, evaluated new forms of knowledge on the basis of old criteria, searching for numeric frequencies and identifiable change between two points in time. The need to stick with the old criteria is even more prominent in the situation where those criteria are the prevalent ones in the institutional environment on which organisations depend, both in terms of financial resources and the identity of being a legitimate "development NGO".

References

Andrews, M., Squire, C. & Tamboukou, M. (eds) (2008) *Doing Narrative Research*. Second edition. London: SAGE.

Alasuutari, P. (1998) *An Invitation to Social Research*. London: SAGE.

Atkinson, R. (1998) *The Life Story Interview*. London: SAGE.

Barthes, R. (1981) Introduction to the structural analysis of narrative. In: Sontag, S. (ed.) *A Barthes Reader*. New York: Hill and Wang, 251–295.

Bold, C. (2010) *Using Narrative in Research*. London: SAGE.

Bruner, J. (1986) *Actual Minds, Possible Worlds*. Cambridge, MA: Harvard University Press.

Chambers, R. (2008) *Revolutions in Development Inquiry*. London: Earthscan.

Chase, S.E. (2005) Narrative inquiry. Multiple lenses, approaches, voices. In: Denzin, N.K. & Lincoln, Y.S. (eds) *The Sage Handbook of Qualitative Research*. Third edition. London: SAGE, 651–679.

Clandinin, J.D. & Rosiek, J. (2007) Mapping the landscape of narrative inquiry: Borderland spaces and tensions. In: Clandinin, J.D. (ed.) *Handbook of Narrative Inquiry. Mapping a Methodology*. Thousand Oaks, CA: SAGE, 35–76.

Cook, S.D.N. & Brown, J.S. (1999) Bridging epistemologies: The generative dance between organisational knowledge and organisational knowing. *Organisation Science*, 10(4), 381–400.

Cortazzi, Martin (1999) Sociological and sociolinguistic models of narrative. In: Bryman, A. & Burgess, R.G. (eds) *Qualitative Research. Volume 3*. London: SAGE, 203–235.

Davies, R.J. (2004) Scale, complexity and the representation of theories of change. *Evaluation*, 10(1), 101–121.

Davies, R.J. (2005) Scale, complexity and the representation of the theories of change. Part II. *Evaluation*, 11(2), 133–149.

Davies, R. & Dart, J. (2005) *The "Most Significant Change" (MSC) Technique. A Guide to Its Use.* https://europa.eu/capacity4dev/iesf/document/%E2%80%98most-significant-change%E2%80%99-technique-davies-dart-2005. Accessed 15.6.2016.

Davis, P. (2011) Exploring the long-term impact of development interventions within life-history narratives in rural Bangladesh. *Journal of Development Effectiveness*, 3(2), 263–280.

Douglas, J.D. (1976) *Investigative Social Research: Individual and Team Field Research.* Beverly Hills, CA: SAGE.

Feldman, M.S. & Orlikowski, W.J. (2011) Theorizing Practice and Practicing Theory. *Organisation Science*, 22(5), 1240–1253.

Gherardi, S. (2000) Practice-based theorizing on learning and knowing in organisations. *Organisation*, 7(2), 211–223.

Glaser, B. & Strauss, A. (1967). *The Discovery of Grounded Theory: Strategies for Qualitative Research.* New York: Aldine

Guba, E.G. & Lincoln, Y.S. (2005) Pragmatic controversies, contradictions, and emerging confluences. In Denzin, N.K. & Lincoln, Y.S. (eds), *The Sage Handbook of Qualitative Research.* Thousand Oaks, CA: SAGE.

Guijt, I. & Roche, C. (2014) Does impact evaluation in development matter? Well, it depends what it's for! *The European Journal of Development Research*, 26(1), 46–54.

Hayman, R., King, S., Kontinen, T. & Narayanaswamy, L. (eds) (2016) *Negotiating Knowledge: Evidence and Experience in Development NGOs.* Rugby: Practical Action.

Horton, K. & Roche, C. (eds) (2010) *Ethical Questions and International NGOs. An Exchange between Philosophers and NGOs.* Dordrecht: Springer.

Joro, V. & Jascent, M. (2015) Narrative Assessment of "Gender Education Programme on Prevention of Domestic Violence" in Kyankwanzi and Wakiso, Uganda. Unpublished report.

Joro, V. (2016) Gender Roles and Domestic Violence: Narrative Analysis of Social Construction of Gender in Uganda. Master Thesis, International Master Degree Programme for Development and International Cooperation, University of Jyväskylä, Finland.

King, A.W. & Zeithaml, C.P. (2003) Measuring organisational knowledge: A conceptual and methodological framework. *Strategic Management Journal*, 24(8), 763–772.

Kontinen, T. & Katsui, H. (2015) Ethical, managerial and methodological perspectives in knowledge creation in two Finnish civil society organisations. *Journal für Entwicklungspolitik – Austrian Journal of Development Studies*, 31(1), 65–82.

Labov, W. (1972) *Sociolinguistic Patterns.* Philadelphia: University of Pennsylvania Press.

Lincoln, Y. & Guba, E. (1999) Establishing trustworthiness. In: Bryman, A. & Burgess, R.G. (eds) (1999) *Qualitative Research. Volume 3.* London: SAGE. 397–444.

Longino, H.E. (2002) *The Fate of Knowledge.* Princeton, NJ: Princeton University Press.

Maguire, S., Hardy, C. & Lawrence, T.B. (2004) Institutional entrepreneurship in emerging fields: HIV/AIDS treatment advocacy in Canada. *Academy of Management Journal*, 47(5), 657–69.

Mäkinen, M., Lager, L. & Tuominen, K. (2014) Tarinoita kehitysyhteistyöstä. [Stories on development co-operation]. *Hallinnon Tutkimus*, 33(2), 182–188.

Ministry for Foreign Affairs of Finland (2017) *Evaluation on Programme-based Support to Civil Society Organisations III.* Evaluation of Finland's Development Policy and Cooperation 5/2017. http://formin.finland.fi/public/default.aspx?contentid=365983&nodeid=49728&contentlan=2&culture=en-US. Accessed 30.5.2017.

Mikkelsen, B. (2005) *Methods for Development Work and Research*. London: SAGE.
Ndidde, A.N. (2015) Evaluation and the leveraging of knowledge: The case of evaluation the gender education program on the prevention of domestic violence in Kyankwanzi and Wakiso districts in Uganda. *Forum for Development Studies*, 41(3), 539–550.
Nonaka, I. & Takeuchi, H. (1995) *The Knowledge-Creating Company: How Japanese Companies Create the Dynamics of Innovation*. New York: Oxford University Press.
Plummer, K. (1995) *Telling Sexual Stories. Power, Change and Social Worlds*. London: Routledge.
Polkinghorne, D.E. (2007) Validity issues in narrative research. *Qualitative Inquiry*, 13(4), 471–486.
Rowland, G. (2004) Shall we dance? A design epistemology for organisational learning and performance. *Educational Technology Research and Development*, 52(1), 33–48.
Seirafi, K. (2012) *Organisational Epistemology. Understanding Knowledge in Organisations*. Berlin: Springer-Verlag.
Spender, J.-C. (1998) Pluralist epistemology and the knowledge-based theory of the firm. *Organization*, 5(2), 233–256.
Tsoukas, H. (2005) *Complex Knowledge: Studies in Organisational Epistemology*. Oxford: Oxford University Press.
Tsoukas, H. & Vladimirou. E. (2001) What is organisational knowledge? *Journal of Management Studies*, 38(7), 973–993.
Tvedt, T. (2002) Development NGOs: Actors in a global civil society or in a new international social system. *Voluntas: International Journal of Voluntary and Nonprofit Organisations*, 13(4), 363–375.
Tvedt, T. (2006) The international aid system and the non-governmental organisations: A new research agenda. *Journal of International Development*, 18(5), 677–690.
von Krogh, G., Roos, J. & Slocum, K. (1994) An essay on corporate epistemology. *Strategic Management Journal*, 15(S2), 53–71.
Watkins, S.C., Swidler, A. & Hannan, T. (2012) Outsourcing social transformation: development NGOs as organisations. *Annual Review of Sociology*, 38, 285–315.
Weick, K.E. & Quinn, R.E. (1999) Organizational change and development. *Annual Review of Psychology*, 50(1), 361–386.

5 Unlearning, forgetting and ignorance

Rarely do NGOs take pride in their organisational "unlearning guidelines", being a "real forgetting organisation", or their excellent capacity to "manage ignorance". However, unlearning, forgetting and ignorance management take place in NGOs, as in other organisations, all the time. Organisations that are effective in learning new approaches also need to unlearn outdated approaches (Haunschild et al. 2015). In the process of changing organisational meanings, routines and practices, it is necessary to unlearn and forget old ones (Tsang & Zahra 2008). As the amount of information and knowledge in the world is limitless, some of it has to be removed from organisational memory systems or left in the sphere of organisational ignorance. Not all forgetting is planned or intentional. It can take place accidentally in different stages of knowledge acquisition, storage and retrieval, or as a result of institutional processes that guide knowledge dismissal. For example, after a successful transfer of knowledge through training, new knowledge achieved might rapidly be forgotten in an organisation, or some well-established knowledge can gradually disappear from organisational memory over a period of time. (Martin de Holan 2011a, 2011b).

In practice, most of us have experienced failures in organisational memory, even in regard to the very recent past. For example, we have participated in meetings where issues already discussed in previous ones are reintroduced as novel items; no one can recall what was already decided, nobody remembered to write a memo, or if a memo was written, it could not be found in the organisational documentation system (Othman & Hashim 2004, 273). Sometimes, storing of information fails; sometimes, as in the case of tacit knowledge, it is impossible to store in the first place (Wettenhall 2011). Unlearning and forgetting can reflect power relations internal to organisations and can be affected by wider societal power constellations. Unlearning and forgetting can also be openly critical, and can include reflection on power effects. For example, ordinary workers in organisations can react critically to expert knowledge or proposals from management that they experience as coming "from above". Reactions may include immediate unlearning and deliberate non-action (Brook et al. 2016, 383). Similarly, in development, communities, partner organisations, or regular staff can ignore expert advice, NGO messages, or management requirements.

It has been suggested that NGOs live in a "perpetual present" and easily forget and ignore the past without learning lessons from it (Lewis 2009, 2016). This tendency to forget, of course, does not mean that the individuals working in development would be less able to remember or less capable of learning than those working in other fields. Rather, development NGOs suffer from the kinds of institutional and organisational amnesia prevalent in our times. The amnesia is triggered by the accelerated pace of experienced change accompanied by exponentially growing access to information (Connerton 2009; Pollitt 2000;), and a common tendency to follow rapidly changing fads and fashions, rather than drawing from the organisation's experience (Wettenhall 2011; Easterby-Smith & Lyles 2011, 314). Moreover, aspects such as a rapid circulation of personnel, the geographical distribution of organisational activities, and the prevalence of project management are factors typical of international development.

In specific institutions, such as international development, there is always an institutional encouragement to remember certain events that strengthen and complement the "right" institutional image (Douglas 1986, 112). For example, in development there is a tendency to forget the colonial roots and their effects on contemporary practices, such as the colonial practice of "community development" being reintroduced under the notions of participation and empowerment (Cooke 2003; Smyth 2004). In a rare case of "radical unlearning" (Hsu 2013), organisations acknowledge the ways in which their institutionalised knowledge and practices serve power, and intentionally aim to forget these practices and seek new and alternative ways of knowing. In development, the debates on alternative development and post-development have called for this kind of forgetting of the existing institutionalised practices.

In addition to forgetting, the notion of ignorance has recently gained attention in fields such as philosophy, social studies of science, sociology, and organisation studies (Gross 2007, 2010; Gross & McGoey 2015; Harvey et al. 2001; Roberts 2012). Forgetting can result in organisational ignorance, but organisation can also be ignorant of knowledge it has never acquired in the first place. In regard to international development, for example, Hirschman (1967/2015) and Fforde (2017) have suggested that the field necessitates working under the condition of certain kinds of ignorance. They argue that development institutions, despite their aspirations, never have enough predictable knowledge about future changes, and cannot be fully aware of all the complexities of social change involved. At times, ignorance about harmful ideas can also be a strategic asset for an organisation, as in the case of ignoring results of scientific research that do not match the goals and values of organisations (McGoey 2007).

In this chapter, I investigate the question of what kinds of forms of forgetting and ignorance are prevalent for development NGOs, and how these are counteracted by different organisational practices.

Organisational unlearning and forgetting

Some authors distinguish unlearning and forgetting on the basis of intentionality. Unlearning is understood as intentional, whereas forgetting refers to unintentional loss of knowledge, action, beliefs, interpretations and routines (Akhshik 2014; Tsang & Zahra 2008). Traditionally, unlearning has been defined as "discarding obsolete and misleading knowledge" (Hedberg 1981, 3), intentionally dealing with organisationally obsolete and harmful issues to be replaced by new ones (Akhshik 2014; Zhao et al. 2013), and to eliminate beliefs, routines and artefacts from organisational memory (Akgün et al. 2007, 797). Some recent discussion has challenged the necessity of replacement and the normative judgement of obsoleteness of the knowledge to be unlearned (Tsang & Zahra 2008). Unlearning can take different forms as part of either episodic or continuous organisational change (Weick & Quinn 1999). In the context of episodic change, certain forms of knowledge can clearly be deemed obsolete and replaced by new ones, often with the support of outside change agents; in the conditions of continuous change, unlearning is more part of the ongoing daily practices.

It has also been suggested that unlearning is a sub-category of organisational forgetting, and in this instance, it refers to intentional forgetting of already established knowledge (Easterby-Smith & Lyles 2011; Martin de Holan 2011a; Martin de Holan & Phillips 2004a, 2004b). Both unlearning and organisational forgetting include behavioural, cognitive and social elements, and their substance can be actions, routines, understandings, meanings, and collectively constructed social perspectives and world views (Easterby-Smith & Lyles 2011, 313; Martin de Holan & Phillips 2004b, 424;). In general, organisational forgetting can be both intentional and unintentional, and refers to the "loss, voluntary or otherwise, of organisational knowledge" (Easterby-Smith & Lyles 2011, 311; Martin de Holan & Phillips 2004a, 1606, 2004b, 425). Different instances of organisational forgetting resonate with the Batesonian levels of learning discussed in Chapter 2 of this book.

Level I forgetting refers to discarding actions and routines; forgetting in level II can be understood as forgetting organisational rules, policies and strategies, while level III refers to forgetting mental models and ways of generating interpretations. (Fernandez et al. 2012, 159). Level III forgetting requires the biggest efforts, as the models and frames enacted through organisational practices are long-term products of institutional history. History shapes the contemporary action, though is rarely actively reflected but typically forgotten (Berger & Luckmann 1966; Fear 2014; Suddaby et al. 2014). Institutions' memory tends to construct the past in terms of the present; thus forgetting can be a means of building social order (Douglas 1986, 70). Some past events and ideas are left in the shadow, and forgotten. This can happen unintentionally, but can also result from active manipulation and silencing of certain stakeholders; for example, silencing civil society actors in the cases of organisational irresponsibility of enterprises (Mena et al. 2016).

Typical of level II forgetting might be to forget both existing policies and strategies, and especially the processes behind those. In the course of changing strategies, organisations might forget what has worked and why, and reinvent solutions that have already proved not to be sustainable (Martin de Holan 2011b). In development NGOs, this can lead to constant reinvention of development ideas, language and goals (Lewis 2009), if the past is a "murky place where failures can be hidden" rather than a space to draw lessons from (Lewis 2016, 86). Level I forgetting refers to discarding new or already established routines that do not match the current policies and strategies. For example, after shifting from a service-delivery approach to an advocacy approach, the NGOs had to forget their past ways of interacting with the communities.

Organisational forgetting can be categorised into four forms on the basis of differences between the degree of intentionality and the type of knowledge discarded (Martin de Holan 2011b, 442; Martin de Holan & Phillips 2004a, 1606; Martin de Holan et al. 2004). Accidental or unintentional forms of forgetting include dissipation and degradation. The former refers to accidental forgetting of new knowledge resulting from a failure to capture and consolidate with organisational memory and routines, and the latter refers to accidental forgetting of established knowledge, memory decay and, thus, failure to maintain knowledge in an organisation. Intentional forms of forgetting include suspension and purging. Suspension means purposeful forgetting of new knowledge, abandoning innovation or aborted learning where organisation avoids new knowledge, including that of avoiding learning bad habits. Purging is a purposeful forgetting and therefore unlearning of established knowledge. Intentional forgetting is a central mechanism of organisational change (Martin de Holan 2011b, 321), and can also be a strategy for managers to shape the organisational knowledge (Martin de Holan & Phillips 2004b).

All in all, organisational forgetting and its consequences are not necessarily either positive or negative. Such normative judgement depends on the context and form of organisational forgetting (Martin de Holan & Phillips 2011, 447). When deemed desirable, organisational forgetting can be facilitated through transformative training (Easterby-Smith & Lyles 2011, 314), whereas the means to counteract forgetting are related to the availability of knowledge assets, existing routines to use the assets, and the structured design of power and tasks (Martin de Holan 2011b).

In the following section, the typical mechanisms of forgetting in development NGOs are discussed on the basis of staff interviews conducted during 2014–2015 in a Finnish organisation which I have decided to call FINGO. The organisation conducts both development and humanitarian activities, and has grown remarkably during the last years. Moreover, it has not only grown in size and budget, but has also transformed from merely a funding organisation for an INGO to an organisation that implements its own programme.

These developments have posed challenges to the organisation, for instance, in terms of dealing with the rapidly increasing number of staff, establishing country offices in challenging and complex environments, designing organisational procedures and guidelines, and establishing knowledge-management systems that could meet the needs of the expanded organisation.

However, according to the organisational meetings and interviews of both headquarters (16) and field office staff (12), the organisation has been successful in establishing a new organisational identity and creating a learning culture in which there is room for joint creation of guidelines and tools, and space for critical reflection. A strong indicator of the existing learning culture was the fact that in the research interviews the staff did not give a "polished picture" of the state of organisational affairs as sometimes might happen in organisations with weaker learning culture. Instead, they provided a wealth of critical reflections about the instances where knowledge can be lost. For a learning organisation, it is necessary to be self-critical and identify the potential pitfalls in order to be able to response to these in a continuous manner.

In what follows, FINGO's strong learning culture and existing learning practices is considered a taken-for-granted starting point, and my analysis focuses exactly on the critical reflections provided in order to illustrate mechanisms of forgetting typical to development NGOs. Therefore, the following section should not be taken as a comprehensive description of the practices and learning in FINGO, but as provision of illustrative examples of the everyday challenges NGOs in general have to deal with when "counteracting development amnesia", and the ways these can be done. Interviewees in headquarters (FINGO) and field offices (FINGOF) are identified with a running number. FINGOM refers to an organisational meeting.

The usual suspects: personnel turnover, action culture, and accountability

> We are only a handful of dinosaurs here, those of us who have been in the organisation for more than five years.
>
> (FINGO3)

> During my seven years I think I have had ten different superiors; you cannot even get to know the previous one before the new one comes in.
>
> (FINGO2)

Certain characteristics in development NGOs are often identified as hindrances for organisational learning and thus contribute to organisational forgetting. These characteristics include high turnover of personnel, an action or activist culture, and focus on accountability rather than learning (Ebrahim 2003BIB-019; Edwards 1997; Lewis 2009, 2016). In FINGO, as in any NGO, the turnover of staff was high, and because of the organisation's expansion many new members of staff kept coming in. Lewis (2016, 88) suggests that in the conditions of high turnover of staff, forgetting is accelerated by a tendency of new personnel to make a break with the work of their predecessors. There are also more mundane forms of organisational forgetting that result from the turnover; for example, the new staff fail to capture existing organisational knowledge and routines, or parts of organisational memory decay when key personnel leave the organisation (Martin de Holan et al. 2004, 47–48).

Even if the organisational memory, by definition, resides in systems and routines, not in the heads of individuals, individuals are the ones to update and use memory and enact institutionalised routines (Martin de Holan & Phillips 2004a, 1605). When individual members of staff continuously change, organisational forgetting is likely to occur as decay of already established knowledge. One of the ways to counteract the decay of organisational memory in the situation of frequent staff turnout is an overall strategy of "avoiding heroes" – individuals whose competence is crucial for the organisation and who leave a huge knowledge gap behind them when changing jobs (Martin de Holan et al. 2004, 49). However, this is easier said than done. Especially in the field offices, competent individuals are crucial for an organisation's reputation and its capacity to act, so often "when a person leaves, the knowledge and competence is lost from the organisation" (FINGO6). Maintaining with individual competencies and avoiding their institutionalisation can also serve individual interests to keep a power position on the basis of expertise (Martin de Holan et al. 2004, 49), and there might be reluctance to spread the knowledge and skills.

An explicit transfer of knowledge between those going out and those coming in is crucial for counteracting memory decay. This transfer is typically mediated by documents and other artefacts, and rarely takes place in face-to-face interaction. Even rarer are instances with an ideal opportunity of having a parallel working period. In FINGO, as in many NGOs, there are explicit organisational procedures for recruitment, introduction and handing over knowledge, but they are not always ideally realised. Members of staff can leave rapidly and as a surprise, and they are already working in another organisation when the recruitment for their replacement begins. It is always unclear whether a "new person will have time to read the documentation" (FINGO6), and how much there will be to read in the first place, as storing information for your follower "depends on your personal interest, time and energy" (FINGO1). Additionally, no documentation can capture experience and tacit knowledge since that "cannot be read from the reports, and we lose this kind of information when people leave the NGO" (FINGO10).

Moreover, established knowledge stored in documents can appear as "outsider knowledge" to new staff. The new members of staff lack the experience of the process behind the acquisition of the knowledge. As one of the interviewees reflected, no matter how good the documentation of the existing ideas is, the "underlying learning processes cannot be transferred to the follower" (FINGO2). What can be transferred is the outcome, not the process, and from the point of view of individuals adapting new knowledge, these two are completely different processes. For example, when we asked about principles behind different organisational guidelines, many interviewees did not know the logic behind them and answered: "I was not here at the time, I cannot answer precisely". The high staff turnover and a high number of incoming new staff due to growth also disrupt the ongoing learning and change processes in organisation as:

> You start to do something, and introducing a new idea to an organisation takes time, and in the meantime a lot of new people have come in you do not know anything even about the previous stage; so we often have to take steps back.
>
> (FINGO7)

Second, an activist culture or preferring action over reflection is one of the most common hindrances to learning, and is a factor contributing to forgetting existing knowledge in NGOs (Edwards 1997). Accordingly, creating a "culture of learning", and the positive attitude of managers, are suggested strategies in support of organisational learning and to overcome internal hindrances to it (Britton 2005; Fowler 1997). Similarly, in FINGO, the positive learning culture and attitudes were frequently cited, and the staff felt encouraged to reflect also the challenges confronted. However, the common phenomenon of privileging the action over reporting and reflection was also discussed (Edwards 1997). According to an evaluation of a senior officer the younger generation in particular were "enthusiastic about making the world a better place", and regarded the institutionalised learning mechanisms such as monitoring being something additional to the "real work" and definitely "not sexy" (FINGO7). While the systematic monitoring and evaluation could be seen as "bureaucracy", the learning zeal was explicated more in a willingness to experiment new things and see how these might work.

Being very active in doing their daily work, NGO staff are often "too busy" to learn new things or to make sure to update or revisit organisational memory systems in order to ensure that knowledge is not degraded. The members of staff reflected that within the hectic flow of everyday tasks they often feel that there is no time to attend training courses, to share new knowledge acquired with their colleagues, or to update the documents due to time constraints. The judgement of relevance of training is connected with the detailed division of labour described above. As one of the headquarters officers stated: "I haven't participated in any training courses; my working time is full already now, so if I would add something extra like training, I should consider it really important in regard to my work" (FINGO12). If the staff in headquarters are very busy, the working life is even more hectic in the field offices. As a field representative stated: "the work load in the field is very high, and field officers, honestly, they barely have time to do everything" (FINGOF1). Those who are really competent and engaged with partners and project participants might be "always so over-booked and busy that they cannot find time, for example, even to read their emails", not to mention to sit down with the office colleagues for reflection (FINGOF10). Additionally, the culture of reflection on successes and failures might represent a "totally new way of learning" (FINGOF4) for the field staff that might have an educational history in institutions where the provision of right answers rather than critical reflection was encouraged. Additionally, the institutional tendency to prove success, which is common to development, might result in a rapid forgetting of challenges, errors and misunderstandings. One of the African field officers explained counteracting this tendency in interaction with partner organisations: "We say we are not in the praising business here. From the very beginning you get people used to this idea" (FINGOF5), and continued to describe how learning from challenges is much more demanding than "praising", but in the end, much more rewarding in everyone's opinion.

Third, being busy and forgetting to learn can be connected to the project management practices if their use for purely accountability purposes is emphasised. Working on the implementation of a project is hectic, and the physical field conditions with security risks, unreliable transport and electricity cuts easily occupy most of the working time. Interestingly, however, the hectic work rhythm and being too busy to learn were often perceived to result not from the field conditions but from the annual rhythm of project management. In other words, the staff felt fully occupied with managing with no time left for learning. Quarterly and annual reporting as well as annual planning offer potential opportunities for learning, but in real life "those processes are usually so hectic that we rarely have time to reflect, there are so many obligatory things to be done" (FINGOF4). Therefore, the institutionalised instances of "learning" can be experienced as disappointing when it comes to learning: "In our annual planning workshop, things are rushed, you really have to move fast, give a brief update on what is happening in the field; I do not take that as learning" (FINGOF8) reflected one of the African field officers. In development, it is a well-acknowledged phenomenon that much information is collected and knowledge produced for accountability rather than learning purposes (Ebrahim 2003). As one of the field workers described: "We have piles and piles of files of documentation; this is a waste of paper, because you would never go back to all these files … you will never have time, you are just documenting and documenting" (FINGOF1). To counteract the practical problems of piles of paper and speeding the analysis process, there had already been experiments with conducting data collection and storage in electronic form by means of mobile phones and tablets in some locations, and further encourage allocating working time for learning, for instance, by introducing digital learning platforms. It is generally acknowledged, that the hectic rhythm of project management seems to accelerate forgetting and leads to failure to capture new knowledge inherent in the recent project experiences since there is no time to share it (Lewis 2009). Similar forgetting can also happen at an organisational level, for instance, in regard to evaluations and their use in the design of further projects. In FINGO, evaluation practices of its self-implemented projects was in its infancy at the time of the interviews, and there were detailed guidelines designed to facilitate their conduct. The results of evaluations are discussed in many organisational levels and utilised in the specific locations. A concern expressed by the staff was about how the accumulated evaluation knowledge could be reflected within the higher levels of the organisation. Taken the relatively large size of the organisation, the internal coordination meetings are very packed with different issues and "the evaluations are merely noted rather than discussed, because it is usually a two-hour meeting with 14 items on the agenda" (FINGO6). Moreover, the past experiences are often forgotten when competing for diminishing donor resources. Development NGOs continuously search for funding for their activities from agencies with different priorities, and in proposals try to combine their own goals with those of potential donors. The lessons learned from different projects funded by other donors might not be the top priority, and learning how to modify the activities according to varying donor agendas is important. As stated by one of the interviewees in the headquarters: "When planning a new project the donor requirements might be the place to start, and not the previous knowledge" (FINGO15). These include the need to learn the latest international "development trends" (FINGOF11) as frequently emphasised by one of the African interviewees. This resonates with the common observation that the need to learn the latest development fads and fashions contribute to forgetting NGOs' past experiences (Cornwall 2007; Lewis 2009). Additionally, the lessons drawn from evaluations are forgotten "because of the changing themes, changing partners; sometimes we just leave some themes, or exit from some programmes, and the lessons are not relevant anymore" (FINGO14). The question of "how much we prioritise the previous lessons and how much those towards future" (FINGO15) becomes relevant. With the changing organisational programmes and themes, or general development fashions, lessons drawn from the previous ones might feel already outdated.

When the tendencies to forget due to turnover, activist culture and bias for accountability were clear, FINGO attempted to find ways to counteract these tendencies. For example, in the preparation of its annual reports a practice of "writeshop" was introduced. A number of members of staff spend several days together for reflection and to write the report (FINGO3). The annual reports of the organisation are very informative, both in terms of description of the contexts as well as reflecting on the programme progress. However, much of this in-depth information can be forgotten for the simple reason that important stakeholders do not have, or do not allocate time to read them in detail. Moreover, while much of the organisational learning effort was geared towards the "official learning" and reporting, there were wishes for more "closed spaces" (FINGO5) in which the staff among themselves could reflect on the lessons learned in an "open and deep way" without a need to report to anyone. The balancing between the limited resources and resource needs is difficult. In development, the question is often "How much time is given to documentation, how much to implementation" (FINGO5). This has direct implications for organisational learning which, to a great extent, depends on the quality of documentation and how well the documentation is used. In terms of monitoring, for example, each sequence of collecting data requires resources, the securing of which was emphasised in the interviews of country staff.

Forgetting being part of a global organisation: memory systems, identity and power

> There should not be many FINGOs all over the world but everyone should have the same principles. However, this is often forgotten due to the context specificity and strengthened by the aspired independence of the country offices.
>
> (FINGO1)

Creating shared organisational structures and common global identity is a challenge for development NGOs whose functions are spread over a wide variety of geographic locations (Watkins el al. 2012). Organisations have to create a certain image in each location, and additionally, have a joint identity as a global entity. The process of establishing a global structure for FINGO entailed a number of steps such as design of the organisational programme with clearly defined thematic areas and definition of global indicators to follow each. At the same time, FINGO had established a number of regional and country offices that either implemented development projects and humanitarian action by themselves, or supported local partners in implementing their projects. At the same time, the number of personnel in FINGO had increased both in the headquarters and in the field offices. In addition to all the practical arrangements related to such reorganising, the organisation had invested a significant effort in building organisational memory systems, and consolidating organisational project management practices into guidelines and templates; as one of the senior officers in headquarters said:

> We have an evaluation guide, then we have our own internal guidelines from 2010, we have our programme manual that has all the operational processes and guidelines such as format for partner assessment, guidelines for project monitoring for partners, quarterly work plan format, quarterly monitoring format, monitoring visit format … and a lot more.
>
> (FINGO13)

In order to consolidate the joint principles and shared identity the organisation also developed systematic learning practices such as annual learning seminars where staff from headquarters and field offices spent a week together discussing joint themes. In 2015, the themes included M&E, programme indicators and data collection for the measurement of programme indicators, human rights-based approach (HRBA), and best failures.

However, despite the deliberate efforts to learn to be one global organisation, there were some instances where this was somehow, mostly unintentionally, forgotten. As an example, the electronic documents archive that was supposed to provide a shared knowledge base was constantly referred to as "the famous Cemetery of Documents" (FINGOM2). The experienced challenges in using the stored knowledge resonated with the common issues related to institutional memory assets and routines to use them, the division of tasks and power, and building coherence in joint organisational understanding (Martin de Holan 2011b). First, the hardware for an organisational memory system was in place and FINGO had both an electronic document archive and a project management system. However, the routines for their use varied both from individual to individual, and from office to office. In the interviews with those working in the field offices, some admitted that they had never read guidelines in the electronic system, while others constantly used them actively: "Some templates are updated and very relevant; some of them need to be contextualised" (FINGOF6). Those working in the headquarters had noticed the variety of uses in field offices, especially in information storage and sharing: "From some you cannot get any information even if you ask; others are very active, and share so that the experience can be used for the entire organisation" (FINGO2). At the same time, some of the headquarters staff was not accustomed to using the system frequently either. Therefore, to counteract a memory decay, in a situation in which it was evident that much new knowledge would be produced and stored in the organisational memory systems, the staff were continuously encouraged to use the system; and the usability of the system itself was continuously improved.

In order to institutionalise organisational practices, developing and storing guidelines in the organisational memory system is often not sufficient as new knowledge, and guidelines also have to be routinised in action (Martin de Holan et al. 2004). Formal guidelines are relatively easy to establish, but their integration with the existing organisational knowledge and practices is harder. In general, formal training or encouragement of the staff "to read" is not sufficient; instead, learning-by-doing and situational training are needed (Martin de Holan & Phillips 2011, 441). In development NGOs, learning by reading guidelines can be difficult for some members of staff in field offices, especially those with relatively little education. For example, during a feedback seminar in 2016 in Helsinki, one of the fieldworkers approached me "for professional advice". He told me that no matter how much he tried, for him it was impossible to read guidelines in such a way that he could apply them in his professional practice, and asked me what he could do to improve his skills. We brainstormed together, and one of the ways of learning we identified was to read through the guidelines with colleagues working in the same office, and continuously discuss their implications together. In the same vein, notwithstanding their origin, many members of staff who worked in country offices distinguished between desk-based and field-based work, and the latter was considered more motivating: “I do not like desk-based work, I like relating to people, I like to talk to people, and people talk to me” (FINGOF3). Sitting at a desk and computer, reading guidelines and other documents was perceived as a less inviting part of the job, and probably was not always done to a sufficient extent.

There were also technical hindrances to the use of digital systems in the field offices as common in the contexts where general infrastructure is unreliable. At times there were not enough computers, the electricity was frequently cut, or internet connections were unreliable or too slow. However, we also encountered similar difficulties in the headquarters in Helsinki when we conducted our research interviews. For example, one of the interviewees wanted to show us something and started to click her computer mouse: “I would show you this manual, if only I could get into the system … well, it seems not to be working right now, I will check it later” (FINGO13). The document management system had been in place since 2011, and its systematic use had taken some time, and there were still some challenges in both storing and retrieving the information. The storage depended on personal preferences and willingness, and the database was not found to be very efficient for information retrieval. All over the organisation, when searching for relevant information staff often did not search the database first. Instead, “the first step would be to try to guess the right persons and start asking where to find the information” (FINGO11).

An additional element that contributes to organisational forgetting is the structure of divisions of tasks. As is typical of organisations, as FINGO had grown it had developed a more detailed and explicit division of tasks and job descriptions. In regard to development programmes, the division of tasks in headquarters followed, on the one hand, geographical lines – desk officers focused on interacting with certain regional and country offices – and on the other, tasks were divided according to thematic expertise, including thematic advisers. In country offices, apart from the directors, the job descriptions of “project officers” were divided along the lines of different projects. While in some large INGOs there are entire units for “accountability and learning”, FINGO did not have such a unit. The systems of learning and accountability were developed by a few persons A director for organisational development did not focus only on development programmes, but was involved in overall human resource management, risks management and leadership development. Therefore, “it is not particularly in my job description” was a typical answer we heard from the headquarters staff interviewed when asked about organisational learning. Against this backdrop, the wealth of design of joint guidelines and indicators, establishing routines of conducting global meetings, and creation of positive learning environment were great achievements that had emerged out of a successful combination of expertise. It was often suggested that "it would be good to have two or three people with a job description that included systematic planning of distribution of information within the organisation" (FINGO3) in resonance with the common observations that the lack of structural division of tasks for ensuring knowledge storage and sharing among the organisation contributes, in general, to failure to capture new knowledge, and accelerates forgetting the knowledge already established (Martin de Holan 2011b).

In addition to guidelines and division of tasks, general organisational identity was called for:

> It is important to have an idea about how *we* do things here, in a positive sense. Even if you do not go back to the guidelines all the time, you should have some shared understanding of why we are doing these things, and that is why I need to pay attention to certain things.
>
> (FINGOM1)

This resonates with the idea than to counteract organisational forgetting, not only are guidelines and their routine use needed, but also a view of the world that explains what the organisation is, what it does, and how it does what it does (Martin de Holan 2011b, 320). These kinds of sets of shared beliefs, even if contested, are essential for organisational integration. In FINGO, the face-to-face meetings were considered important for such identity-building. As one of the African project officers reflected:

> You meet in occasional meetings, and then people keep implementing programmes in different countries; we have an intranet, but it is not adequate because you can only talk so much with somebody on the internet; you can store the data, send an email or two to someone, but you cannot really learn much.
>
> (FINGOF8)

The occasional field visits from the headquarters to country offices, and the annual programme meetings offered face-to-face leaning opportunities for the staff from different offices. However, to consolidate the global organisational identity, and thus reduce the tendency to forget of being part of a larger organisation, more face-to-face meetings and other kinds of interaction between the field offices were called for.

Finally, building one global organisation is not only a question of identity, but also a question of power and autonomy. In organisations, some old knowledge can be discarded, and new knowledge may not be captured as a result of internal struggles for power and interests (Martin de Holan & Phillips 2004a, 1612). New knowledge can be purposefully suspended, innovations abandoned and learning aborted; for example, when templates and job descriptions are brought, or even imposed, from "outside" as might be the case in multinational firms, international chains, and INGOs, the local actors can deliberately choose not to learn those, or to opt for non-action as a response (Brook et al. 2016; Martin de Holan & Phillips 2004a, 2011). In INGOs, certain tensions regarding power and autonomy between headquarters and field offices are common (see also Chapter 4). In knowledge production, headquarters tend to seek standardised practices, while field offices and partner organisations have a greater need to contextualise according to projects and locations. At times, field offices feel they are continuously asked to provide more information, and get frustrated, as exemplified by one of the regional directors: "But there is already a lot of information; sometimes in the field you start to ask how much information you need here [in HQ]; we do not always know what info is needed and what is the right way to report it" (FINGOM1).

Organisational ignorance

The classical account of the connections between learning and ignorance emphasises that the more we learn the more we realise our ignorance. From the point of view of accumulative science, a kind of "functional ignorance" motivates scientific inquiry to turn current ignorance into knowledge (Merton 1987). In the same vein, from the sociological perspective, ignorance can refer to knowledge about the limits of knowing in a certain area (Knorr Cetina 1999, 63), ignorance of the risks brought by modernisation (Beck 1996), or uncertainty about the future (Luhmann 1988). In the contexts of organisations, ignorance often refers to unavoidable ignorance of an organisation about its constantly changing environments. Organisational decisions have to be made under conditions of ignorance of complex and changing environments, and the unavoidable disorder outside an organisation must be turned into an order inside, in order for the organisation to be able to act (Bakken & Wiik 2017; Harvey et al. 2001).

Furthermore, organisational ignorance can result from an absence of knowledge, from an organisation's ignorance about existing knowledge, or from suppression of knowledge, as in the case of taboos and secrecy (Roberts 2012, 277–229). Additionally, organisations and institutions can use ignorance as a strategic resource and ignore unpleasant information in order to maintain their organisational capacity (McGoey 2007). Organisational ignorance is related to time and space; through time, ignorance can be transferred into knowledge, or what is known in one place is not necessarily known in another. In parallel with organisational forgetting, also ignorance can be institutionally produced.

In the following, I discuss some manifestations of ignorance in development NGO, and in development in general on the basis of literature. Additionally, I draw some illustrative examples from a number of case studies used in this book.

Ignoring the uncertainty

Development NGOs work in highly uncertain and complex environments, often with both ambiguous and ambitious goals (Watkins et al. 2012). Due to these uncertainties, NGOs remain partly ignorant about the variety of processes taking place in the environments and the social change they have promoted. More generally, modern life has been seen as characterised by ignorance resulting from the unpredictability of the future (Luhmann 1988). At the same time, growing standardisation and measurement systems aim to reduce complexity and ambiguity, and thus, increase certainty about the past and future (Best 2012). In development literature, drawing from the principle of uncertainty in quantum physics, Uphoff (1992, 324) argues that there are significant uncertainties in regard to knowing about social life in the context of development interventions. In physics, even the smallest particles are inherently unknowable, as they are always affected by attempts to measure them. When it comes to human and social behaviour in natural contexts, attaining full knowledge about them is a much more demanding task. Upphoff's (ibid.) analysis of a project on farmer's associations in Gal Oya provides a convincing example of a discrepancy between the "known" assumption of individual rationality in project design, and the actual interdependence of people's attitudes and practices that was revealed during the project implementation.

A certain level of ignorance can be seen as necessary for a development industry to continue. For example, Fforde (2017, 177) argues that management tools such as LFA and accountability mechanisms particular to development assume the project designers are able to predict the consequences of interventions, while in real-life complexities, "nobody has a predictively reliable clue". To analyse all the complexities involved might not be possible at all, and in any case, it would require resources far beyond the capacity of development NGOs. Additionally, Hirschman (1967/2015) suggests that some kind of "hiding hand" is necessary for development practice. He argues that if the project designs really draw thorough lessons from the past experiences and take into account all the complexities and uncertainties previously encountered, it would be hard to believe in any project designs and, in practice, the proposed projects would never get funded.

The tendency to counteract uncertainty with standardised institutionalised practices, notwithstanding different contexts, is common not only in development, but in all contemporary management. However, despite the efforts, the tension between standardisation and "simplicity" required for management, and the complexity of realities remains. The attempts to solve this challenge typically include trying new ways of formalising knowledge (Best 2012). An additional solution would be to accept complexity and have a right to assume that change processes are more or less unpredictable, and act according to the best knowledge (Fforde 2017, 1). In all the case organisations there was a tendency to reduce uncertainties by means of more elaborate management practices, even if the staff had a number of experiences of situations where the prediction of people's future behaviour had not covered the variety encountered in practice. For example, in their narratives of not very successful empowerment processes, the WV staff (see Chapter 3) described how similar kinds of intervention models could result in different outcomes in different communities due to interdependency of attitudes. A case in point was support for girls' secondary education. In some communities, an NGO's initial support for secondary education produced young female professionals that could act as role models for younger girls in their community. While in others, after receiving secondary education, girls returned home, remained unemployed, and even started to drink as they were continuously discouraged, disempowered and even snubbed by the community members for being "educated, but useless" persons. The probabilities of such disempowering effects articulated by the surrounding communities had not been taken into account in project designs, and there was little to do to counteract them afterwards.

While the contexts in which NGOs work vary, change at different paces, and are complex, NGOs need to make rapid decisions and select strategies to be able to act. In this kind of situation, where knowledge is not available, or there is no time or resources to achieve it, NGOs, like other organisations, might employ so-called pragmatic ignorance (Harvey et al. 2001). The decisions are not made on the basis of predictable knowledge or documented evidence, but draw from "institutional common sense" concerning what could be expected to happen or what is reasonably foreseeable (ibid. 457). In the above example, the common-sense expectation was that the community would be supportive of education to some of its members rather than trying to actively put them down. With standardised approaches, NGOs tend to conduct practices common in the industry without detailed knowledge about their effectiveness in given contexts. A similar kind of pragmatic ignorance can be used in policy formulation if the scientific and practice-based evidence is too complex or abstract (Dunn 1997). Therefore, pragmatic ignorance contrasts with the ideals of evidence-based decision making. Some organisational literature suggests that rather than being evidence based, design should actually be understood as a "practice of ignorance" that investigates possibilities and generates flexible and variable solutions (Bakken & Wiik 2017).

NGOs' impact and the long-term consequences of their interventions are often left in a shadow of ignorance. Measuring impact is challenging and needs considerable resources long after the end of programmes and projects. All the case NGOs acknowledged this challenge, for example: "We know about a lot of results and outcomes, but we need more information about the simple question of what differences we made in the long run" (FINGO3). The acknowledged ignorance considered also the organisational value-added from the perspective of the "right-holders and grassroots" (FINGO7). From the perspective of the staff in all the case NGOs, the ignorance was seen partly as a result of incomplete information, inadequate tools, and the complexity of the intended impact such as attitude change. This ignorance could be addressed by developing more proper methods or collecting more information. A more profound ignorance was related to the uncertainty about the future, especially in relation to risks that could not be predicted notwithstanding the quality of risk assessments. Moreover, the staff acknowledged ignorance about the nature and impact of an NGO's own relationships with its partners and communities. As one of the interviewees in headquarters put it: "We still do not get much information about how our own partnership behaviour is experienced by partners and communities; I would say the experience of our partners on us, our conduct, is the most important knowledge lacking" (FINGO10). In the Evaluation Everyday project, similar challenges were identified. For example, the Zambian organisation Green Living Movement (GLM) initiated an idea together with its Finnish partner TUO to develop mutual reporting practices. Not only would GLM send its reports to the Finnish NGO, but the Finnish NGO would also report about their activities and the challenges to GLM. In the same vein, the mutual reporting practice took place between GLM and some of the farmers' clubs they supported in rural communities.

Ignorance of the "other"

Development is rich with binaries despite continuous calls to abandon them. Among others, binaries such as developed and developing, high income and low income, donors and recipients, facilitators and beneficiaries, and global north and global south are commonly used. These binaries are both material and discoursive constellations and, to a great extent, echo those pervasive to colonialism in which a difference between "us" and the "other" includes an inescapable power relationship (Loomba 1998). The postcolonial literature asks whether the subaltern can speak (Spivak 1988). In the same vein, development literature continuously enquires about whose voice is heard and whose knowledge counts (Chambers 2014). While there is a normative tendency to prioritise local and participatory knowledge along with expert knowledge (Green 2012), in the practical design processes, "attribution of ignorance" to others is common (Hobart 1993, 1–2). In planning for or with the "beneficiaries", they are attributed ignorance; about their rights, efficient farming practices, or treatments for HIV/AIDS. Consequently, expert knowledge, often attributed to NGOs, easily remains ignorant about the local knowledge, or perceives it merely as an "obstacle to designed rational processes" (ibid.). For example, in their narratives about empowerment processes, the field staff in the partners of WV Finland identified "ignorance in communities" as one of the main obstacles to successful empowerment. Additionally, in project design and implementation, knowledge typically revolves around a particular part of life that is in the focus of the project, considering others as not relevant for the particular instance, and thus leaving them in the shadow of ignorance.

In organisational processes, for instance in an attempt to build a coherent programme for international NGOs, participatory knowledge that does not fit the organisational categories will easily be ignored. For example, in the "best failures" session in the FINGO learning seminar in Kampala 2015, one of the country offices presented a failure in a community education project that had suffered from the lack of a participatory design and as a consequence, lacked interest among the community members. One of the presenters said in an interview:

> It is not easy for people to take part in project activities without something in return; so if you want a community to be involved in the project you have to sensitise them. If you do not do so, we do not have any community participation.
>
> (FINGOF7)

In order to learn from the experience, the presenters were producing a participation guideline to be shared within the entire organisation. This example hints to a general tendency in development interventions to ignore the local logics of social organising and the community expectations towards NGOs (Olivier de Sardan 2005). For example, in many contexts patron-clientelism is among the main logics of social organisation (Kellsall 2008; Swidler 2009), and NGOs need to respond to this particular logic in their interaction with their environments and beneficiaries. Community members often offer NGOs the role of patron whose responsibility is to continuously take care of and provide for their clients (Swidler 2009), resulting in disappointment in NGOs' empowerment aspirations. For instance WV field staff described their challenge in balancing between an empowerment approach and community members' demands for charity and continuous help. These challenges resonate with the moral discord identified within NGO grassroots workers in Bangladesh who continuously struggled to address the beneficiaries' questions of "what is our benefit" in projects that did not meet their immediate need, and felt frustrated and even angry with the "ungrateful villagers" (Arvidson 2008, 124).

The ignorance about the particular local realities in development NGOs is typically more distributed the larger and more international they are. For the international ones, the relationship of headquarters staff with the local realities is usually mediated by field offices and partner organisations. At the same time, even the relationships between NGO headquarters and field offices can be distant. NGOs' need to develop strategies and tools universal to all the locations where they work can lead to forgetting and ignoring the special conditions and needs in each location. In turn, from the perspective of field offices, this can be experienced as lack of interest, and can lead to explicit resistance. The International Solidarity Foundation had its one-week programme meeting in the Helsinki headquarters in 2012, where field coordinators and programme staff participated. The headquarters had prepared a five-day agenda on organisational issues. The country coordinators were critical of the content of the agenda and decided to arrange an ad hoc meeting addressing their everyday concerns, such as dealing with multiple realities, logics and cultures, avoiding the role of "Santa Claus", strategies to deal with power struggles inherent in project implementation, and fear of inadequacy of own expertise in the face of growing demands. They experienced that headquarters could provide good support for project management, but that coordinators needed more peer support in dealing with the everyday realities of their work. Similar ideas about the need for more sharing of experiences between different field offices were articulated by FINGO field staff after their programme meeting in Helsinki in 2014 where the agenda was filled with presentations by headquarters staff. The criticism was taken seriously and in 2015 most of the seminar time was allocated to field staff presentations and assignments in breakout groups. These forms created apparent learning enthusiasm among participant, and reduced the ignorance of headquarters staff of the field realities and the ignorance of field offices about each other.

Regarding institutional memory, those working in the field offices often feel that large amounts of their everyday work is never stored in organisational memory, and is left in a shadow of ignorance when it comes to indicators and reports. In turn, headquarters staff acknowledge their ignorance as a natural consequence of the number of projects and contexts they have to deal with; it is impossible and unnecessary to know every detail. As one of the directors of a field office in Africa said:

> It is very little part of the daily work that actually shows in reports, often we report only activities, like we visited this or that project, but we do not report the discussions, the problems and how we solved them together. (FINGOF4)

In the reports, the activities conducted seem quite simple and technical while they actually are quite complex and require a lot of negotiations. Much of the back-and-forth visiting, phone calls and text messages between the field officers, partner organisations and beneficiaries, which might fill a significant portion of the daily working time, are left in the sphere of organisational ignorance. Continuous problem solving, conflict management and dealing with surprises are typical ways to describe the daily work in the field offices. For instance, a Zambian environmental NGO representative described the realities of organisational practice of "monitoring visits" in the following way:

> We conduct monitoring visits, review what project activities they have done, but sometimes, instead of normal project management meetings you are going into conflict management meetings; sometimes the chairperson of the group has been seen to practice witchcraft, sometimes maybe some money was lost … so we monitor not only project achievements, but also the social constellation of the clubs, and general events in the villages, the conflicts. (workshop 12.3.2009)

Ignoring the unpleasant

Organisations and institutions can benefit from "strategic ignorance", which refers to deliberate efforts to ignore information that is unsettling to an organisation and, thus, in some situations "cultivating ignorance is more advantageous than cultivating knowledge" (McGoey 2007, 555). For example, ignorance about the lack of safety of antidepressants or the health risks of cigarettes serves the organisational goals of respective industries. Surprisingly, the bureaucratic regulatory bodies as well might have a "will to ignorance" resulting from their need to maintain relationships with industries by not establishing a firm knowledge about the harmfulness of certain products (McGoey 2007, 232). In addition to ignoring the results of science, organisations might use strategic ignorance to protect organisational interests in a "process of rendering facts inert" through sequestered knowledge and distributed ignorance (Heimer 2012, 18). In sequestered knowledge, inconvenient contextual facts that do not fit the rules are separated from the reported knowledge. For example, the staff can produce "piles of papers" in order to align with rules and regulations. In distributed ignorance, everyone focuses on a certain task only, and a larger and systemic perspective is not known by anyone; facts might be shared, but connections between them can remain unclear (ibid.). Cultivation of strategic ignorance can be a resource, both for those in a position of power and those subject to it (McGoey 2012b). For example, Ebrahim (2003) showed how in north-south development partnerships, southern NGOs have power of information, as their donors depend on the knowledge delivered to them – and consequently, suffer from knowledge held back and are left in the space of ignorance.

Strategic ignorance can be institutionally mobilised, and therefore hard for organisations and individuals to expose, reflect upon or deliberately discuss (McGoey 2012a, 570). Ignorance also has implications for experts' position in regard to their responsibility. When we do not know, we do not have to take responsibility, according to Luhmann's (1988) suggestion that: "Who communicates certainty has to take responsibility, who communicates ignorance, is excused." In development, one of the institutional forms of strategic ignorance is related to "praising culture" and the systematic tendency to ignore failures and challenges, often related to having too ambitious goals in the first place (Watkins et al. 2012). While the challenges are frequently discussed unofficially, in organisational and institutional knowledge production such as evaluations, there is a bias for identifying success. In the discussions concerning empowerment in Chapter 3, the Finnish project coordinators were enthusiastic to hear about the potential unintended consequences of empowerment interventions in Kenya and Uganda. This revealed the organisational ignorance as: "We never hear about these negative outcomes." In a similar vein, presenting the "best failures" from different programmes in the joint FINGO seminar in 2015 was an attempt to reduce ignorance about the challenges encountered. The failures were successfully discussed; not for the sake of judging, but for learning purposes. The culture of praising, bias for success and accepting unrealistic goals in the first place also reflects the nature of the prevalent power relationships and resource dependency in NGO relationships. For example, the Zambian organisation GLM reflected that only through certain trustful donor relationships had they learned to be open and "even with other donors, when we see that certain expectations are not realistic we would rather sit down and tell them that this is not realistic".

Another area of strategic ignorance concerns the issues related to corruption and financial mismanagement. Development NGOs work in environments where everyday corruption is common. Institutionally, corruption in development projects is not accepted in any form (e.g. the Finnish Ministry for Foreign Affairs has anticorruption guidelines for development cooperation). NGOs are openly against corruption and for transparency and good governance. However, in everyday practice there might be issues that could be labelled as "corruption" (Blundo et al. 2006). For example, the author's own experiences in Tanzania and Uganda over the years have shown how according to local practices, in some instances, extra money had to be paid to official guests of honour when they attended project functions. This money is often drawn from personal pockets of the staff of partner organisations, and is not shown in the budgets or books because such expenses are against the logic that public servants should not charge extra for attending such events. When it comes to mismanagement, clear instances of misuse of funding by partner organisations are usually openly addressed. In extreme cases, for example, a few of my case organisations encountered situations in which bookkeepers of partner organisations had run away with project money. While these incidents are handled by the courts, there are also more mundane issues related to financial management that often remain in the domain of ignorance, especially if the bookkeeping is in order. However, as an experienced Finnish NGO professional reflected, in the contexts where "corruption is everywhere" one has to be alert to possibilities of a kind of "virtual bookkeeping" that can be hard to identify. In general, however, the theme of corruption was not brought up in the interviews neither as an issue about which the NGOs should learn more nor as sharing experiences of tackling this everyday phenomenon.

Field visits and the illusion of the everyday practice

One of the most common complaints among the headquarters staff in the case of NGOs was that they knew too little about their partner organisations and beneficiaries due to the limited opportunities for field visits. Most interaction in all case NGOs was through emails, Skype or other web-based platforms that left much knowledge untouched while it typically concentrated on certain details concerning project plans and reports. Both the headquarters and field staff agreed that field visits offered good opportunities to acquire knowledge. However, field visits might also contribute to ignorance through creating an "illusion of truth". For example, Heimer (2012, 35) reports on a large-scale study on strategic ignorance in the context of HIV clinics in the USA, Uganda, South Africa and Thailand, and examines how clinics employ strategic ignorance in their relationship with donors. During field visits, the main task was to assure donors that their requirements were fulfilled and provide them with opportunities to familiarise themselves with the "actual practice". However, the actual practice shown for the visitors was "fixed" in a way that was more streamlined than the actual practices and routines that include much "shoving, nipping and tugging" (ibid.) in interaction with the patients and larger community.

The routine structures of NGO field visits support ignorance while not providing much opportunities to see the actual, normal practice. For the hosts, the visits are deviations from normal, and thus specific efforts are made to show the success of NGO activities and provide normal hospitality for guests. The field visits are time constrained. In a number of case organisations, during their field visits lasting a maximum of one week, Finnish coordinators rushed from one meeting to another and from one field location to the next. Moreover, they also felt that most of their time was used in meetings with partner organisations dealing with administrative issues. Getting to know the experiences of beneficiaries and learning about new issues were allocated less time. The project communities, naturally, did their best for the visitors and arranged welcoming celebrations with speeches, dancing and beverages, and expressed overwhelming gratitude towards the Finnish NGOs. When a new school library in Kenya was visited, about a hundred children waited for hours to greet the guests with songs. After the welcoming ceremony, most of the children went to "use" the library while the guests observed them. In an urban slum in India, visitors were taken to visit the small businesses of the successful entrepreneurs who had received support from the NGO, while the stories of the other, less successful, entrepreneurs were not heard. All hospitality, certainly, is enjoyable and shows good spirit in communities. However, experience in everyday life and the potential consequences of project activities on daily conduct merely remains in the sphere of ignorance.

During the visits, Finnish coordinators made a great effort to interact with as many and as diverse a set of people as possible, although the time available did not allow much participation or getting to know each other properly. In order to counteract this kind of ignorance, some of the coordinators in case organizations made frequent efforts to stay in the participant communities for an extended period of time. Those who were able to do that emphasised the importance of a stay. Participating in everyday community life and having relaxed chats in the evenings around the bonfire reduced mutual ignorance. Additionally, it made the relationships more normal and human, and decreased the effect of institutionalised donor-beneficiary positions.

Denial of critical reflection of the current development trends

Organisational taboos and denials are potential sources of organisational ignorance (Roberts 2012, 223). Taboos refer to areas of knowledge that should not be entered in an organisation. They might be internal to organisations or derive from its external environment. Organisational denials occur when the values and norms embedded in the organisation "blind its members to knowledge that does not fit easily with the existing framework of understanding" (Roberts 2012, 43). Denials might also hinder learning lessons from past action; if failures or challenges are denied, an organisation might stubbornly stick with its old strategies that do not work in the way wished. Furthermore, when the uncertainty about tasks and environments increases, both individuals and organisations tend to commit to their work world view rather than draw from information available (Harvey et al. 2001, 456). For example, universalistic organisational approaches can lead to similar ways to promote quality education in Nepal and Liberia, or to support livelihoods in Haiti and Uganda, and thus lead to ignorance about the diversity of actual mechanisms of the project activities in different contexts.

In development NGOs, training and other learning opportunities for staff typically concentrate on management tools and development approaches. Over the years, NGO staff all over the world have been trained in LFA, PRA, HRBA, ToC, OM, RBM, MSC, gender analysis, power analysis, and other approaches on the basis of which they could structure their work in different contexts and in order to do the work in improved ways. The issues learned have also functioned as tools for building coherence in NGOs, and in the field of development in general. Each new approach opens novel insights and carries a promise of improvement vis-á-vis the old one. Often, from the point of view of an individual member of staff, these learning opportunities are initiated outside, by the organisation or wider development community, and they are presented as ready-made approaches to be implemented. The experiences and lessons learned – for example on the question of why to move from needs-based to rights-based approach, or why to shift from building schools to promote citizen engagement – are not considered. This might lead to mechanical implementation of templates in different contexts such as, "This is how we should do it". Harvey et al. (2001, 455) suggest that there is often probabilistic ignorance in organisations when managers choose what learning opportunities to offer. The opportunities offered change employees' cognitive understanding of the issue, but at the same time, they are not provided with a chance to validate that knowledge based on their own practical experience. Standardised learning opportunities increase ignorance as those trained might expect to experience a situation similar to those explained in training, which they might not come across in their particular professional conduct. Therefore, manager-chosen learning outcomes might hinder learning from their experience.

The staff of the case organisation were provided with quite a large number of training opportunities, both chosen by the management and of their own choice. However, much of the training content was institutionally defined, and not always based on the experienced need. There was not much reflection whether and in what ways new institutional approaches and novel fads were useful to the particular organisations. Over the course of our 2009–2010 OD project supporting M&E improvement, none of the ten organisations questioned the relevance of an M&E system or tried to find alternatives to the prevailing indicator-based model (Kontinen & Onali 2017). In one of the case organizations, the participants in our feedback meeting confirmed that the prevailing development approaches and fads were not usually subject to critical reflection. In the meeting, these approaches were not referred to as taboos, but as "development mantras that have significant statue in development" or "development doctrines". Another participant added that development approaches are

> something very hard to question, even if history shows that there have been problems with different approaches. For example, a lot of effort is put into explaining what the rights-based approach is and how to best use it, but its pitfalls and challenges, or its basic assumptions are less discussed. We do it now because it is considered good, and we perform results-based management because donors say so and everyone else is doing it as well.

Experiential learning that would change organisational world views and assumptions is rare in organisations with a strong culture (Harvey et al. 2001, 456). In building a new, expanded organisation, FINGO aimed to build a strong organisational culture and establish standardised organisational practices. While the majority of the respondents regarded guidelines and standardisation of knowledge and information as the best ways to promote learning, alternative opinions were also articulated. One of the interviewees in the headquarters reflected,

> I do not believe that we could have a kind of static knowledge which we would then distribute to the field offices. The best learning is to experiment; in development cooperation we have a tendency to believe in rather universalistic solutions, and of course there might be some principles, but my experience is that real development and change happens quite intuitively, through applying and experimenting.
>
> (FINGO9)

This quote reflects an idea that standardised organisational knowledge can produce ignorance and hinder learning from experience and experimenting. From the organisation's point of view the dilemma is that if everyone in the organisation is acting intuitively and experimenting with different things in a vast variety of contexts, the organisation, in a traditional sense, disappears, or it becomes a totally different, probably some kind of network-formed organisation.

Conclusions

This chapter suggested that in addition to organisational learning, attention should be paid to the processes of unlearning, forgetting and ignorance in development NGOs. The chapter provided examples of the dynamics of forgetting and ignorance. The usual suspects identified when it comes to forgetting both new and established knowledge were continuous personnel turnover, an action culture, and prioritising accountability over learning. These especially facilitate forgetting when it comes to the institutionalised mechanisms of M&E. The tendency to forget of being part of the entire organisation was related to access and the routines of using organisational memory systems, the need to build an organisational identity and the struggles over autonomy in an organisation.

Ignorance was mainly related to institutional characteristics of international development. These included ignoring uncertainties, ignorance of the "other", the partners, the beneficiaries, the headquarters or field offices, ignorance produced in field visits, and ignoring the criticisms of the mainstream approaches of any time, which are all systemic features circulating in development. Ignorance about the unpleasant or the actual impacts can serve as strategic ignorance that keeps the development industry going. As the literature cited in this chapter showed, phenomena of organisational forgetting or ignorance are not typical of development NGOs only. Rather, they are wider organisational and institutional processes of our times. More research on organisational forgetting and ignorance is needed to give a more elaborate account of their specificities in development.

References

Akgün, A.E., Byrne, J.C., Lynn, G.S. & Keskin, H. (2007) Organisational unlearning as changes in beliefs and routines in organisations. *Journal of Organizational Change Management*, 20(6), 794–812.

Akhshik, S.S. (2014) Organisational unlearning: An analytical literature review. *International Journal of Economics & Management Sciences*, 3(3). Online at dx.doi.org/10.4172/2162–6359.1000190

Arvidson, M. (2008) Contradictions and confusions in development work. Exploring the realities of Bangladeshi NGOs. *Journal of South Asian Development*, 3(1), 109–134.

Bakken, T. & Wiik, E.L. (2017) Ignorance and organisation studies. *Organization Studies*, Online first, doi; 10.1177/0170840617709312

Bateson, G. (1987/1964) The logical categories of learning and communication. In: Bateson, G. (ed.) *Steps to an Ecology of Mind*. Baum, WC, NJ: Jason Aronson Inc.

Beck, U. (1996) *The Reinvention of Politics. Rethinking Modernity in the Global Social Order*. Cambridge: Polity Press.

Berger, P.L. & Luckmann, T. (1966) *The Social Construction of Reality. A Treatise in the Sociology of Knowledge*. London: Penguin.

Best, J. (2012) Bureaucratic ambiguity. *Economy and Society*, 41(1), 84–106.

Blundo, G., Olivier de Sardan, J.-P., Arifari, N.B. & Alou, M.T. (2006) *Everyday Corruption and the State in Africa: Citizens and Public Officials*. London: Zed Books.

Britton, B. (2005) *Organisational Learning in NGOs: Creating the Motive, Means, and Opportunity*. Praxis Paper No 3. UK: INTRAC.

Brook, C., Pedler, M., Abbott, C. & Burgoyne, J. (2016) On stopping doing those things that are not getting us to where we want to be: Unlearning, wicked problems and critical action learning. *Human Relations*, 69(2), 369–389.

Chambers, R. (2014) Knowing in development: A radical agenda for the twenty-first century? *Forum for Development Studies*, 41(3), 525–538.

Connerton, P. (2009) *How Modernity Forgets*. Cambridge: Cambridge University Press.

Cooke, B. (2003) A new continuity with colonial administration: Participation in development management. *Third World Quarterly*, 24(1), 47–61.

Cornwall, A. (2007) Buzzwords and fuzzwords: Deconstructing development discourse. *Development in Practice*, 17(4/5), 471–484.

Douglas, M. (1986) *How Institutions Think*. Syracuse, NY: Syracuse University Press.

Dunn, W.N. (1997) Probing the boundaries of ignorance in policy analysis. *The American Behavioral Scientist*, 40(3), 277–298.

Easterby-Smith, M. & Lyles, M.A. (2011) In praise of organisational forgetting. *Journal of Management Inquiry*, 20(3), 311–316.

Ebrahim, A. (2003) Accountability in practice: Mechanisms for NGOs. *World Development*, 31(5), 813–829.

Edwards, M. (1997) Organisational learning in non-governmental organisations: What have we learned? *Public Administration and Development*, 17(2), 235–250.

Fear, J. (2014) Mining the past: Historicizing organizational learning and change. In: Bucheli, M. & Wadhwani, R.D. (eds) (2014) *Organizations in Time. History, Theory, Methods*. Oxford: Oxford University Press, 169–191.

Fernandez, V., Sallan J.S., Simo, P. & Enache, M. (2012) Organisational forgetting/unlearning: The dark side of the absorptive capacity. In: Hou, H.T. (ed.) *New Research on Knowledge Management Applications and Lessons Learned*, 155–170.

Fforde, A. (2017) *Reinventing Development. The Sceptical Change Agent*. Cham, Switzerland: Palgrave Macmillan.

Fowler, A. (1997) *Striking a Balance: A Guide to Enhancing the Effectiveness of Non-Governmental Organisations in Development*. London: Earthscan.

Green, M. (2012) Framing and escaping. Contrasting aspects of knowledge work in international development and anthropology. In Venkatesan. S. & Yarrow, T. (eds) *Differentiating Development. Beyond and Anthropology of Critique*. New York: Bergham Books.

Gross, M. (2007) The unknown in process. Dynamic connections of ignorance, non-knowledge and related concepts. *Current Sociology*, 55(5), 742–759.

Gross, M. (2010) *Ignorance and Surprise. Science, Society, and Ecological Design*. Cambridge, MA: the MIT Press.

Gross, M. & McGoey, L. (eds) (2015) *Routledge International Handbook of Ignorance Studies*. Oxon: Routledge.

Harvey, M.G., Novicevic, N.N., Buckley, M.R. & Ferris, G.R. (2001) A historic perspective on organisational ignorance. *Journal of Managerial Psychology*, 16(6), 449–468.

Haunschild, P.R., Polidoro, F. Jr & Chandler, D. (2015) Organisational oscillation between learning and forgetting. *Organization Science*, 26(6), 1682–1701.

Hedberg, B. (1981) How organisations learn and unlearn. In: Nyström, P.C. & Starbuck, W.H. (eds) *Handbook of Organisational Design, Volume 1.* New York: Oxford University Press, 3–27.

Heimer, C. (2012) Inert facts and the illusion of knowledge: Strategic uses of ignorance in HIV clinic. *Economy and Society*, 41(1), 17–41.

Hirschman, A.O. (1967) Reissued with new preface in 2015. *Development Projects Observed.* Washington, DC: The Brookings Institution.

Hobart, M. (1993) Introduction: the growth of ignorance? In: Hobart, M. (ed.) *An Anthropological critique of development. The growth of ignorance*. London: Routledge, 1–30.

Hsu, S-w (2013) Alternative learning organisation. In: Örtenblad. A. (ed.) *Handbook of Research on the Learning Organisation: Adaptation and Context*. Cheltenham and Northampton, MA: Edward Elgar, 358–371.

Kelsall, T. (2008) Going with the grain in African Development? *Development Policy Review*, 26(6), 627–655.

Knorr Cetina, K.(1999) *Epistemic Cultures: How the Sciences Make Knowledge*. Cambridge, MA: Harvard University Press.

Kontinen, T. & Onali, A. (2017) Strengthening institutional isomorphism in development NGOs? Program mechanisms in an organisational intervention. *Sage Open*, 7(1).

Lewis, D. (2009) International development and the "perpetual present": Anthropological approaches to the rehistoricisation of policy. *European Journal of Development Research*, 21(1), 32–46.

Lewis, D. (2016) Abandoned pasts, disappearing futures: Further reflections on multiple temporalities in studying non-governmental organisation worlds. *Critique of Anthropology*, 36(1), 84–92.

Loomba, A. (1998) *Colonialism/Postcolonialism*. London: Routledge.

Luhmann, N. (1988) *Observations on Modernity*. Stanford, CA: Stanford University Press.

Martin de Holan, P. (2011a) Organisational forgetting, unlearning, and memory systems. *Journal of Management Inquiry*, 20(3), 302–304.

Martin de Holan, P. (2011b) Agency in voluntary organisational forgetting. *Journal of Management Inquiry*, 20(3), 317–322.

Martin de Holan, P. & Phillips, N. (2004a) Remembrance of things past? The dynamics of organizational forgetting. *Management Science*, 50(11), 1603–1613.

Martin de Holan, P. & Phillips, N. (2004b) Organizational forgetting as strategy. *Strategic Organisation*, 2(4), 423–433.

Martin de Holan, P. & Phillips, N. (2011) Organizational forgetting. In: Easterby-Smith, M. & Lyles, M.A. (eds) *Handbook of Organizational Learning and Knowledge Management*. Second edition. Chichester: John Wiley & Sons, 433–452.

Martin de Holan, P., Phillips, N. & Lawrence, B.T. (2004) Managing organizational forgetting. *MIT Sloan Management Review*, 45(2), 45–51.

McGoey, L. (2007) On the will to ignorance in bureaucracy. *Economy and Society*, 36(2), 212–235.

McGoey, L. (2012a) The logic of strategic ignorance. *The British Journal of Sociology*, 63(3), 553–576.

McGoey, L. (2012b) Strategic unknowns: towards a sociology of ignorance. *Economy and Society*, 41(1), 1–16.

Mena, S., Rintamäki, J., Fleming, P. & Spicer, A. (2016) On the forgetting of corporate irresponsibility. *Academy of Management Review*, 14(4), 720–738.

Merton, R.K. (1987) Three fragments from a sociologist's notebooks: Establishing the phenomenon, specified ignorance, and strategic research materials. *Annual Review of Sociology*, 13(1), 1–29.

Olivier de Sardan, J.-P. (1995) *Anthropology and Development. Understanding Contemporary Social Change*. London: Zed Books.

Othman, R. & Hashim, N.A. (2004) Typologizing organizational amnesia. *The Learning Organization*, 11(3), 273–284.

Pollitt, C. (2000) Institutional amnesia: A paradox of the "information age"? *Prometheus*, 18(1), 5–15.

Roberts, J. (2012) Organizational ignorance: Towards a managerial perspective on the unknown *Management Learning*, 44(3) 215–236.

Smyth, R. (2004) The roots of community development in colonial office policy and practice in Africa. *Social Policy and Administration*, 38(4), 418–436.

Spivak, G.C.(1994/1988) Can the Subaltern Speak? In Williams, P. & Chrisman, L. (eds) *Colonial Discourse and Post-Colonial Theory. A Reader*. London: Pearson Education, 66–111.

Swidler, A. (2009). Dialectics of patronage. Logics of accountability at the African AIDS-NGO Interface. In Hammack, D.C. & Heydemans, S. (eds) *Globalization, Philanthropy, and Civil Society. Projecting Institutional Logics Abroad*. Bloomington, IN: Indiana University Press, 192–220.

Suddaby, R., Foster, W.M. & Mills, A.J. (2014) Historical institutionalism. In: Bucheli, M. & Wadhwani, R.D. (eds) (2014) *Organisations in Time. History, Theory, Methods*. Oxford: Oxford University Press, 100–123.

Tsang, E.W.K. & Zahra, S.A. (2008) Organisational unlearning. *Human Relations*, 61(10), 1435–1462.

Uphoff, N. (1992) *Learning from Gal Oya. Possibilities for Participatory Development and Post-Newtonian Social Science*. London: IT Publications.

Watkins, S.C., Swidler, A. & T. Hannan, T. (2012) Outsourcing social transformation: Development NGOs as organisations, *Annual Review of Sociology*, 38(1), 285–315.

Weick, K.E. & Quinn, R.E. (1999) Organizational change and development. *Annual Review of Psychology*, 50, 361–386.

Wettenhall, R. (2011) Organizational amnesia: a serious public sector reform issue. *International Journal of Public Sector Management*, 24(1), 80–96.

Zhao, Y., Lu, Y. & Wang, X. (2013) Organizational unlearning and organizational relearning: a dynamic process or knowledge management. *Journal of Knowledge Management*, 17(6), 902–912.

6 Learning as legitimation and synchronisation

In this chapter, I approach learning from the perspective of institutionalism through notions of learning as legitimation and synchronisation. The chapter scrutinises not only organisational learning but also learning to be an organisation. For a long time, it has been argued that development NGOs all over the world have turned out to be various types of modern organisations (Banks et al. 2015; Dar 2014; Howell 2000). From the point of civil society, such modern organisations differ from the ideal of civil society being a place for counter-hegemonic action and platform for alternative, transformative development (Mitlin et al. 2007). However, the increased support for civil society since the late 1980s has produced an international field of development NGOs that aligns with the characteristics of modern organisations. The question is therefore why do groups of people all over the world adapt such a model – in other words, how do they learn to be organisations. This chapter proposes that they do so, first, to be legitimate in the field of development NGOs and adapt to its isomorphic trends (Claeyé & Jackson 2012; Tvedt 1998); and second, through adaptation to the global cultural model of organisation (Bromley & Meyer 2017; Meyer & Bromley 2013).

In both cases, organisational learning does not necessarily lead to better effectiveness of what the organisations are doing – promoting development in diverse locations – but to increased legitimacy in the global world of development NGOs characterised by increased isomorphism (DiMaggio & Powell 1983; Powell & DiMaggio 1991). It is easy to observe such isomorphism while reading the mission statements, project proposals and annual reports of NGOs from countries as diverse as Nepal, Sierra Leone or Nicaragua, not to mention those from Germany, Sweden and the UK. Isomorphic tendencies are not, however, mechanically adopted, but organisations edit, translate and domesticate them in a process of synchronisation (Alasuutari 2015; Alasuutari & Qadir 2014). For example, NGOs can use the isomorphic management and reporting models flexibly, according to their interest and cultural practices, as illustrated in examples from South Africa (Claeyé & Jackson 2012) and Uganda (Girei 2016).

This chapter tackles the question of organisational learning and legitimation and synchronisation in the context of the field of development NGOs and the cultural model of modern organisation. The empirical examples in this chapter consist of organisational development (OD) processes in different locations and times: in Finnish NGOs in 2009–2010 and in small Tanzanian NGOs in 2000. The material on Finnish NGOs includes OD processes in the Towards Evaluation for Everyday Use project, and the material from Tanzania includes two organisational workshops, organisational analysis of 11 NGOs, and individual interviews conducted in a framework of needs analysis for a capacity-building project.

Learning for legitimation and synchronisation: responding to isomorphic pressures

Legitimacy of development NGOs is often discussed in relation to the question of representativeness vis-á-vis those, often marginalised, groups they claim to present; and their moral legitimacy as "good organisations" contributing to the common good on a voluntary basis (Atack 1999; Edwards & Hulme 1995; Ossewaarde et al. 2008, 51). The professionalisation of NGOs has been seen as a threat to their legitimacy when it comes to their assumed role addressing grassroots interests and being agents of alternative development (Banks et al. 2015; Walton et al. 2016). From the organisation theory point of view, in the search for legitimacy, organisations tend to align with the practices and perceptions that are assumed to be desirable in a certain socially constructed system (Suchman 1995, 574). For the development NGOs, in addition to their immediate societal environments, this system appears to be an organisational field with a common meaning system and "production of similar goods or services", which, in the case of NGOs, is development (DiMaggio & Powell 1983; Tvedt 1998). NGOs struggle between being legitimate grassroots representatives on the one hand, and competent and legitimate members of the international field on the other (Walton et al. 2016). They aspire to part of the international field where certain organisational practices, meanings and vocabularies circulate along with the resources allocated for "NGO development" channel (Tvedt 1998, 2002, 2006); they are not only competent in one of the international languages such as English or French, but also fluent in "developmentalese" (Mueller-Hirth 2012).

Learning for legitimacy means that organisational routines, behaviours, meanings and practices are changed in such a way that they better align with the expectations of appropriateness shared in the organisational field (Haunschild & Chandler 2008, 624; Powell & DiMaggio 1991, 3). This change can be triggered, for example, by particular change agents such as consultants, and spread in workshops, seminars and trainings that all promote normative isomorphism, that is constructing professional standards (Beckert 2010, 155; DiMaggio & Powell 1983; Haunschild & Chandler 2008, 626). Like in other non-profit fields, the global professionalisation of NGOs has led to a situation where the institutional pressures are directed towards proficiency in shared management practices rather than towards any substantial areas (Hwang

& Powell 2009, 269–270; Lister, 2003). In development, changes are often instigated by international development policies, approaches and guidelines. The long-standing hegemony of LFA as an appropriate development management tool, the ongoing change in organisations to align their strategies with Sustainable Development Goals rather than the previous Millennium Development Goals, the adaptation of HRBA, and the spread of theories of change for evaluation purposes are all examples of field level changes that NGOs all over the world adopt, often through training, capacity building and consultancies, in their quest to be real, and better, development NGOs.

NGOs do not, however, mechanically adopt similar objectives, structures and approaches, but respond to these pressures in different ways; and a wealth of meaning-making and translation takes place during adaptation (Chandler & Hwang 2015, 1447; Ramanath 2008). On the surface, the practices and ideas might look similar, but they can be "edited" in such a way that they provide an answer to any organisational problem existing at the time (Sahlin-Andersson 1996). In the course of learning, organisations can routinely imitate the local or distant "best practices" as ready-made packages, but these can also be deliberatively refigured to fit the organisational context and its current needs and practices (Argote 2013, 47; Chandler & Hwang 2015, 1458). The process of learning narrative approaches to M&E described in Chapter 4 is an example of a reconfiguration process in which an organisation familiarised itself with the narrative evaluation models of distant others, but instead of straightforwardly adapting one of those, went through a process of its own design and experimentation. However, it is common that "early adopters", those NGOs on the edge of new developments, are more reflective in the process of refiguring. When something, for example HRBA, is already considered as best practice in the field by actors such as Oxfam (Offenheiser & Holcombe 2003), it is often taken as such by the "late adopters" (Chandler & Hwang 2015, 1459). In this process, such "organisational fashions" can be institutionalised in organisations through a process of "translation" in texts and action, or they can be simply adopted as a label for already existing practice (Czarniawska & Joerges 1996); for instance in situations where NGOs begin to label their approach as HRBA even if they continue similar needs-based practice.

Taken into account the different organisational responses, instead of isomorphism we could speak of domestication or synchronisation (Alasuutari 2015, 13; Alasuutari & Qadir 2014). In synchronisation, organisations continuously keep an eye on what others are doing – their neighbours, competitors and other reference groups – and then synchronise their actions with others. For example, NGOs do not only "adapt symbolic frames without substantive meanings" (ibid. 15) when they adopt the above-mentioned international development goals, project management models and practices; they adapt these through continuous dialogue with different actors, and both the models and the organisations change during the process. Therefore, from the point of view of synchronisation, travelling ideas are often reasons for change, but not proof of isomorphism. Rather, trendy ideas are like waves that cause an organisation to take a new turn in their specific locations

In the processes of synchronisation and translation of international models, power works merely in a form of "epistemic governance" (Foucault 1991). The adaptation of a model is not forced, but epistemic governance acts upon the aspirations of organisations that come to believe that it is desirable. In the networks on development NGOs and international development, epistemic governance works while actors convince each other about what is "rational, necessary, or the morally right thing to do" (Alasuutari & Qadir 2014, 8). Organisations start to perceive the world in a similar way and talk about it through similar vocabularies. In organisations, epistemic governance is embedded in the ways organisations make sense of their environments; for example, what categories are used in interpreting events (Taylor & van Every 2000; Weick 2001, 2009). In development NGOs, for example, the world is now interpreted through ideas such as "duty bearers" and "rights holders", and empowerment is the morally right thing to do. At the same time, speaking of "charity" or "help" is not considered rational any more, as these concepts do not fit with the prevailing ideas of empowerment. Moreover, the world is depicted through LFAs, performance indicators, and organisational goals, and made sense of through baseline studies, power analysis, gender analysis, and other frameworks.

From improving M&E to multiple synchronisations

An example of learning for legitimation and synchronisation comes from the Towards Evaluation for Everyday Use project we conducted in ten Finnish NGOs engaged in development cooperation in 2009–2010 (Kontinen 2012). At that time, improvement of M&E systems for NGOs and the introduction of HRBA were among the main issues promoted in the international field. Much was discussed about the possibilities to combine accountability and learning (Guijt 2010). Some of the largest INGOs were the "first adopters". For example, Action Aid developed a comprehensive accountability and learning system in the early 2000s (Owusu 2004), and Oxfam International clearly articulated HRBA in its strategy for 2001–2004 (Offenheiser & Holcombe 2003). World Vision developed a global indicator tracking system, and Oxfam GB later opted for developing a Global Performance Network (Hutchings 2014). All these developments were partly responses to the global spread of results-based management and the introduction of ideas of evidence-based decision making to development policy.

However, while the large and resourceful INGOs allocated resources to designing strategies and establishing M&E systems for accountability and learning, the majority of the smaller ones, both in the global north and south, continued to implement projects and conduct M&E on a project basis. However, while keeping an eye on the other NGOs in the international field, and listening to their governmental donors, who, in turn, observed the global developments, many NGOs became convinced that they needed to develop a programmatic approach instead of implementing individual projects, and also needed to improve their organisational M&E systems and performance follow-up. A number of training courses, workshops and consultancies played a role in this process. In Finland, the umbrella organisation, KEPA, was actively introducing new global models to Finnish NGOs by means of training. It also provided OD services to NGOs, one of which was the Towards Evaluation for Everyday Use project in which I was one of the facilitators. At that time, I had a double role as a KEPA employer and an academic researcher, and from the beginning of the project it was agreed with the NGOs that the material collected in the OD process could be further used in academic publications.

Each NGO participated in a series of six to ten organisational workshops over a period of one year. The organisations first analysed their existing M&E practices, identified their strengths and weaknesses, and then gradually decided what would be their particular learning task during the OD process. The final learning tasks included, for instance, development of programme indicators, accomplishing a development cooperation programme, and designing M&E guidelines for the organisations. Therefore, the learning tasks the organisations selected echoed the isomorphic trends of the field in regard to moving from a project to programme approach and designing more elaborate M&E tools (Kontinen & Onali 2017). However, despite the isomorphic trends, the learning process was not the same in all organisations. Our OD process had quite a straightforward aim to support the design of M&E systems, but in the course of the processes, NGOs synchronised their needs in relation to other processes that were going on in the organisations. Moreover, much of the learning expanded from learning to do better M&E to learning to be better organisations. In many cases, the NGOs first identified a need to develop better indicators for the purposes of M&E, after which they realised that better indicators would first require more focused goals and, further, that developing indicators for a development programme or the entire organisation instead of individual projects required internal synchronisation of all organisational activities.

The idea for a need to improve M&E was first synchronised with the historical situation and identity of each organisation. By definition, all the participating organisations were development NGOs. They implemented development cooperation projects and received funding from the development aid budget from the Ministry for Foreign Affairs. However, their historical trajectories of becoming what could be called development NGOs were different. For most of the organisations, the identity of a development NGO was quite new, and for the last two decades they had modified into being legitimate ones. For example, Interpedia was established in 1974 as an organisation to coordinate international child adoption. Only later did it start to engage in development cooperation projects, mostly service-delivery projects related to children such as orphanages in Nepal; first with funding from individual sponsors and later, funding from the Ministry for Foreign Affairs. In the late 1990s Interpedia started to move away from implementing individual projects, began to draft its first development cooperation programme, and to take the first steps in adopting HRBA, specialising in child rights. The international child adoption continued along with development work, but these two organisational functions were kept quite separate.

Another NGO established in 1974, The Finnish Lutheran Overseas Mission had completely different history, and an explicit mission for Christian proclamation connected with improving the lives of the poor. One of its challenges was to separate development work from the missionary work in terms of planning and measurement when it came to funding from development aid funds. However, in the field countries, typically, the same persons conducted both missionary and development work. As the missionaries mainly followed their Christian calling, the substance the particular project ideas derived often from their individual professional backgrounds. However, with regard to the development projects the organisation was eager to develop a development programme and comprehensive measurement system based on an idea of a scorecard inspired by the private sector. Two of the organisations, the National Union of University Students in Finland (SYL) and the Student Union in Turku University of Applied Sciences (TUO) were student unions, for which engaging in development cooperation was a small addition to their core activities related to students' welfare and interests in Finland. They worked typically with one partner organisation at a time, and wanted to include student interns in their projects as much as possible in order to provide learning opportunities. For them, the programmatic approach was not relevant, but they had strong aspirations to improve the equal partnership.

Among those with a clear identity of a development NGO was the International Solidarity Foundation (ISF) (see also Chapter 3). It was established in 1970 as part of the international solidarity movement and at that time was affiliated with the Finnish Social Democratic party. It had started by arranging demonstrations, collecting money to support different liberation movements in Africa. In the 1980s it had adopted a development project approach, and later, a programmatic approach. Thus, it had gradually developed from a political movement to a professional development NGO that implemented development projects related to sustainable livelihoods and gender equality in Uganda, Somaliland and Nicaragua with some employed staff in the field countries. Another organisation with a background in the third world movement was Operation a Day's Work, Finland (ODW). It is a youth NGO in support of global solidarity. The organisation had its roots in a Swedish movement that originated in 1961 to honour for the memory of Dag Hammarskjöld, the Swedish Secretary General of the UN. The foundational idea of the movement was that for one day each year, students and pupils work and donate their payment to development projects. Later, ODW started to implement more long-term development cooperation projects supporting youth with funding from its member organisations and the Ministry for Foreign Affairs of Finland. The Finnish Refugee Council

(FRC) was founded in 1965 in order to collect money for UNHCR and disseminate information about the issues related to refugees. It had a long experience in working with refugees in post-conflict areas as well as in Finland. FRC started its first development project in early 1990s, and has since expanded development cooperation activities with Ministry for Foreign Affairs funding. Its development activities revolved around adult literacy among refugees and returnees in countries such as Uganda, Sierra Leone, Liberia and Thailand.

Despite the different backgrounds, value bases and scope of work, when it came to the development cooperation, all of these organisations had adopted certain isomorphic trends related to project planning and management over the years. These were mostly related to their undertaking of development projects with funding from the Ministry for Foreign Affairs and implemented with partners in the south. Some had only one partner and one project at a time, while some implemented development programmes in a number of countries with many partner organisations, and had their own staff in the field countries. In the Towards Evaluation for Everyday Use, therefore, the NGOs synchronised their ideas of development of their M&E with their historical stage as "development NGOs". While the organisations were, at least partly, development organisations, they also had other functions to synchronise with. In some organisations, such as the student unions, there were no efforts to combine the M&E in development cooperation with the other activities, whereas some kind of internal synchronisation was relevant in others. For example, in ODW our project workshops brought all the organisational activities to plan together for the first time, as the development cooperation had usually been planned and managed only by those officers dedicated to it. Additionally, the FRC put great effort into harmonising development cooperation projects with domestic projects with refugees in Finland, as well as communication activities and financial administration. The representatives of all these activities participated in every workshop, and in the course of the project, the question of what kinds of indicators and M&E practices and frequencies would suit all the activities was continuously revisited. Additionally, in the discussion, the participants continuously returned to the ongoing strategy process implemented by the board of the organisation, and argued that it would not be possible to define organisational indicators without the finalisation of strategic goals. In the workshops it was relatively easy for the staff to articulate that both development and domestic work shared an overall objective of "realisation of the rights of refugees, returnees, and immigrants", whereas the strategy process in the board took over one and half years due to differences in the political opinions of the board members. Among the staff as well, some kind of tension between the "domestic" and "development" activities emerged throughout the process. There were suspicions about the suitability of similar guidelines. There seemed to be more positive attitudes towards M&E in development partners than in domestic staff not used to as detailed follow-up as typical in development cooperation. The difficulties in synchronisation between development and domestic projects were also related to their different donors. While the development cooperation was funded by the Finnish Ministry for Foreign Affairs, the projects with refugees and immigrants in Finland received funding mainly from the Finnish Slot Machine Association with different guidelines and demands.

In addition to the time and energy needed for the internal synchronisation within NGOs in Finland, additional effort was invested in alignment between the so-called headquarters in Helsinki and field offices. The ISF had Finnish coordinators in Nicaragua, Uganda and Somaliland who, along with a few local staff, constituted the personnel of their field offices. Similarly, the FRC had expatriate coordinators in Liberia, Sierra Leone and Uganda while most of the staff of the field offices were local. Some other organisations, such as TUO and Interpedia did not have their own staff in the field and worked directly with partner organisations. In the course of conducting the learning tasks in the project, it became evident that the field offices often perceived the headquarters to demand much "extra bureaucracy" and not to understand the particularities of the countries or the everyday work. Similarly, at times, the headquarters could perceive field offices as taking too many liberties from organisational practices, and withholding some of the interesting information. In FRC, at the start of the project the staff in the headquarters held the view that: "I am sure they [the field offices] do a lot of monitoring, but it is not documented or sent to us". In order to synchronise the understanding of the M&E and the tools used, a one and a half hour meeting with the country coordinators was arranged during their visit to Helsinki in August 2009. The meeting revealed that the perspectives of the field staff concerning monitoring of the progress of the project differed from the organisational ideas of the staff in Helsinki. The field staff perceived M&E in more practical terms compared to the more abstract ideas discussed in the headquarters. Under "assessments" the field officers spoke about assessing the capacity and literacy level of the beneficiaries. Under "monitoring", it was about the monitoring of the attendance of the students in literacy circles, the building of latrines, or adapting new farming technologies depending on the scope of individual projects. Moreover, monitoring also included checking whether the partners were performing the activities according to the plans. For example, when the representatives of partner NGOs had promised to visit all the reading circles with a certain frequency, this could be verified by looking at the visitor's books of village literacy management committees. In the meeting, when Helsinki staff brought the discussion back to the organisational guidelines for monitoring that were being designed, one of the coordinators wondered with laughter: "Are we then implementing the guidelines, or are we going to use the guidelines in implementing our programme, or implementing an assessment of the programme? I am a bit lost."

The synchronisation of M&E systems was not only needed within the NGOs, but also with the systems of the partner organisation. For example, in FRC, much of the time was used during the process to collect the tools already used by partner organisations: partner organisations in Sierra Leone were quite strong, and had their own M&E systems. Synchronisation of their processes with FRC's M&E systems proved to be difficult while also the partner organisations disagreed with each other about the focus of measuring adult literacy. One emphasised traditional tests while the other focused on approaches that would take into account functional literacy and the use of the acquired skills in many fields of activity. Interestingly, in terms of mastery of the buzzwords and frameworks prevalent in the field, the stereotypical north-south knowledge differences were challenged in the course of the project. For instance, in the case of FRC described above, some of the partner organisations were more conversant with the latest development approaches than their Finnish partner. The clearest case of the primacy of southern expertise was the partnership between the student union TUO and the Zambian environmental NGO Green Living Movement (GLM) that had much development expertise. One of the coordinators of GLM was invited to provide an eye-opening training for all the Finnish NGOs participating in the Towards Evaluation in Everyday Use project on their participatory M&E approaches with farmers groups in rural Zambia.

Donor accountability demands and the managerialism attached as a source of isomorphism have gained much attention in the literature. However, in most of the NGOs participating in the Towards Evaluation for Everyday Use project, certain demands from the Ministry for Foreign Affairs, such as the use of LFA model, annual reporting, or a programmatic approach for larger NGOs were considered merely as taken-for-granted starting points. The motivation for developing M&E addressed more an organisational drive to know more and be more well-established organisations, rather than trying to meet the donor demands as well as possible. Overall, the experience of Finnish NGOs was that the Finnish Ministry for Foreign Affairs was quite a flexible donor with which you could discuss modifications during funding periods. Most of the organisations had an adequate competence level and routines when it came to producing project proposals and reports. Furthermore, in the discussions, the NGO staff did not challenge or question the overall need for reporting and aligning with donor objectives if they could work under their own specific missions. There was also consideration of whether there was a need for a further dialogue with the donors. In a TUO workshop in March 2009, the representative of the Zambian partner NGO said that they actually slightly missed the discussions with the donor and would be delighted to hear something about the dialogue between the Finnish NGO and the Ministry. The response, in this instance, was laughter and a description: "It is like a one-way communication; we send the report and do not get any feedback." Despite the wealth of policy talk about the importance of results, outcomes and impacts, the NGOs felt that after the funding had been granted, the Ministry for Foreign Affairs were not very interested in the substance of their work if the spending and financial management had progressed according to the plans and requirements. The dialogue, if any, concerned typically the financial issues rather than the results of outcomes.

The examples of the Finnish NGOs showed how, instead of adopting any M&E model circulating in the in the international field and developed by one of the first adopters, the organisations actively took their own change directions. Through joint analysis of their history, existing practices and strengths and weaknesses, the idea of M&E developed in continuous synchronisation not only with the donor demands, but also with the historically evolved situations, the domestic and development activities, and partners of the organisation. None of these appeared to be a strong coercive isomorphic force, nor did the NGOs directly imitate others, but all seemed to be convinced that improving M&E is what they wanted and needed. Furthermore, in the course of starting to develop M&E, some of the NGOs realised that designing "better indicators" was not the right place to start, but a polished programme, objectives and goals, as well as harmonisation of different organisations were needed first. All in all, while the processes did not represent straightforward adoption of ready-made models, all the participating NGOs moved in the direction of being even more legitimate development NGOs with M&E systems considered to be appropriate and, further, towards alignment with the ideals of rational organisation in which all the branches of activities should contribute to organisation's overall mission.

Learning to be an organisation

> In this rationalised world, there is no alternative to rationalised planning or action, planning gains even more legitimacy; the world is a stage where everyone plays the role of a planner.
>
> (Hwang 2006, 89)

Whereas learning and adoption of different management practices and development models can be perceived as an attempt to be a legitimate member of the international field of development, a further analytical step can be taken when it comes to the idea of rationalised organisation. The overall spread of rationalisation and the model of modern organisation in NGOs have been seen as effects of global neoliberalism (Mueller-Hirth 2012), managerialism (Girei 2016), and instances of global audit culture (Power 1997). The world culture approach to institutionalism would suggest that the spread of accountability, transparency, M&E and other organisational principles familiar to development NGOs are examples of a general global expansion of the model of modern organisation (Meyer & Bromley 2013). The spread of the cultural model of modern organisation, in this perspective, is more than a response to donor demands by NGOs. It is argued that the model of organisation is a cultural principle that shapes private firms, government agencies and third sector alike (ibid. 941). Everywhere in the world, there is an increasing number of entities that call themselves "organisations" in a variety of areas such as science, religion and communal life, and organisation has become a kind of global field of its own (Bromley & Meyer 2017, 952; Drori et al. 2006).

For example, the empowerment work of development NGOs often revolves around supporting community groups (see Chapter 3) that can gradually develop into organisations. They can first be informal and loose constellations of people, but gradually start to adopt a model of formal organisation; define organisational positions, draft plans and start to report on their activities. This is partly due to the donor requirements for results-based management, and partly as a consequence of the motivation of members of the organisation to learn new practices (Mueller-Hirth 2012).

The model of modern organisation partly draws from the more "traditional" forms of social organising, when traditional is defined vis-á-vis the societal development in the global north, as to a large extent, is done in the world culture approach. For instance, an organisation has clear boundaries of ownership common with family enterprises and formalised rules typical to traditional bureaucracies (Drori et al. 2006, 15). There are, however, also new standards of appropriateness. These standards are based on an assumption of rights and capabilities of individuals, belief in scientific and professional knowledge, and the need to follow principles of rationality (ibid.; Meyer & Bromley 2013, 369–373). Individuals, the assumed locus of rights and actions, are supposed to join each other through participation in formal organisations instead of being integral members of communities. For example, in the case of INGOs, the cultural conception of organisation has constituted identities in which individuals rationally organise internationally to pursue their interests (Boli & Thomas 1999, 14). For development INGOs, identities revolve also around promoting others' interests; of those being impoverished and marginalised.

The main elements of the contemporary model of organisation entail that an organisation is an actor with a legitimate capacity to make decisions while pursuing organisational goals. According to the model, organisations are rational actors with goals explicated in mission statements and strategies; they have an elaborate structure through which the goals are to be achieved; they track their resources through counting and accounting; they incorporate individuals to certain organisational roles through spirit rather than control; and they have clear symbolic boundaries that limit their actorhood shown in contracts, mandates, and accountabilities (Bromley & Meyer 2017, 950; Meyer et al. 2006, 45). In this model, all kinds of organisations, ranging from Microsoft to churches to universities, should conduct formal planning or use outcome evaluation to assess their goal achievement (Bromley & Meyer 2017, 954). These general characteristics of an organisation clearly resonate with the tendencies in development NGOs. For example, Crewe (2014, 100–101) argues that currently in development "all self-respecting organisations should have a vision". She provides an example of an NGO that deliberately refused to have a detailed plan with a mission, vision and goals in its attempt to give its southern partner NGOs as much decision-making power as possible; and how, as a consequence, some of its donors considered the approach "amateurish".

The overall rationalised cultural environment facilitates the translation of existing forms of social organising towards a form of modern organisation, in every country, and in every social sector (Meyer et al. 2006, 48). In development, for instance, the somewhat mythical entity of "community" as an agent of development (Guijt & Shah 1998) is turned into manageable community-based organisations. In voluntary organisations, attempts to follow this model have led to a situation in which organisations adapt strategic plans with no financial means to implement them, just because their funders require such plans, and because they assume such a plan has to exist in order to be legitimate (Hwang 2006, 84–86). In development NGOs, it sometimes seems that legitimacy cannot be gained with any kind of goals or plans, but there is an additional requirement of goals being ambitious enough in regard to social change (Mowles 2007; Watkins et al. 2012). The ambitious goals do not always resonate with the everyday practice. For example, Mowles (2008, 11) describes a development INGO meeting where the atmosphere created by a director was that "only the impossible was deemed ambitious enough", and the feeling was that strategy could be "viable only if it could deliver the Promised Land". The ambitious goals provided excitement and motivation to the members of staff who previously had complained about their difficulties in implementing the existing, already ambitious plans. Therefore, in development NGOs of all sizes, often the rational planning is merged with idealistic hopes and goals that – rationally considered – are far beyond the reach of the organisation.

All in all, it is very hard to go against the global wave of rational organising even if in the field of development NGOs the rationalisation pressures often contradict with other institutionalised goals such as ownership. Building comprehensive M&E systems often means that southern partner NGOs are mainstreamed with the visions, strategies and goals of their northern partners rather than their own. The southern NGOs, in their part, are under contradictory pressures when it comes to their focus and competencies. On one hand, there are requirements to work with grassroots in a democratic manner; on the other, the activities have to be represented and reported in rationalised forms and in global languages. NGOs end up translating between the local group activities and LFAs or reducing narrative accounts into results indicator matrices (Mueller-Hirst 2012; Dar 2014). However, much of NGOs have adapted some of the cultural features of modern organisation.

Small NGOs in Morogoro, Tanzania

In order to reflect the adoption of the model of a modern NGO, I return to recent history in a Tanzanian town of Morogoro; a town located in the central part of the country with some 200,000 inhabitants at that time. In the early 2000s I was conducting fieldwork for my PhD in Morogoro (Kontinen 2007). During that time, I also participated in a commissioned study under the title "NGO Quality Performance and Collaboration Improvement Through Capacity Building" in the town of Morogoro (Kontinen et al. 2001) The title of the study, commissioned by a Finnish NGO in order to design a capacity-building project, really captured the catchwords of the era. Together with my Tanzanian colleagues, we conducted a so-called participatory performance analysis in 11 NGOs, and two seminars with representatives of a total of 16 organisations. The analysis discussion in each NGO took some three hours, and discussed the history, objectives, achievements, obstacles and capacity-building needs of the organisations.

The first observation was that while the organisations continuously referred themselves as "NGOs", none of them was an "NGO" in legal terms. Such a legal framework and the associated registration procedures were just in the process of being established in Tanzania where the first NGO Act was issued in 2002. The organisations were registered under the Societies Ordinance dating from colonial era, as trustees, or as companies. All the organisations participating in our study were relatively fresh at that time; the earliest registration year was 1995, while most had registered in 1997–1998. These registration dates echoed the general increased establishment of NGOs in Tanzania affected by the introduction of a multi-party democracy, the implementation of larger retrenchment schemes connected to structural adjustment programmes, and the international NGO boom in development (Gibbon 2001).

In the 2000s, we were definitely not the only ones to conduct organisational analysis and design organisational capacity-building projects in Tanzania. For example, the British Council issued a large "Civil society support programme" in 2001 for which the NGOs we interviewed were interested to submit proposals. At the same time, NGOs were built and supported in many local contexts all over the world, consultants and OD professionals travelled around, organisational training programmes and institutes flourished. One could hear the "babble of organisational talk" everywhere (Meyer et al. 2006, 45–46). Moreover, the NGO capacity-building programmes typically promoted the general form of rationalised formal organisation in which goals, plans, capacities, and competencies were outlined in standardised ways (ibid.). Also in our study, we looked at different elements of organisational capacity and investigated whether the organisations were able to define their goals, and make logical connections between their activities and goals. It became clear that the small organisations tended to define their goals and objectives in terms of intended activities: convening seminars, establishing schools, assisting members with revolving funds. However, during the analysis, most of the organisations were able to define their goals in terms of a problem or challenging situation they would like to address with their activities.

When the standardised type of organisation is promoted in different contexts, the phenomenon of loose coupling between the good-looking goals and real actions and purposes of organisations often occurs (Meyer et al. 2006, 47). In the late 1990s in Morogoro, organisations produced different documents and structures according to a variety of requirements. For example, constitutions were required for registration, and their contents depended on the requirements of the legislation under which the organisation was registered. In addition, small NGOs produced different kinds of organisational profiles and project proposals in order to present themselves to the public, and especially to potential partner organisations. In general, the goals and profiles of the organisations depicted much of what they would like to be and do, compared to what they currently were. In a sense, they were ambiguous ideas for future action that could be realised if the financial resources were there. This had implications also for budgeting. Most of the organisations budgeted only on project basis according to their action plan that was "never over 50 per cent realised". In the smallest organisations there were no organisational budgets as the only financial resources came from the pockets of the founder members on ad hoc basis. Therefore, at the moment of designing the organisational profiles, descriptions were decoupled from the actions.

The ideas of establishing an organisation had often occurred to individuals or small groups of people in a face of observed challenges. For example, a group of ten female widows had established a mutual self-help group to seek support for their own challenging situations. They started with joint poultry keeping, and established a small-scaled loan scheme among themselves. The scheme proved to be successful in increasing capital, and the group gradually registered itself as a women's NGO. It started to conduct livelihood-related activities, and later, with the support of external donors, established an English-medium pre-school. Another organisation addressing HIV/AIDS, registered as trust fund, was established by a few members who were already working with the issue in other institutions. They had motivation to focus on preventive training through songs, dance and leaflets, and provide counselling and small-scale financial support for those affected. They worked voluntarily in a number of communities in which they had trained over 200 peer educators. These two examples exemplify how NGOs were established both for primarily addressing the needs of those involved in the organisation, or primarily for addressing needs of others.

A story of an environmental organisation illustrates well the general patterns of emergence of small-scale "NGOs". The organisational profile depicted that the organisation is a "dynamic NGO that seeks to enhance human development, other species and land conservation towards the twenty-first century", and that defined its aims as to "build the capacity of all communities and institutions to manage changes" in order to achieve "peace, equity, and human empowerment leading to improved welfare of all communities in Tanzania, Africa, and the rest of the world". While these goals were extremely wide and ambitious, what the organisation actually did was to take care of a shared field, *shamba*, to produce food for its members, and to undertake subcontracts from the Morogoro municipality to clean roads, to do *usafi*, in certain town areas. When we look at the story behind the establishment of the NGO, the discrepancy between goals and action can be understood as part of gradual learning to be an NGO.

The history of the organisation told by its chairperson (I will call by the name of Charlie) in an interview in February 2000 illustrates well the typical pattern of establishing an "NGO" at the time when it was on everyone's lips but there was uncertainty of its meanings. For a start, the chairperson had worked as a civil servant in a government office until the year 1990, when he resigned and started a private firm dealing with timber and food crops. He shifted sectors as he "saw that the business sector is better than being employed in government". He learned from the transnational model of NGO while still in office. One of his clients had been a person from the USA who "had an NGO". This person argued that at the time, the theme of the environment was becoming prevalent, and suggested "Why don't you try environment, start an NGO parallel to you company". The chairman became interested in the establishment of an NGO, and when "the World Environment Day was celebrated in Morogoro, I established an NGO with one of my friends, and we registered it" (Charlie 02/2000). There were certain requirements concerning the registration under the Societies Ordinance, and additional members were invited: "We needed 12 members, so it was my wife, a wife of my friend, and some other friends. Together we were 15" (ibid.). These accounts illustrate how both businesses and NGOs were seen as different from the government bureaucracy; providing opportunities both to do new things and gain access to livelihood strategies. In this case, the idea of an "NGO" was received through a personal interaction in which such a transnational model was introduced. Moreover, in this instance, as in many others, in the course of establishing and registering the NGO, informal family and friendship relationships were re-defined in organisational terms.

Before the day to celebrate the World Environment Day in Morogoro in 1999, this particular NGO was allocated the task of cleaning the big road, as the chairperson proudly said, showing some photos: "The inaugural street for the environmental day, the very day the president came, people were waiting along this street; so we cleaned it when President Mkapa came to explore" (Charlie 02/2000). This comment illustrates how the organisation took pride in being recognised by the municipal authorities and being requested to contribute to a significant event with an esteemed guest. In our organisational analysis, many mentioned the importance of good relationships with the government officials. It was an asset to have a member of parliament or district commissioner as a guest of honour is any of the NGO functions. Important guests brought prestige but sometimes also came with financial support. Rather than being a kind of watchdog for government or a space for citizen mobilising, the newly established NGOs searched for recognition from the authorities and "big men" in politics. They also tried to establish patronage relationships with the influential business men in order to receive supports. Many organisations had received financial assistance, T-shirts and other items. NGOs eagerness to engage with political and business elites partly exemplifies how NGO logics were embedded in the prevailing social order of patron-clientelism in which mutually beneficial loyalty relationships are important (Kelsall 2008).

For the environmental NGO, engaging in cleaning and sanitation activities was still part of the NGO's activities at the time of the interview in

2000. By then, the NGO had some 75 members of different ages. Usually those members who had already retired from their formal employment did the sub-contracted cleaning activities in order to receive a small income. Additionally, the NGO had a field with a tree nursery and an area for food production: "The *shamba* is for the food, for the members who are interested" (Charlie 02/2000). In a similar vein, many NGOs engaged with small-scale production of food or other items in order to get in income. Moreover, when NGOs discussed their planned activities such as training and seminars, the overall idea was that these would provide short-term employment opportunities for the members. An organisation in support of retired professionals wanted to establish a secondary school in order to provide employment opportunities. The characteristics of small NGOs in Morogoro resonate with Fowler's (2012) analysis of civil society in African contexts. He argues that civil society organisations are often hybrids that both address the common good and support the livelihood strategies of their members. The legitimacy of NGO vis-á-vis its members was often constructed on the basis of the potential benefits the organisation could provide. In the analysis discussion, many NGOs complained about members leaving the organisation, "when they see NGO means voluntary work and not big profit" (Kontinen et al. 2001). On the contrary, those NGOs who had been successful in attracting donor funding told that they had had to set very high membership fees for new members as the interests to join had grown exponentially after the establishment of partnership.

In this context, however, it would not be appropriate to judge the small NGOs in Morogoro with their over-ambitious plans as "briefcase organisations", established only for the sake of attracting donor money with "fake" documents. They genuinely believed – as often repeated by local consultants – that the objectives of an NGO should be ambitious and preferably global. Additionally, organisations were seriously trying to "do good" – both for their members living in challenging life situations and for the wider public. It was clear that the ideal of NGOs as a voluntary organisation doing good for others, often cherished in development policies, was challenged by the lack of time and financial resources of the active individuals to do such things without combining NGO activities with possibilities for earning their own income Establishing a structured organisation was one potential way to get access to income – for both the members and beneficiaries.

The aim of NGOs serving as a source of income for members was sometimes an alien idea for the northern partners. For example, an immediate need for income for members created many tensions when designing a project in collaboration with the NGO for retired professionals and a Finnish NGO with a strong training orientation. The planning process also showed how the rational planning tool of LFA became the means in the struggle to include and exclude different project components. Before joint planning, the Tanzanian NGO had produced a project proposal, with an LFA and a problem tree attached, and delivered it to the Finnish NGO. As a response to retired professionals' need of capital for starting small businesses, the Tanzanian NGO recommended that a micro-credit component should be attached to a training course for retired professionals that the Finnish NGO wanted to implement. The argument was that "if you are getting skills, those skills should be put into practice in order to solve the problems you have; suppose you come back from five weeks of training, you are still poor and you cannot apply those skills". The idea of micro-credit was continuously excluded by the Finnish NGO that considered it to be outside of its competence. While micro-credit was included in the LFA in a rational way to address the needs identified, the Finnish NGO had chosen another box – that of "training". Further, the need for income came up in other discussions. First, it was argued that the members of the organisation of the retired professionals should be employed as trainers, whereas the Finnish NGO gave this responsibility to the staff of selected training institutions. Second, the issue of participant allowances was discussed. The Finnish NGO considered it strange to pay allowances to training participants, whereas the Tanzanian NGO wanted to maximise them in order to provide at least some small capital for the participants, and compensate them for their absence from their daily small businesses. On the second day of training course implemented, some of the participants loudly complained about the small amount of "incidental money" and a few left training. The Tanzanian NGO negotiated the issues directly with the training institution, and suggested cutting down the services, such as meals, and distributing the saved money as additional participant allowances. An agreement was made to cut the morning and afternoon teas and refund the money to be used for the allowances. (Kontinen 2007, 99–134). The described negotiations illustrate how rational planning and proposal writing can function as a means for restricting the scope of collaboration according to the mission of the donor organisation.

In late 1990s and early 2000s, the mushrooming of NGOs contributed to the emergence of a new organisational field in Tanzania. Among the small NGOs at that time there was a lot of uncertainty about the meaning of NGO: "actually, we are going with any direction, even the senior officers within the government are not aware of these NGOs, what they are doing" (Charlie 02/2000). In this situation, the newly established NGOs were very willing to learn from others, and were interested in the information they had received from the Finnish NGOs, "which have provided some ideas of what an NGO is". The organisations were also eager to receive training and capacity building "so that we could manage our own organisation, in order to be on a modern track" (Charlie 02/2000). The main capacity-building needs mentioned in every NGO concerned financial management and proposal writing, office space and equipment such as computers, and only a few mentioned the need for training material, medicine or tools related to the actual substance of their activities. Afterwards, many did receive such capacity building, and over the years have grown to be "real NGOs", with well-functioning management systems, outside funding, and more realistic profiles and plans. They have adapted well to the model of modern organisation and are competent in required rational planning, proposal writing, measurement and reporting.

Conclusions

In this chapter, conceptualisations of learning as legitimation and synchronisation were introduced. It was argued that while development NGOs all over the world seek legitimacy vis-á-vis the international field of development NGOs, they do not simply adapt or imitate the models and approaches. The analysis of the Finnish NGOs illustrated how developing M&E was not primarily about seeking and adapting the best practices of early adopters in international NGO field, but rather a process of internal parallel synchronisation between different organisational functions, between headquarters and field, and between the NGOs and their partner organisations. In the course of all these processes of synchronisation, the initial idea of improving M&E often expanded into the development of the entire organisation with clearer and more measurable goals, in alignment with a rational global model of organisation.

The case of small Tanzanian NGOs in the early 2000s illustrated how the idea of an NGO was first embedded in already existing social forms of organising, such as family and state bureaucracy and gradually through training and capacity building, started to adopt more practices of "organisation". Organisations learned to define their goals and activities in a way that described organisational actorhood vis-á-vis certain societal problems rather than simple activities, partly in order to provide income for the members. In that way, the small NGOs became more legitimate both regarding the international field of development NGOs and the global cultural model of a modern organisation. Both of the examples showed how organisations not only learn new ideas and practices in order to do what they do, but they also learn to be more of an organisation.

References

Alasuutari, P. (2015) The discoursive side of new institutionalism. *Cultural Sociology*, 9(2), 162–184.

Alasuutari, P.O. & Qadir, A. (2014) Introduction. In: Alasuutari, P. & Qadir, A. (eds) (2012) *National Policy-Making. Domestication of Global Trends*. London: Routledge.

Argote, L. (2013) *Organizational Learning. Creating, Retaining and Transferring Knowledge*. New York: Springer.

Atack, I. (1999) Four criteria of development NGO legitimacy. *World Development*, 27(5), 855–864.

Banks, N., Hulme, D. & Edwards, M. (2015) NGOs, states, and donors revisited: Still too close for comfort? *World Development*, 66, 707–718.

Beckert, J. (2010) Institutional isomorphism revisited: Convergence and divergence in institutional change. *Sociological Theory*, 28(2), 150–166.

Boli, J. & Thomas, G.M. (eds) (1999) *Constructing World Culture. International Nongovernmental Organisations since 1975*. Stanford, CA: Stanford University Press.

Bromley, P. & Meyer, J.W. (2017) They are all organizations: The cultural roots of blurring between the nonprofit, business and government sectors. *Administration and Society*, 49(7), 939–966.

Chandler, D. & Hwang, H. (2015) Learning from learning theory: A model of organizational adoption strategies and microfoundations of institutional theory. *Journal of Management*, 41(5), 1446–1476.

Czarniawska, B. & Joerges, B. (eds) (1996) Travels of ideas. In: Czarniawska, B. & Sevón, G. (eds) *Translating Organisational Change*. Berlin: Walter de Gruyter, 13–48.

Claeyé, F. & Jackson, T. (2012) The iron cage re-revisited: Institutional isomorphism in nonprofit organizations in South. *Journal of International Development*, 24(5), 602–622.

Crewe, E. (2014) Doing development differently: Rituals of hope and despair in an INGO. *Development in Practice*, 24(1), 91–104.

Dar, S. (2014) Hybrid accountabilities: When western and non-western accountabilities collide. *Human Relations*, 67(2), 131–151.

DiMaggio, P.J. & Powell, W.W. (1983) The iron cage revisited: institutional isomorphism and collective rationality in institutional fields. *Annual Review of Sociology*, 16(2), 137–159.

Drori, G.S., Meyer, J.W. & Hwang, H. (2006) Introduction. In Drori, G.S., Meyer, J.W. & Hwang, H. (eds) *Globalization and Organisation. World Society and Organizational Change*. Oxford: Oxford University Press, 25–49.

Edwards, M. & Hulme, D. (eds) (1995) *Non-governmental organisations – Performance and accountability. Beyond the Magic Bullet*. London: Earthscan.

Fowler, A. (2012) Measuring civil society: Perspective from afro-centrism. *Voluntas* 23(1), 5–25.

Foucault, M. (1991) *Discipline and Punish: the Birth of a Prison*. London: Penguin.

Gibbon, P. (2001) Civil society, locality and globalization in rural Tanzania: A forty year perspective. *Development and Change*, 32(5), 819–844.

Girei, E. (2016) NGOs, management, and development: Harnessing counter-hegemonic possibilities. *Organization Studies*, 37(2), 193–212.

Guijt, I. (2010) Accountability and learning. Exploding the myth of incompatibility between accountability and learning. In: Ubels, J., Acquaye-Baddoo, N.-A. & Fowler, A. (eds) *Capacity Development in Practice*. London: Earthscan.

Guijt, I. & Shah, M.K. (1998) *The Myth of Community, Gender Issues in Participatory Development*. London: ITDG Publications.

Haunschild, P. & Chandler, D. (2008) Institutional-level learning: Learning as a source of institutional change. In: Greenwood, R. & Oliver, C. & Sahlin, K. & Suddaby, R. (eds) *The Sage Handbook of Organizational Institutionalism*. Los Angeles, CA: SAGE, 624–649.

Howell, J. (2000) Making civil society from the outside: Challenges for donors. *The European Journal of Development Research*, 12(1), 3–22.

Hutchings, C. (2014) Balancing accountability and learning: A review of Oxfam GB's global performance framework. *Journal of Development Effectiveness*, 6(4), 425–435.

Hwang, H. (2006) Planning development: Globalization and the shifting locus of planning. In: Drori. G.S., Meyer, J.W. & Hwang, H. (eds) *Globalization and Organization. World Society and Organisational Change*. Oxford: Oxford University Press, 69–90.

Hwang, H. & Powell, W.W. (2009) The rationalization of charity: The influences of professionalism in the nonprofit sector. *Administrative Science Quarterly*, 54(2), 268–298.

Kelsall, T. (2008) Going with the grain in African Development? *Development Policy Review*, 26(6), 627–655.

Kontinen, T. (2007) *Learning Challenges of NGOs in Development: Co-operation of Finnish NGOs in Morogoro. Tanzania*. Helsinki: Helsinki University Press

Kontinen, T. (2012) *Towards Evaluation for Everyday Use*. Helsinki: Service Center for Development Co-Operation KEPA, report series 117.

Kontinen, T. & Onali, A. (2017) Strengthening institutional isomorphism in development NGOs? Program mechanisms in an organisational intervention. *SAGE Open*, 7(1).

Kontinen, T., Abel, J. & Saqware, J. (2001) *NGO Quality Performance and Collaboration Improvement through Capacity Building*. Planning and Analysis Mission in Morogoro, Tanzania. Unpublished report delivered to National Research and Development Center for Welfare and Health (STAKES), May 2001.

Lister, S. (2003) NGO legitimacy: Technical issue or social construct? *Critique of Anthropology*, 23(2), 175–192.

Meyer, J.W. (2010) World society, institutional theories, and the actor. *Annual Review of Sociology*, 36, 1–20.

Meyer, J.W. & Bromley, P. (2013) The worldwide expansion of "organisation". *Sociological Theory*, 31(4), 366–389.

Meyer, J.W., Drori, G.S. & Hwang, H. (2006) World society and the proliferation of formal organisation. In: Drori, G.S., Meyer, J.W. & Hwang, H. (2006) *Globalization and Organization: World Society and Organizational Change*. Oxford: Oxford University Press, 25–49.

Meyer, J.W., Boli, J., Thomas, G.M. & Ramirez, F.O. (1997) World society and the nation state. *American Journal of Sociology*, 103(1), 144–181.

Mitlin, D., Hickey, S. & Bebbington, A. (2007). Reclaiming development? NGOs and the challenge of alternatives. *World Development*, 35(10), 1699–1720.

Mueller-Hirth, N. (2012) If you don't count, you don't count: Monitoring and evaluation in South African NGOs. *Development and Change*, 43(3), 649–670.

Mowles, C. (2007) Promises of transformation: Just how different are international NGOs? *Journal of International Development*, 19(3), 401–411.

Mowles, C. (2008) Values in international development organisations: Negotiating the non-negotiables. *Development in Practice*, 18(1), 5–16.

Offenheiser, R.M. & Holcombe, S.H. (2003) Challenges and opportunities in implementing a right-based approach to development: An Oxfam America perspective. *Nonprofit and Voluntary Sector Quarterly*, 32(2), 268–306.

Ossewaarde, R., Nijhof, A. & Heyse, L. (2008) Dynamics of NGO legitimacy: How organizing betrays core mission of NGOs. *Public Administration and Development*, 28(1), 42–53.

Owusu, C. (2004) An international NGO's staff reflections on power, procedures and relationships. In: Groves, L. & Hinton, R. (eds) *Inclusive Aid: Changing Power and Relationships in International Development*. London: Earthscan, 108–122.

Powell, W.W. & Colyvas, J.A. (2008) Microfoundations of institutional theory. In: Greenwood et al. (eds) *Handbook of Organizational Institutionalism*. London: SAGE.

Powell, W.W. & DiMaggio, P.J. (eds) (1991) *The New Institutionalism in Organizational Analysis*. Chicago: University of Chicago Press.

Power, M. (1997) *The Audit Society: Rituals of Verification*. Oxford: Oxford University Press.

Ramanath, R. (2008). Limits to institutional isomorphism: Examining internal processes in NGO government interactions. *Nonprofit and Voluntary Sector Quarterly*, 38(51), 51–75.

Sahlin-Andersson, K. (1996) Imitating by editing success: The construction of organisational fields. In: Czarniawska, B. & Sevón, G. (eds) *Translating Organisational Change*. Berlin: Walter de Gruyter, 69–92.

Suchman, M.C. (1995) Managing legitimacy: Strategic and institutional approaches. *Academy of Management Review*, 20(3), 571–610.

Taylor, J.R. & Van Every, E.J. (2000) *The Emergent Organization: Communication as its Site and Surface*. Mahwah, NJ: Erlbaum.

Tvedt, T. (1998) *Angels of Mercy or Development Diplomats? NGDOs and Foreign Aid*. Oxford: Africa World Press.

Tvedt, T. (2002) Development NGOs: Actors in a global civil society or in a new international social system. *Voluntas: International Journal of Voluntary and Nonprofit Organizations*, 13(4), 363–375.

Walton, O.E., Davies, T. Thrandardottir, E. & Keating, V.C. (2016). Understanding contemporary challenges to INGO legitimacy: Integrating top-down and bottom-up perspectives. *Voluntas: International Journal of Voluntary and Nonprofit Organizations*, 27(6), 2764–2786.

Watkins, S.C., Swidler, A. & Hannan, T. (2012) Outsourcing social transformation: Development NGOs as organisations. *Annual Review of Sociology*, 38, 285–315.

Weick, K.E. (2001) *Making Sense of the Organization*. Oxford: Blackwell.

Weick, K.E. (2009) *Making Sense of the Organization. Volume 2*. Chichester: Wiley.

7 Conclusions

The task set for this book was to explore whether discussions and conceptualisations in the organisational theory could contribute to the understanding of learning and change in development organisations. The concepts drawn from the organisational theory in different chapters included those of organisational meanings, scripts and schemata; organisational knowledge and epistemology; organisation forgetting and ignorance; and organisational legitimacy and synchronisation. Each chapter analysed learning from different conceptual perspectives. However, every perspective drew from the overall understanding of first, organisations as practices; second, learning as social rather than individual phenomenon; and third, continuous interaction between individual organisation and cultural-cognitive elements of wider institutional fields.

The emphasis of the book was on everyday life in NGOs. The chapters illustrated the dynamics of learning at different scales; ranging from situational institutionalised learning events in Chapter 3 and a few years' learning trajectory in Chapter 4, to more enduring phenomena of forgetting and ignorance in Chapter 5, and finally, to the ongoing global spread of the model of organisation in Chapter 6. The empirical examples were from particular organisations that mostly presented small and medium-size NGOs when measured on a global scale. The dynamics of learning are different in every empirical context. However, a detailed analysis of some can trigger examination of similar kinds of phenomena in other NGOs that would add to the variety. In general, the organisational theory perspectives provided conceptual frameworks that contributed to understanding the organisational live in entities called development NGOs (Watkins et sl. 2012), provided additional vignettes of the dynamics of *NGO-ing* within the field of development (Hilhorst 2013), and illustrated how organisational categories such as empowerment and M&E are used to make sense of organisational work in development (Crewe & Axelby 2013, 86).

At the same time, the chapters showed that many of the phenomena often discussed specifically in regard to development NGOs, are typical trends widely discussed in organisational literature and contemporary phenomena in any field. These include the issues such as decoupling between rhetoric and practice (Cyert & March 1963), professionalisation in management rather than substance of organisation's work (Hwang & Powell 2009), and attempts to tackle uncertainties with increasingly detailed management procedures (Heimer 2012). Moreover, the close connection between organisational learning and management practice is common to many areas of social life, and a typical example of the overall rationalisation of any social formations into modern organisations (Meyer et al. 2006). In the current context, the ideas of organisational visions, plans and measurements have become taken-for-granted to the extent that they are followed in many fields of life, ranging from small farmers' associations in rural Zambia to large international companies.

The book circulated, in a quite eclectic way, between organisational theory and management literature combined with development research. The connection between these works of literature was established by focusing on the learning as a social, organisational and institutional phenomenon. In what follows, I argue that there are three main messages to take out from the book. None of these is completely new when compared with the existing literature on NGOs. It might perhaps have been surprising to find something completely different from the existing literature taking into account the prevalence of the institutional features attached to development. However, the findings of the book contribute, on their part, to further analysis and reflection of the emerging issues. The first message is related to many faces of learning and forgetting in development NGOs. The second message points to the continuous balancing between control and contexts in learning related to management. The third message reminds about the need to tackle the politics of learning.

Many faces of learning and forgetting

The first lesson learned is that there are many faces of learning in development NGOs that need to be distinguished. In practitioners' everyday talk learning is, of course, often used in a loose way, but when it comes to analysis, more nuanced notions are needed. The categorisation of learning in development suggested in Chapter 2 provides one option for distinguishing different forms of learning. In this categorisation, it was done on the basis of different learners and the qualitatively different levels of learning. Learning in NGOs can range from almost automatic adoption, imitation and repetition of routines and managerial procedures to highly conscious reflection and change in organisational world views, assumptions, goals and practice. The categorisation revealed how assumed agents of learning can move from individual person to overall historically formed institution, and how the types of learning can refer to quite taken-for-granted maintenance of existing meanings, routines and practices up to their fundamental transformation. Obviously, theories and methods addressing learning in each category are different, and all the aspects cannot be captured simultaneously. Therefore, in this book, analysis focused on organisational learning. Institutional learning was discussed in connection to the organisational one, and detailed analysis of individual learning was excluded.

On the basis of the chapters we learned that much of organisational learning in development NGOs tends to be maintaining organisational practices or to change some of the practices to better achieve existing goals. In the context of personnel turnover, geographical distance of parts of an organisation and challenges with maintaining and using organisational memory, these kinds of learnings are often hampered by organisational forgetting. Learning in an organisation is a combination of cognitive, behavioural and social aspects, and thus learning is shown in changes in organisational meanings and schemata, organisational routines and practices, and the way members of an organisation interact and make sense of what they are doing. In realities of development NGOs, from the above-mentioned reasons, much of the learning work is done to simply construct, achieve and maintain shared understandings, routines and practices, rather than to change them on the basis of reflecting experiences.

When changes take place, they are often triggered by so-called development fads rather than an analysis of an organisation's own prior practices and experiences (Lewis 2009, 2016). Learning from the experience of other NGOs can mean adapting ready-made "best practices", without considering the historical background of these practices and with no attempt to reconfigure them with the organisation's own experiences and context. In the instances where such reconfiguration is done, as in the case of introducing the story-based M&E analysed in Chapter 4, learning is hard to identify as it takes place through a long-term process of negotiation and experimentation embedded in the everyday practices rather than as a rapid change in organisational guidelines as a result of intentional learning events such as training in "best practices". Moreover, as the analysis of the search for the shared meaning of empowerment in Chapter 3 showed, institutionalised learning events such as workshops are often constructed and acted upon according to institutionalised scripts in such a way that they reinforce the existing routines and meanings rather than provide real spaces for critical reflection on the taken-for-granted assumptions that could lead to learning at levels II or III. For example, in the discussions of empowerment in the Chapter 3, the idea of "empowerment, of course" was not changed in any occasion into the question of "empowerment, why?" in order to reflect the basic organisational assumptions behind the approach.

Often these common but modest and mundane forms of learning do not gain as much attention as those labelled transformative learning, supposedly being of levels II or even III in Bateson's categorisation discussed in Chapter 2. At times, transformative learning takes place. However, the literature often rather includes prescriptions for these kinds of learning, than actual empirical evidence of fundamental changes in organisational assumptions, identity, or world views and paradigms. The discussions of transformation and transformative learning in NGO literature emphasise becoming aware of prevailing power relations, and deliberation and action towards their change (Johnson & Wilson 2009). In organisational literature, transformation often refers merely to fundamental changes in organisational identities, epistemologies and paradigms – not necessarily discussed at all in terms of power (Tosey et al. 2011). I suggest that in investigation of organisational learning in NGOs, a variety of different meanings and manifestations of transformation should be further explored; for example, analyse instances where NGO's worldviews and value-base change as a consequence of learning.

All the learning processes depicted in this book scrutinised organisational learning as an ongoing practice rather than a one-time event, perhaps facilitated by outside change agents such as consultants (Weick & Quinn 1999). Nevertheless, consultants contribute to learning processes and, together with training courses and workshops, they are important carriers of institutionalised terminologies and practices. However, as shown in Chapter 3, enduring organisational learning typically requires a long process of organisational experimentation and internal interaction that gradually lead to changes in organisational knowledge, understandings, routines and practices. It requires some kind of organisational memory system, and systematised learning practices in order to counteract unintentional organisational forgetting discussed in the Chapter 5. Moreover, continuous organisational learning is accompanied by organisational unlearning and intentional forgetting; sometimes for the benefit of learning, sometimes hindering it. Nevertheless, some issues are always left in the sphere of ignorance, and these are often affected by institutional processes that direct attention to certain events and issues and encourage ignoring the others (Douglas 1986). The bias for success and the tendency to ignore challenging complexity and unpleasant issues as discussed in Chapter 5 were examples of the ways the institution of development constructs its image. In the current context where NGOs need to adapt to changing development fads, approaches and policies, the questions of unlearning and forgetting would need more scrutiny.

However, while development fashions seem to change, there are more enduring assumptions that endure. NGOs have a taken-for-granted stance towards the goals related to change in a variety of arenas of life. NGOs aim is to promote development; a change towards a presumably better direction that needs support, contribution, or triggering from the organisations. This basic belief in change that can be somehow externally promoted and planned is the basis of the organisational identities of development NGOs, and the entire field. Similarly, the basic model of an NGO or that of modern organisations in general, was not questioned. Rather, NGOs had an aspiration to be better organisations in terms of their capability to plan, implement and measure. Thus, considering the Batesonian levels of learning discussed in Chapter 2, much learning in NGOs takes place in level I and occasionally in level II in their attempts to learn the institutionalised practices and become more effective and legitimate. However, commonly, learning III rarely takes place as NGOs remain with their world views according to which some kind of change is needed, the kind of change needed can be identified, planned, implemented and measured within constellations of modern organisations. The learning III, which would include the reflection and change of these basic assumptions, would be challenging, as it would mean a complete change in identities, meanings and practices, and perhaps learning and change in the entire institution of development.

Management as balancing between coherence, control and contexts

Much of the explicit and documented organisational learning in NGOs takes place within the institutionalised learning mechanisms embedded in M&E. At the same time, these mechanisms seemed to keep the NGO staff too busy to learn when it came to learning defined as a reflection of not only whether the right things were done when compared to plans, but also whether the plans were addressing the right issues or had proper assumptions in regard to the aspired change in the lives of the people. However, even if there were occasional frustration with the increased M&E procedures, the overall need for such institutionalised knowledge production was rarely questioned. Therefore, the chapters showed that much organisational learning is intertwined with the practice of management of both organisation and development projects. From the organisational perspective, in order to be able to effectively manage organisational structures and goals, there is a need to control the use of organisational resources, the division of labour, and to measure the achievement of organisational goals. In order to hold together, organisation also needs to have certain coherence in its practices. For that purpose, NGOs have a certain hierarchical division of labour, and an existing reporting mechanism. Additionally, more mundane control mechanisms work through organisational rules, routines and alignment of individuals with organisational identity.

However in resonance with the idea of the modern organisation discussed in Chapter 6 (Meyer et al. 2006), the members of staff were merely expected to "control themselves" by adhering to the organisational guidelines and routines, rather than by obeying orders given by directors. The intertwining personal motivation and organisational goals of "doing good" provided a good platform for individuals to be committed to NGOs. However, the commitment to management procedures varied. Organisational memory systems were of great importance in the efforts to control the conduct of management. However, as discussed in Chapter 5, individual variations in their use enabled derivations from the organisational guidelines, and were therefore disturbances from the point of view of management. The perspective of an NGO, often explicated by headquarters, emphasises coherence and standardisation. The focus on coherence can clash with the contextual needs of the field offices, as well as their necessary aspirations to have an image of autonomous actors recognised in their specific contexts. The mutual tendencies to forget and ignore the everyday life in field offices by headquarter staff and the nature of work in the headquarters by those working in the field, as discussed in Chapter 5, revealed the challenges of organisational management. In a similar vein, the negotiations in the course of developing new M&E approaches in Chapter 4 showed how, under the general banner of story-based M&E, individual field locations strived for different solutions that would address their particular needs.

The challenges of managing the organisational structure and following up the achievement of the organisational goals are greater when it comes to partnerships between different organisations. One of the pervasive questions is whether the southern partner organisation should act "as if" it was part, or an extension, of its northern donor organisation, and attempt to follow its strategic goals and M&E procedures, or whether the partner organisations are able to keep their autonomy, goals and follow-up procedures. Often, the coherence is mainly imposed by donor NGOs (Mueller-Hirth 2012), while combining different organisational goals and measurement practices requires more flexibility and endurance of uncertainty on the part of the northern NGO and its donors (Crewe 2014). Regarding the organisations discussed here, World Vision had most well-established coherence between northern and southern organisations as they were all part of the international federative network. In other instances, for example, Finnish NGOs had a principle to prioritise partner organisations' own M&E systems; however, they had to negotiate ways in which the information needed for their organisational indicators could be received.

An additional layer that contributes to complexities of measurement is brought by so-called beneficiaries. In the systems of results-based management, they should also constitute a part of the NGO system and produce knowledge about their results according to the reporting needs of the NGO. The chapters showed how for the headquarters of northern NGOs, the interaction with so-called beneficiaries is often quite sporadic. The everyday encounters with beneficiaries are mainly conducted by the the field offices or southern partner organisations, and the knowledge from beneficiaries is often mediated by their reports. In many instances, the local NGOs have to translate the local accounts into development management language (Dar 2014; Mueller-Hirt 2012). As argued in Chapter 5, the short-term field visits that were experienced as crucial learning events by the staff in northern NGOs might add to their knowledge, but can also contribute to ignorance about the real everyday life of the beneficiaries. In the organisational realities, knowledge-management systems tend to discard and forget much knowledge from the beneficiaries as irrelevant (Ferguson et al. 2010).

Critical development management literature has advocated post-rational management and learning to counteract the spread of isomorphic and rationalistic management models and to emphasise social learning vis-á-vis local knowledge (Dar & Cooke 2008; McFarlane 2006). For example, Ferguson et al. (2010) argue for "situated mutual learning" that could allow for innovative management different from the prevalent models. However, in the everyday life of NGOs there seems to a tendency to move towards increasing rationality, goal-setting, planning, and measurement. As illustrated by the example of small Tanzanian NGOs in 2000 discussed in Chapter 6, this trend has led to the modification of existing social forms such as government bureaucracies, friendship and family into organisations, and thus has increased the organisational way of acting and speaking about what is being done. The suggested alternatives such as post-rational thinking (McFarlane 2006), dialogue in global solidarity (Dar & Cooke 2008), drawing from romanticism (Guljarani 2010), and returning from professionalised NGOs to more local member-based organisations (Banks et al. 2015), do not necessarily speak to the everyday challenges of contemporary development NGOs. However, they open potential spaces for learning to change the world view of management, and seeing differently.

Recently, the need for NGOs and CSOs to adapt to the overall global disruptive changes has been increasingly debated (Gnärig 2015). Disruptive changes refer to, for instance, the change in development policy framework to Sustainable Development Goals, increasing implications of climate change all over the world, changing geopolitical architecture, and the shrinking of the space for civil society in a number of countries, that all affect the need for NGOs to reconsider their agendas and activities. The shifting emphasis to private sector in international development and the political atmospheres in donor countries have already affected the financial resources of the NGOs, as in the case of ISF in Chapter 4. Detailed analysis of the learning in NGOs vis-á-vis these processes is needed to identify how organisations can adapt to ongoing changes through changing their meanings, practices and routines.

Politics of learning

From the organisational and institutional perspectives, learning is not only an individual cognitive and behavioural phenomenon, but is also social and societal. Therefore, relations of power and the politics of learning become increasingly relevant. Social learning in organisations is embedded in the organisational power relations as well as those prevalent in wider society (Contu & Willmott 2003). For example, when interaction and joint reflection is essential for organisational learning, the asymmetries in organisational status effect the learning situations in which knowledge perspectives of those in a higher position might gain more legitimacy than those in a lower organisational rank (Bunderson & Reagans 2011). The scripts of the NGO workshop analysed in Chapter 3 showed how directors and researcher were positioned to provide more legitimate knowledge about empowerment than those participants who engage in empowerment every day. This echoed also the prevalent power imbalances between north and south and NGOs. Further, not much voice from the beneficiaries was heard in these particular discussions on empowerment (Ferguson et al. 2010). In the case discussed in Chapter 4, the story-based approach was seen as potential means to change the power relations between NGOs and their beneficiaries by giving more voice to people's experiences. At the same time, the very negotiations over the status of story-based M&E included struggles over right definitions and over the extent of the autonomy of field offices from the headquarters. The effects of power in organisational meaning-making, knowledge creation and learning, thus, should receive increasing attention (Contu & Willmott 2003; Heizmann 2011).

However, among the most visible power effects was the power of institutional practices, meanings and routines over individual organisations. The approaches institutionalised in international development and the overall idea of possibility of intentional development, were merely taken for granted. Organisational institutionalism has been criticised for not engaging with power (Clegg 2010; Munir 2015). According to critique, institutional theory focuses on taken-for-granted meanings and routines while neglecting the role of power in naturalising these meanings (Willmott 2015), and the political struggles that are part of the legitimacy process (Hirsch & Lounsbury 2015). In response, Lawrence (2008) has proposed a notion of institutional politics to analyse the interplay between power and institutionalism. Institutional politics entails power as institutional control over actors' behaviours, as institutional agency of actors to disrupt and transform institutions, and as institutional resistance in which actors attempt to limit the institutional control.

In the cases analysed, there was not much open resistance towards the institutionalised practices. Rather, in most of the instances they were experienced as good and desirable. While this can be an indication of institutional control, it merely resonates with the idea of systemic power (Lawrence 2008), or epistemic power (Alasuutari 2015) that modifies the behaviour of actors through the "myths of appropriate conduct" (Suddaby 2015, 93). In Chapter 3, the routine script of an organisational workshop and the tendency to talk about empowerment with a vocabulary of LFA showed the power of institutional vocabularies. In Chapter 4, the new ideas related to story-based M&E continuously clashed with the taken-for-granted ideals of measurability prevalent in development. In Chapter 5, institutionalised ideas of certainty and success guided what was left in the sphere of ignorance. Finally, the Chapter 6 showed the epistemic power of the model of modern organisation in ways in which NGOs were eager and willing to learn to be better organisations. The approaches used in the organisations such as HRBA, management tools such as LFA, and commitment to empowerment can all be understood as examples of carriers of cognitive-cultural elements of the international institution of development, and thus, its epistemic power. They can be understood as examples of transnational governance that modify the agendas of NGOs all over the world, as an example of the human rights agenda in Malawian NGOs illustrates (Englund 2006). In organisation theory, power is a contested concept (Haugaard & Clegg 2009). In this context, the conceptualisation of power as governmentality (Foucault 1991) in analysis of the taken-for-granted institutional meanings and routines, as struggles over hegemony (Gramsci 1971) in investigating the strategies by which certain ideas become hegemonic in both organisation and institution, or as power effects of material artefacts (Latour 2005) such as institutionalised measurement devices, among others, would be relevant.

Moreover, the chapters of the book showed that while the north-south power relations are prevalent in international development, the power of institutionalised models transcends the north-south divide. NGOs engaged in development activities both in the global south and north are subject to similar kind of epistemic power as a consequence of which they shape their activities according to the pressures of the field and global models of a rational "organisation". However, the north-south divide remained significant from the point of view of resource dependency, as power related to financial resources divided unevenly. An example of coercive institutional power was shown in Chapter 4, in the decision by the Ministry for Foreign Affairs of Finland to drastically cut NGO funding, which ended large parts of the ongoing organisational learning. These cuts did not have anything to do with the evidence of organisational performance as exactly similar cuts were done over the sector, but resulted from the change in the political constellation of the Finnish parliament and government. While the NGOs in the global north depend on individual sponsors and governmental donors to operate, they nevertheless have a more secure position than their southern partners. For example, the cuts in funding hit the ISF hard but had even more drastic consequences for those Ugandan NGOs that ISF had to remove from its partnerships. For ISF it meant cutting some of its activities; for the smaller Ugandan NGOs, perhaps it was losing the majority of their foreseen resources.

From learning in NGOs towards of learning of citizens

In this book, my deliberate choice was to focus on learning that takes place within organisations and not in their relationships and encounters with so-called beneficiaries of the organisations; those whose lives or life-conditions are supposed to be changed as a result of NGO activities. It is well known that beneficiaries' participation in the design, implementation and assessment of NGO activities and interventions, and engagement with local knowledge, are crucial for any lasting change to occur. My decision to leave learning with beneficiaries outside the focus of the book, by no means indicates that I would not consider such learning extremely important. However, my own institutional hindrances limited the research projects to focus on learning in organisation with no resources to expand the analysis to include beneficiaries. Therefore, I did not have sufficient empirical material and evidence to analyse and discuss the dynamics of mutual learning or non-learning in NGO-beneficiary encounters, and the encounters with beneficiaries were discussed to the extent it came up in the interaction within the NGOs.

We learned that from the point of view of northern NGOs the encounter with the beneficiaries is often mediated by local partner organisations. The headquarter staff learn from the situation on the ground mostly on the basis of reports and accounts of the partner organisations. Those having field offices might have more direct and frequent contact with beneficiaries, but their experiences often stay with individual members or in particular offices and it is hard to share through organisational knowledge production mechanisms and memory systems. Therefore, the complexities, social orders and multiple processes going on in the beneficiaries' lives are easily forgotten and ignored. In the organisational discourses people living their everyday lives are categorised as "beneficiaries" or "project participants" who have to be empowered and helped to take care of their own development, and whose knowledge, attitudes and practices are changed as an outcome of the NGO interventions. From the perspectives of ordinary people, being a beneficiary in an NGO project is only one of their many roles and life activities. They, however, learn not only about their development, but also about how to be beneficiaries, clients or participants in NGO interventions in an attempt to combine their life logics with the one inherent in interventions (Olivier de Sardan 2005). The complexities of learning in NGOs' encounters with beneficiaries are worth further examination.

The categorisation of learning suggested in Chapter 2 could be further adapted to analyse the learning of people that takes place around NGO interventions. Currently, the trend is to emphasise learning of active citizenship by means of social accountability and citizen engagement programmes using the HRBA approach. The goals of these programmes are often ambitious and seek for increasing political engagement of people that would, in turn, lead to transformative change. Sometimes, questions to be asked include why people do not become active, why the occurrence of change is often incremental rather than transformational, and whether people are more interested in being engaged with activities with economic empowerment than in activities involving mainly political participation (King 2015). Factors such as acknowledging the local social orders and power relations (Gaventa & Barret 2012), the tendency to align with authorities (Dorman 2014), and an overall democratic habitus (Pettit 2016) have been identified as potential hindrances to learn to be active citizens.

In this context the intertwined categories of learning of types I, II, and III, performed by individuals and communities might be able to facilitate analysis of how learning to be an active citizen takes place as a combination of reproduction and critical reflection on routines, practices and assumptions in one's life. Paying attention to different types of learning does not imply being sceptical or cynical about the possibilities of transformative change towards more just societies, but could provide a wider spectrum of change trajectories, and realistic account of the pace and means of transformation.

In the same vein, in this conclusion, I do not want to take a normative stand towards the NGOs analysed and judge whether they learn in the "right" way, whether they learn the "right things", or whether they have become the "right" kinds of organisations, nor do I want to suggest what NGOs in general should do. Rather, I wanted to offer a detailed analysis of the everyday learning in NGO, and encourage more research on different types of organisational learning and forgetting in a wide diversity of contexts. Adapting institutionalised practices and meanings is not inherently good or bad, and many of today's institutionalised ideas have been gradually developed in order to address some perceived challenges. Institutionalised practices, such as HRBA, have brought new ideas for the older institutionalised ways of doing development, as well as the institutionalised attempts to measure the outcomes have facilitated learning of what works and what does not. However, they need constant critical reflection and, at times, reformulation. In regard to learning in NGOs, my main recommendation would be to acknowledge different types of learning, and sometimes, allocate resources also for the more demanding reflective learning processes and bold experimentation of new ways of doing things. As learned from the organisational institutionalism (Powell & Colyvas 2008), on the one hand, institutional pressures shape directions of organisational learning; but on the other, institutions can be changed through resistance and agency, through modification of local meanings and practices, by doing differently.

References

Alasuutari, P. (2015) The discoursive side of new institutionalism. *Cultural Sociology*, 9(2), 162–184.

Banks, N., Hulme, D. & Edwards, M. (2015) NGOs, states, and donors revisited: Still too close for comfort? *World Development*, 66, 707–718.

Bunderson, J.S. & Reagans, R.E. (2011) Power, status and learning in organisations. *Organization Science*, 22(5), 1182–1194.

Clegg, S. (2010) The state, power and agency: Missing in action in institutional theory? *Journal of Management Inquiry*, 19(1), 4–13.

Contu, A. & Willmott, H. (2003) Re-embedding situatedness: The importance of power relations in learning theory. *Organization Science*, 14(3), 283–296.

Crewe, E. (2014) Doing development differently: Rituals of hope and despair in an INGO. *Development in Practice*, 24(1), 91–104.

Crewe, E. & Axelby, R. (2013) *Anthropology and Development. Culture, Morality and Politics in a Globalised World.* Cambridge: Cambridge University Press.

Cyert, R.M. & March, J.G. (1963) *A Behavioral Theory of the Firm.* Englewood Cliffs, NJ: Prentice Hall.

Dar, S. (2014) Hybrid accountabilities: When western and non-western accountabilities collide. *Human Relations*, 67(2), 131–151.

Dar, S. & Cooke, B. (eds) (2008) *The New Development Management.* London: Zed Books.

Dorman, S.R. (2014) Citizenship in Africa. In: Isin, E.G. & Nyers, P. (eds) *Routledge Handbook of Global Citizenship Studies*. London: Routledge, 161–172.

Douglas, M. (1986) *How Institutions Think*. Syracuse, NY: Syracuse University Press.

Englund, H. (2006) *Prisoners of Freedom. Human Rights and the African Poor*. Berkeley, CA: The University of California Press.

Ferguson, J., Huysman, M. & Soekijad, M (2010) Knowledge management in practice: Pitfalls and potentials for development. *World Development*, 38(12), 1797–1810.

Foucault, M. (1991) *Discipline and Punish: the Birth of a Prison*. London: Penguin.
Gaventa, J. & Barrett, G. (2012) Mapping the outcomes of citizen engagement. *World Development*, 40(12), 2399–2410.
Gnärig, B. (2015) *The Hedgehog and the Beatle. Disruption and Innovation in the Civil Society Sector*. Berlin: International Civil Society Center.
Gramsci, A. (1971) *Selection from the Prison Notebooks*. Edited and translated by Hoare, Q. & Smith, G.N. London: Lawrence and Wishart.
Guljarani, N. (2010) New vistas for development management: Examining radical-reformist possibilities and potential. *Public Administration and Development*, 30(2), 136–148.
Haugaard, M. & Clegg, S.R. (eds) (2009) *The Sage Handbook of Power*. Los Angeles, CA: SAGE.
Heimer, C. (2012) Inert facts and the illusion of knowledge: Strategic uses of ignorance in HIV clinic. *Economy and Society*, 41(1), 17–41.
Heizmann, H. (2011) Knowledge sharing in a disperse network of the practice: Zooming in on power/knowledge struggles. *Management Learning*, 42(2), 379–393.
Hillhorst, D. (2003) *The Real World of NGOs. Discourse, Diversity and Development*. London: Zed Books.
Hirsch, P. & Lounsbury, M. (2015) Toward a more critical and "powerful" institutionalism. *Journal of Management Inquiry*, 24(1), 96–99.
Hwang, H. & Powell, W.W. (2009). The rationalization of charity: The influences of professionalism in the nonprofit sector. *Administrative Science Quarterly*, 54(2), 268–298.
Johnson, H. & Wilson, G. (2009) *Learning for Development*. Zed Books: London.
King, S. (2015) Political capabilities for democratisation in Uganda: Good governance or popular organisation building? *Third World Quarterly*, 36(4), 741–757.
Lawrence, T.B. (2008) Power, institutions and organisations. In: Greenwood, R., Olivier, C. & Suddaby, R. (eds) *The Sage Handbook of Organizational Institutionalism*, 170–197.
Latour, B. (2005) *Reassembling the Social: an Introduction to Actor-Network-Theory*. Oxford/New York: Oxford University Press.
Lewis, D. (2009) International development and the "perpetual present": Anthropological approaches to the rehistoricisation of policy. *European Journal of Development Research*, 21(1), 32–46.
Lewis, D. (2016) Abandoned pasts, disappearing futures: Further reflections on multiple temporalities in studying non-governmental organisation worlds. *Critique of Anthropology*, 36(1), 84–92.
McFarlane, C. (2006) Knowledge, learning and development: a post-rationalist approach. *Progress in Development Studies*, 6(4), 287–305.
Meyer, J.W., Drori, G.S. & Hwang, H. (2006) World Society and the proliferation of formal organization. In: Drori, G.S., Meyer, J.W. & Hwang, H. (2006) *Globalization and Organization: World Society and Organizational Change*. Oxford: Oxford University Press, 25–49.
Munir, K.A.(2015) A loss of power in institutional theory. *Journal of Management Inquiry*, 24(1), 90–92.
Olivier de Sardan, J.-P. (2005) *Anthropology and Development. Understanding Contemporary Social Change*. London: Zed Books.
Pettit, J. (2016). Why citizens don't engage? Power, poverty and civic habitus. *IDS Bulletin*, 47(5), 89–102.

Powell, W.W & Colyvas, J.A. (2008) Microfoundations of institutional theory. In Greenwood, R., Oliver, C., Suddaby, R. & Sahlin-Andersson, K. (2008). *The Sage Handbook of Organisational Institutionalism.* London: SAGE.

Suddaby, R. (2015) Can institutional theory be critical? *Journal of Management Inquiry*, 24(1), 93–95.

Tosey, P., Visser, M. & Saunders, M.N.K. (2011) The origins and conceptualizations of "triple-loop" learning: A critical review. *Management Learning*, 43(3), 291–307.

Watkins, S.C., Swidler, A. & Hannan, T. (2012) Outsourcing social transformation: Development NGOs as organisations. *Annual Review of Sociology*, 38(1), 285–315.

Weick, K.E. & Quinn, R.E. (1999) Organisational change and development. *Annual Review of Psychology*, 50(1), 361–386.

Willmott, H. (2015) Why institutional theory cannot be critical? *Journal of Management Inquiry*, 24(1), 105–111.

Index

Note: References such as '178–9' indicate (not necessarily continuous) discussion of a topic across a range of pages. Wherever possible in the case of topics with many references, these have either been divided into sub-topics or only the most significant discussions of the topic are listed. Because the entire work is about 'learning' and 'development', the use of these terms (and certain others which occur constantly throughout the book) as an entry point has been restricted. Information will be found under the corresponding detailed topics.

accountability 2, 7, 104, 107–8, 111, 114, 131, 137–8
acronyms 49, 72
active citizenship 17, 62, 158
activist culture 2, 16, 104, 106, 108, 124
actors 26, 28, 32, 39, 63, 130–1, 138, 156; rational 37, 138
adaptation 6, 11, 16, 36, 38, 128, 130–1
adoption, international 132–3
agency 27, 34, 46, 56, 58–9, 62–3, 108, 159
agents: change 14, 36, 46, 82, 95, 102, 129, 152; of learning 23, 26–32, 150; of transformation 7, 30
aidland 3
alignment 10–11, 38, 86–7, 95, 135, 137, 145, 153
alternative development 29, 33, 46, 101, 129
amnesia 13, 101
annual plans 2, 4, 13, 49, 107
annual reports 4, 77–80, 93–4, 107–8, 136
artefacts 36, 40, 49, 52, 102, 105, 157
aspirations 1–2, 7, 67, 101, 117, 131, 133, 152–3
assumptions 16, 25, 28, 30–5, 41, 123, 150–3, 158
asymmetries 10, 12, 28, 51, 155
attitude change 80–1, 85, 91–2, 94, 96, 115
attitudes 26, 61, 84, 86, 93–4, 106, 115, 134
autonomy 82–3, 112–13, 154, 156

Bangladesh 36, 88–9, 117
baseline studies 4, 6, 74, 92, 131
beliefs 6, 30, 35, 60, 74, 102, 112, 138
beneficiaries 34–5, 75–6, 85–6, 93, 116–18, 120–1, 154–5, 157–8
best failures 110, 119
best practices 11, 38, 130, 145, 151
bias 88, 95, 108, 119–20, 152
bookkeeping 120
bridging: between organisations and institutions 37–41; between projects and programmes 82–3
briefcase organisations 143
budgets 75, 103, 120, 132
bureaucracy 106, 135, 142, 155
buzzwords 27, 47, 49, 136

capacity building 3, 11–13, 59, 85, 129–30, 139–40, 144–5
caste 61, 63
categorisation of learning 15–16, 23–4, 32–5, 41, 150–1, 158
change 14–16, 24–36, 58–9, 62–7, 79–83, 85–7, 92–7, 149–53; agents 14, 36, 46, 82, 95, 102, 129, 152; attitude 80–1, 85, 91–2, 94, 96, 115; continuous 3, 102; depiction 92–4; disruptive

155; first-order 50; fundamental 33, 86, 151–2; incremental 30–1; organisational 4–5, 9–10, 12, 14, 31, 82, 102–3; in organisational epistemology 15, 71–97; paths 92, 94; positive 35, 49, 87; processes 36, 75, 106, 114; second-order 50; stories of 77–8, 80–1; third-order 50, 66; trajectories 92, 95, 158; transformative 3, 17, 30, 158
children 47–8, 52, 58, 65–6, 121, 132–3
civil society 6–7, 11, 30, 41, 85, 103, 128, 143; organisations (CSOs) 8, 143, 155
cognitive frameworks 49, 56–7, 59
coherence 41, 82, 153–4
collaboration 11, 34–5, 48, 53, 95–6, 143–4
community development 4, 63–4, 68, 101
community empowerment 63–4, 66
community members 59, 73, 115, 117
community-based organisations 61, 139
competence 26–7, 78, 91, 105, 136, 144
competencies 78, 105, 139–40
conceptualisations 7, 9, 11, 14, 41, 145, 149, 156
conflicts 51, 85–6, 118
consultants 77, 79, 82, 84, 87, 89, 129–30, 152
continuous change 3, 102
control 138, 150, 153, 156
cooperatives 76, 84
coordinators 78–9, 82–5, 88, 90–2, 117–18, 121, 135–6
corruption 120
Counteracting Development Amnesia 13, 104
country coordinators 78–9, 82–5, 90, 92, 117, 135
country offices 82, 109, 111–12, 117
credibility 89–91
critical reflection 3, 5, 15–16, 28, 34, 104, 122–3, 158–9
CSOs (civil society organisations) 8, 143, 155
cultural barriers 63–4
cultural model of modern organisation 129, 137
cultural-cognitive elements 8, 37, 40, 149
cultures 8, 49, 107, 118; activist 2, 16, 104, 106, 108, 124; learning 104, 106

data collectors 84, 89–90
decent work 71, 76, 84
decoupling 8, 38, 149
democracy 3, 7, 140
denials 122
depoliticisation 3, 11, 37
desk officers 111
development: cooperation 56, 58, 64, 67, 85, 87, 92, 131–5; discourse 11, 29, 36; intentional 41, 156; literature 6, 11, 26–30, 34, 36, 46, 114, 116; management 4–6, 16, 59, 154; NGOs 2–10, 14–16, 28–9, 71–6, 103–4, 128–34, 137–9, 149–52; NGOs, legitimate 10, 137; NGOs, professional 13, 75, 133; partnerships 9, 28, 34–5, 87, 119; *see also Introductory Note*
dialogue 14, 23, 28, 54, 56, 130, 136, 155
digital systems 40, 111
disability 51, 53
disempowerment 46, 60, 64–5, 67, 115
disruptive changes 155
division of labour 81–4, 96, 106, 153
division of tasks 110–12
documentation/documents 13, 71, 74–5, 105–7, 109, 111, 140, 143
domestic violence 76, 80, 85–6, 91
donor–recipient relationships 31, 48
donors 9–10, 35, 74, 76, 78, 95, 119–21, 135–6; demands 136–7; governmental 131, 157
double-loop learning 5, 25–6, 29, 31
duty bearers 80, 131
dynamics 5, 7, 9, 37, 51, 67, 149, 157

early adopters 130, 145
economic empowerment 65, 158
education 30–1, 47, 74, 94, 110–11, 115; *see also* learning; training
effectiveness 25, 28, 30, 96, 115, 128
emancipation 31, 46
empirical realities 6, 24, 41
Empowering Leadership in an International NGO 13
empowerment: as change in individuals, communities or structures 62–4; as change in power balance or in people's inner strength 64–6; community 63–4, 66; definition 46–8, 51, 53, 56–7, 62, 64, 67; economic 65, 158; goals 66, 86; as guiding principle 86–7; indigenous 61; locus 15, 62; monitoring 13, 48, 67; pathways 48, 53–5; processes 47–8, 53, 56, 59, 61, 67, 116; schemata 15, 56–62, 67;

scripts for discussing 51–6; shared meaning for 15, 46–68; *see also Introductory Note*
environmental NGOs 118, 136, 142
environments 8–9, 24, 27, 62, 64, 120, 122, 142; complex 104, 114; institutional/organisational 5, 9, 14, 32, 35–8, 41, 71–2, 87; material 52, 74; working 34, 71
epistemic governance 131
epistemic power 156–7
epistemological criteria 71, 76, 80, 87, 91
epistemology, *see* organisational epistemology
equality, gender 71, 76, 84–5, 96, 133
established knowledge 102–3, 105, 124
evaluation 1, 13, 82, 84–5, 89, 91, 94–5, 106–8
everyday life 5, 14, 24, 57, 88, 121, 149, 153–4
everyday practices 3, 8, 14, 16, 51, 68, 75, 120
evidence-based decision making 96, 115, 131
experience 25–6, 37–9, 87–8, 100, 105, 110, 116–17, 121–3; individual 36, 62; personal 48, 89
experiential learning 29, 39, 123
experimentation 15, 55, 72, 79, 84, 87, 130, 151
expert knowledge 36, 100, 116
expertise 26, 28, 72, 105, 111–12, 118, 136
experts 4, 26–7, 95, 119
external change agents 36, 46

face-to-face interaction 105, 112
facilitation 60–1
facilitators 46, 54, 78–9, 116, 132
fads 2, 28, 101, 108, 123, 151–2
failures 95, 103, 107, 112, 117, 119–20, 122; best 110, 119
faith-based organisations 35
families 58, 62, 64–5, 85–6, 145, 155
feedback 4, 27, 34–5, 83, 110, 123, 136
FGM (female genital mutilation) 76, 89, 93–4
field coordinators 82, 117
field offices 105–6, 109–13, 117–18, 123–4, 135, 153, 156, 158
field visits 51, 112, 120–1, 124, 154
financial management 120, 136, 144
financial resources 97, 141, 143, 155, 157
Finland 12–13, 48, 57, 75–6, 78, 80, 96, 132–5
Finnish NGOs 13, 95–6, 116, 120–1, 129, 131–2, 136–7, 143–5
first adopters 131, 137
first-order change 50
flexibility 2, 6, 16, 27–8, 154
flipcharts 52, 54
food 64–6, 89, 141–3
forgetting 2, 13–14, 16, 40, 100–24, 149–52, 159; level I and II 102–3; organisational 16, 40, 102–5, 111–13, 124, 151–2; *see also* unlearning
funding 7–8, 34, 36, 76, 80, 95, 132–4, 136; negotiations 81, 95; systems 29, 95

gender 51, 65, 76, 91; analysis 122, 131; equality 71, 76, 84–5, 96, 133; roles 74, 76, 94
generalisability 89, 91
girls 62, 65, 89, 93, 115
GLM (Green Living Movement) 116, 120, 136
global organisations 16, 109–10, 112
global solidarity 3, 5, 7, 35, 133, 155
goals 8–10, 25–6, 33–5, 37–8, 71–4, 83–6, 137–41, 150–4; institutional 29, 33; organisational 5, 8, 33, 71, 73–5, 81, 84–7, 153–4; project 27, 34, 93; strategic 134, 154
governance 4, 47, 120; epistemic 131; transnational 7, 156
governmentality 32, 156
grassroots 3, 9, 129, 139
Green Living Movement, *see* GLM
group assignments 53–5, 59, 67
group work 52–3, 56, 66
guests 120–1, 142
guidelines 72–3, 76, 78–9, 104, 108–12, 120, 123, 134–5; organisational 84, 106, 135, 151, 153

habits 25, 62–3, 72, 76, 86, 95, 103
headquarters 80, 82–4, 94, 108–13, 117–18, 123–4, 135, 153; staff 78, 96, 106, 110–11, 117–18, 120, 153, 157
hegemonies 4, 11–12, 31, 40, 130, 156
hierarchies 11–12, 51, 55, 82, 153
hindrances 7, 63–4, 104, 106, 111, 157
history 102, 107, 123, 133, 137, 139–41

HIV/AIDS 116, 121, 141
HRBA (human rights-based approach) 4, 6, 122, 130–1, 133, 156, 158–9

identity 35, 49, 51, 109, 112, 132, 151, 153; organisational 26, 33, 35, 40, 47, 104, 112, 152–3
ignorance 2, 14, 16, 63, 100–24, 149, 154; organisational 16, 100–1, 113, 118–19, 122; shadow of 115–16, 118; sphere of 16, 100, 118, 121, 152, 156; strategic 119–21, 124
imitation 38, 130, 137, 145, 150
impact assessment 2, 80, 86, 88–9, 91
implementation 4, 27, 34, 107, 109, 114, 116, 118
income 65, 76, 84–5, 88, 96, 116, 143–5
incremental change 30–1
India 12–13, 15, 47, 51–5, 59, 61, 63–4, 121
indicator-based approach 75–6, 83, 92, 97, 123
indicators 75, 79–83, 92, 97, 110–11, 132, 134, 137; numeric 80, 94; programme 80, 82–3, 90, 94, 110, 132
indigenous empowerment 61
indigenous processes 15, 59–61
INGOs (international non-governmental organisations) 1, 13, 103, 111, 113, 131, 138, 140
innovation 61, 103, 112
institutional approaches 37, 123
institutional environments 5, 9, 14, 32, 35–8, 41, 71–2, 87
institutional goals 29, 33
institutional isomorphism 5, 38
institutional knowledge criteria 95–6
institutional learning 1, 23, 26, 29, 32, 35, 41, 150
institutional memory 102, 110, 118
institutional pressures 10, 81, 129
institutional processes 100, 124, 152
institutional repertoires 50–1
institutionalisation 35, 50, 55–7, 72, 105, 107, 110, 121
institutionalised knowledge 15, 101, 153
institutionalised learning: events 3, 15, 149, 151; mechanisms 106, 153
institutionalised practices 15, 95, 97, 114, 152, 156, 159
institutionalised schemata 49–50, 57
institutionalised scripts 10, 51–2, 56, 66, 151
institutionalised vocabularies 57, 59
institutionalisms 8–10, 23–41, 128, 137, 156, 159
intentional development 41, 156
intentionality 102–3
interaction 8, 14–15, 32, 34–7, 40–1, 49, 120–1, 154–5; face-to-face 105, 112
internal synchronisation 132, 134–5, 145
international child adoption 132–3
international development, *see Introductory Note*
international non-governmental organisations, *see* INGOs
International Solidarity Foundation, *see* ISF
Interpedia 132–3, 135
intervention approach 15, 59–60, 66–7
interviewees 60–2, 64–5, 88, 105–6, 108, 111, 116, 123
interviewers 88, 90
interviews 1, 14, 56–60, 62–3, 67, 88–9, 104, 108–11; individual 13, 47–8, 56, 129; narrative 80, 88–9
ISF (International Solidarity Foundation) 13, 15, 71–2, 75–87, 92, 94–7, 133, 157; country coordinators 83, 96; headquarters 76, 83, 91
isomorphism 5, 16, 38, 128–32, 134, 136

job descriptions 111–12

Kenya 13, 15, 47, 51–5, 63–7, 84–5, 119, 121
KEPA 12, 78, 132
knowledge 36–7, 39–41, 71–5, 90–3, 100–8, 112–16, 119–23, 154; established 102–3, 105, 124; expert 36, 100, 116; local 2, 47, 82, 85, 116, 154, 157; narrative 39, 73, 79; needs 40, 51, 79, 82, 96; new 1–2, 36, 39–40, 96–7, 103, 106–7, 110, 112; organisational 15, 39, 71–5, 79, 102–3, 149, 152, 158; participatory 116; propositional 39, 73, 78; tacit 39, 73, 100, 105
knowledge-management systems 2, 29, 39–40, 73, 154

language 10, 40, 49, 73, 75, 83, 103; organisational 48–9, 58, 72
late adopters 130
leadership 2, 56, 81

learning 1–6, 8–17, 23–32, 34–41, 106–8, 110–13, 128–45, 149–59; agents of 23, 26–9, 32, 150; to be an organisation 137–9; categorisation of 15–16, 23–4, 32–5, 41, 150–1, 158; as change in organisational epistemology 71–97; double-loop 5, 25–6, 29, 31; experiential 29, 39, 123; I 24–6, 34–5, 38, 40–1, 75; II 24–5, 30, 32, 34–5, 38, 40–1; III 23–6, 30, 32, 34, 40–1, 102, 151–3, 158; institutional 1, 23, 26, 29, 32, 35, 41, 150; as legitimation and synchronisation 128–45; mutual 11, 28, 31, 35, 154, 157; organisational 2–9, 11–15, 24–6, 31, 35–40, 47–9, 75–6, 150–3; organisations 1–2, 28, 104; in partnerships 2, 34; processes 3, 23, 27, 97, 105, 152, 159; as search for shared meaning for empowerment 15, 46–68; single-loop 5, 25, 29; trajectories 15, 75–81, 149; transformative 30–2, 41, 151; triple-loop 26; zero 24, 26, 32–4
legitimacy 4, 9, 128–9, 137, 139, 143, 145, 155; learning for 37–8, 41, 129
legitimation 128–45
lessons 1–2, 16, 29, 103–4, 108, 114, 122
LFA (logical framework approach) 4, 6, 55–6, 75–6, 95, 130–1, 143–4, 156
life stories 75, 88, 91
literacy 134–6
livelihood strategies 142–3
livelihoods 71, 76, 85, 96; sustainable 133
local knowledge 2, 47, 82, 85, 116, 154, 157
locus of empowerment 15, 62
logical framework approach, *see* LFA

management 3–7, 100, 114, 123, 134, 150, 153, 155; financial 120, 136, 144; practices 3–4, 7, 27, 38, 109, 114, 129, 137; project 3–4, 27, 29, 34, 92, 95, 107, 118; systems 6, 27, 144
managerialism 4–5, 11, 32, 136–7
M&E (monitoring and evaluation) 1–2, 53–5, 74–5, 81, 86–8, 132, 134–5, 137; approaches 12, 75, 84, 136, 154; indicator-based 75–6; qualitative 76, 78; story-based 15, 71, 76, 78–83, 85–7, 92–7, 151, 154–6
meaning perspectives 30, 33–4
meanings 27–8, 32–3, 40–1, 47–52, 66–8, 71–3, 149–53, 155–6
memory 37, 41, 133; decay 103, 105, 110; organisational 36, 38–40, 100, 102–3, 105, 110, 118, 151–3; systems 16, 100, 110, 124, 152–3
micro-credit 61, 144
micro-foundations of institutions 9–10
Millennium Development Goals 29, 130
Ministry for Foreign Affairs of Finland 48, 76, 78, 80, 82, 95–6, 132–4, 136
modern organisations 4, 6, 10, 16, 128–9, 137, 139, 152–3; model of 5, 137–8, 144, 156
modernisation 6, 10, 46, 113
monitoring 1, 4–5, 73, 77, 95, 106, 109, 135; and evaluation, *see* M&E; story-based 15, 78, 93, 96; visits 4, 118
Morogoro 13, 139–43
motivation 62, 136, 138–9, 141, 153
MSC (most significant change) 75, 78, 87, 122
muddling through 3, 10
multiple synchronisations 131–7
mutual learning 11, 28, 31, 35, 154, 157

narrative analysis 79, 92
narrative interviews 80, 88–9
narrative knowledge 39, 73, 79
narratives 79–80, 85, 87–8, 90–4, 115–16
negotiations 50–2, 56, 59, 72, 75, 151, 154, 156
neoliberalism 4, 11, 32, 47, 137
Nepal 122, 128, 132
new knowledge 1–2, 36, 39–40, 96–7, 103, 106–7, 110, 112
NGOs (non-governmental organisations) 1–16, 35–8, 64–7, 71–5, 114–17, 120–2, 128–45, 149–59; environmental 118, 136, 142; Finnish 13, 95–6, 116, 120–1, 129, 131–2, 136–7, 143–5; northern 10, 154, 157; small 13, 79, 96, 141, 143–5; southern 2, 7, 10, 119, 138–9; staff 2, 4, 13, 47, 89, 106, 122, 136; workshops 5, 13, 15, 155
Nicaragua 71, 75–6, 80, 82–4, 90, 94, 133, 135
north–south partnerships 11–12, 119
numeric indicators 80, 94

objectives 3, 13–14, 32, 34, 130, 137, 140, 143
objectivity 84, 89–90
OD, *see* organisational development
open questions 53, 76, 80, 88, 94

organisational action 52, 73, 82
organisational analysis 50, 129, 142
organisational change 4–5, 9–10, 12, 14, 31, 82, 102–3
organisational contexts/environments 9–10, 36, 38–9, 49, 58, 74, 130
organisational development (OD) 1, 3, 11–12, 28, 111, 129
organisational epistemology: challenges in changing 81; change in 15, 71–97; confirmation by organisational goals 84–5
organisational forgetting 16, 40, 102–5, 111–13, 124, 151–2
organisational functioning 5, 47, 57
organisational goals 5, 8, 33, 39, 71, 73–5, 81, 153–4; confirmation of organisational epistemology 84–5; problematisation 85–6
organisational guidelines 84, 106, 135, 151, 153
organisational hierarchies 11–12, 55, 82
organisational identities 26, 33, 35, 40, 47, 104, 112, 152–3
organisational ignorance 16, 100–1, 113, 118–19, 122
organisational institutionalism 8–10, 23–41, 156, 159
organisational knowledge 15, 39, 71–5, 79, 102–3, 149, 152, 158
organisational language 48–9, 58, 72
organisational learning 2–9, 11–15, 24–6, 31, 35–40, 75–6, 128, 150–3; as negotiating meanings 48–51
organisational meanings 8, 40–1, 47–9, 51, 66, 71, 149, 151; shared 15, 56, 72
organisational memory 36, 38–40, 100, 102–3, 105, 110, 118, 151–3
organisational practices 10, 36–7, 40, 66, 71–2, 79, 81, 101–2
organisational schemata 15, 49, 63–4, 66
organisational structures 8, 40, 73–4, 81, 84, 109, 153–4
organisational theory 2–4, 8, 14, 31, 149–50, 156
organisational unlearning 102, 152
organisational vocabularies 36, 58, 66
organisational workshops 104, 132, 156
organisations 1–16, 35–41, 47–51, 71–6, 108–15, 121–4, 128–45, 151–8; global 16, 109–10, 112; modern, *see* modern organisations
outcomes 53, 57, 80, 94, 96, 115, 136, 158–9
outsiders 49, 59, 61, 67, 89
ownership 34, 46, 59, 89, 138–9
Oxfam 130–1

participant observation 72
participation 12–13, 27, 32, 34, 51–2, 81, 101, 121
participatory knowledge 116
participatory performance analysis 13, 140
partner countries 48, 51, 76, 82, 84, 89
partner organisations 13, 75–9, 81–4, 86–7, 89, 117–18, 120–1, 133–6
partnerships 7–8, 23, 26, 28, 33–4, 67–8, 154, 157; equal 28, 133; learning in 2, 34; north-south 11–12, 119
perceptions 47–8, 50, 56, 67, 81, 83, 91–2, 94
performance analysis, participatory 13, 140
perpetual present 2, 101
personnel turnover 16, 104–6, 108, 124, 151
planning 61, 73, 76, 134–6, 138–40, 143–4, 150, 152–3; annual 2, 4, 13, 49, 107; formal 138; rational 27, 139, 143–4; strategic 1, 37, 139
politics 11–12, 51, 142, 150, 155
post-development 6, 33, 41, 101
poverty 29, 41, 58, 64, 76
power 10–12, 31, 51, 56–7, 64–5, 109–10, 112–13, 155–7; analysis 122, 131; effects 11, 100, 156–7; epistemic 156–7
presentations 52–4, 66, 118
pressures 10, 130, 139, 157; external 28, 62; institutional 10, 81, 129; isomorphic 16, 38, 129
prioritisation 26, 47, 108, 116, 124, 154
professional development NGOs 13, 75, 133
professionalisation 3, 7, 10, 129, 150, 155
programme approaches 49, 53, 60, 66, 76, 82–3, 132–3, 136
programme indicators 80, 82–3, 90, 94, 110, 132
project activities 59, 76, 86, 93, 117–18, 121–2
project goals 27, 34, 93
project implementation 4, 34, 114, 118
project management 3–4, 27, 29, 34, 92, 95, 107, 118
propositional knowledge 39, 73, 78
psychological theories 26, 62

qualitative M&E 76, 78
qualitative research 14, 90–2
questionnaires 76, 78, 87–8, 91

rational planning 27, 139, 143–4
rationalisation 137, 139–40, 150
RBM, *see* results-based management
reconfiguration 38, 130, 151
refugees 134–5
reports, annual 4, 77–80, 93–4, 107–8, 136
research interviews, *see* interviews
researchers 13–14, 54–6, 66–7, 89, 132, 155
resource dependency 8, 120, 157
resources 34, 37, 56–7, 60, 109, 114–15, 157, 159; financial 97, 141, 143, 155, 157
responsibilisation 47
responsibility 59, 65, 117, 119, 144; shared 57, 61
results-based management (RBM) 1, 4, 122–3, 131, 138, 154
rhetoric 10, 29, 34, 38, 149
rights-based approaches 4, 29, 36, 53, 95, 110, 122–3
role expectations 50, 52, 54–6, 67
roles 14, 16–17, 46–8, 50–2, 55, 64, 84, 117–18; gender 74, 76, 94
routines 32–41, 79, 81, 102–3, 105, 110, 150–3, 155–6
rules 8, 28–9, 37–8, 40, 72–3, 119

saturation 92
schemata 48–50, 64, 66–7, 149, 151; of empowerment 15, 56–62, 67; institutionalised 49, 57
scripts 48, 149, 155; for discussing empowerment 51–6; institutionalised 10, 51–2, 56, 66, 151
second-order change 50
sense-making 3, 10, 50
shadow of ignorance 115–16, 118
shared meanings 15, 28, 35, 46–68, 72, 151
shared responsibility 57, 61
shared understandings 37, 47, 112, 151
Sierra Leone 128, 134–5
single-loop learning 5, 25, 29
skills 36, 39, 91, 93, 96, 105, 110, 144
small businesses 121, 143–4
small NGOs 13, 139–43
social change 5, 75, 101, 114, 139
social epistemology 74
social learning theories 12, 26
societal power relations 11, 30–1
societal structures 31, 47, 62–4, 66
solidarity, global 3, 5, 7, 35, 133, 155
Somaliland 75–6, 78–80, 82, 84–5, 88–9, 93–4, 133, 135
South Africa 121, 128
southern expertise 136
southern NGOs 2, 7, 10, 119, 138–9
sphere of ignorance 16, 100, 118, 121, 152, 156
Sri Lanka 13, 15, 47, 64
stability 37, 40
staff 13–14, 47–8, 66–8, 82–5, 104–12, 114–16, 122–3, 134–5; field 13, 106–7, 110, 116–18, 121, 135; headquarters 78, 96, 106, 110–11, 117–18, 120, 153, 157; *see also* personnel
stakeholders 4, 27, 34, 103, 108
standardisation 82, 88, 114–15, 122–3, 153
story collection 78, 82, 84, 87–9
story-based M&E 15, 71, 76, 78–83, 85–7, 92–7, 151, 154–6
strategic goals 134, 154
strategic ignorance 119–21, 124
structures 35–6, 38, 53–4, 56, 62–4, 71, 74–5, 138; societal 31, 62–4, 66
student interns 80, 133
success stories 3, 62, 78, 80, 95
sustainable development 30, 57, 66
Sustainable Development Goals 29, 35, 130, 155
synchronisation 128–45, 149

taboos 113, 122–3
tacit knowledge 39, 73, 100, 105
taken-for-granted elements 5, 34–5, 37, 40, 50, 54, 150–1, 156
Tanzania 12–13, 58–9, 120, 129, 139–41, 143–4
templates 72–3, 109–10, 112, 122
terminologies 3–4, 29, 49, 58, 60, 66, 152
Thailand 121, 134
Theology of Change 58
third-order change 50, 66
Towards Evaluation for Everyday Use 12, 129, 131–2, 134, 136
traditions 9, 37, 65, 90; positivistic 89; qualitative 89–91
training 36, 93–4, 106, 122, 129–30, 132, 143–5, 151–2; *see also* learning

transformative change 3, 17, 30, 158
transformative development 29–30, 128
transformative learning/education 30–2, 41, 151
translation 38, 130–1, 139
transmissional education 30
transparency 120, 137
triple-loop learning 26
trustworthiness 15, 89
truth 11–12, 36, 90–1, 121
turnover, personnel 16, 104–6, 108, 124, 151

Uganda 13, 75–6, 79, 84–5, 87–8, 96, 119–22, 133–5
Uganda Women Media Association (UMWA) 78–80, 96
uncertainties 74, 113–14, 116, 122, 142, 144, 150, 154
universalistic approaches 6, 122–3
unlearning 2, 14, 16, 100–24, 152; *see also* forgetting

values 27–8, 30, 32–3, 35, 37–8, 47, 73, 101
violence, domestic 76, 80, 85–6, 91
vocabularies 1, 46, 57, 59, 64, 66–7, 129, 131; *see also* terminologies

wealth 34, 36, 76, 78, 104, 111, 130, 136
women 30, 46, 63, 65, 67, 74, 93, 141
working time 3–4, 106–7, 118
workshops 3–4, 12–13, 35–6, 52, 55–7, 66, 79–80, 134
world culture approach 10, 137–8
World Vision (WV) 13, 15, 47–54, 56–8, 60–1, 63–8, 116, 121
worldviews 27, 30, 35, 41, 152

Zambia 12, 36, 118, 136, 150
zero learning 24, 26, 32–4

Taylor & Francis Group
an **informa** business

Taylor & Francis eBooks

www.taylorfrancis.com

A single destination for eBooks from Taylor & Francis with increased functionality and an improved user experience to meet the needs of our customers.

90,000+ eBooks of award-winning academic content in Humanities, Social Science, Science, Technology, Engineering, and Medical written by a global network of editors and authors.

TAYLOR & FRANCIS EBOOKS OFFERS:

- A streamlined experience for our library customers
- A single point of discovery for all of our eBook content
- Improved search and discovery of content at both book and chapter level

REQUEST A FREE TRIAL

support@taylorfrancis.com

Routledge
Taylor & Francis Group

CRC Press
Taylor & Francis Group

For Product Safety Concerns and Information please contact our
EU representative GPSR@taylorandfrancis.com Taylor & Francis
Verlag GmbH, Kaufingerstraße 24, 80331 München, Germany